HOW TO GET A JOB IN AMERICA

GW00703471

In this Series

GET A JOB IN AMERICA

A guide to employment opportunities and contacts

Roger Jones

How To Books

By the same author

How to Get the Job you Really Want
How to Get a Job Abroad
How to Teach Abroad
Languages and How to Master Them

British Library Cataloguing-in-Publication data
A catalogue record for this book is available from the
British Library.

Cartoons by Mike Flanagan

First published in 1992 by How To Books Ltd, Plymbridge House,
Estover Road, Plymouth PL6 7PZ, United Kingdom.
Tel: Plymouth (0752) 735251/695745. Fax: (0752) 695699. Telex: 45635.

Typeset by Kestrel Data, Exeter
Printed and bound in Great Britain by
Dotesios Ltd, Trowbridge, Wiltshire.

Contents

Illustrations

Fig. I. The United States of America

Preface

Each year thousands of people toy with the idea of working in the United States of America, but many are uncertain how to set about it. This book aims to provide some of the answers as well as some useful contacts for people who have never worked in the country before, whether they are applying for jobs from a foreign base or from inside America. I hope it will also be of benefit to employees who are being posted to the United States for the first time.

One characteristic of this book is the quantity of 'mays' and 'mights' you will find, the reason being that in many cases the situation is far from clearcut. This is particularly true with respect to immigration practice where there is uncertainty even among the experts as to how the 1990 Immigration Act will work out.

I also have to sound a word of caution. As I write, the United States is experiencing a recession, so jobs are not as plentiful as they have been in the past. As a consequence even if you follow up every lead in this book assiduously, you may experience disappointment. Fortunately, recessions do not last for ever, and if you do not succeed this year, there is always a chance that next year you will fare better. Bear in mind, however, that fortune favours the well qualified.

In another book of mine, *How to Get a Job Abroad*, I place emphasis on the need for adequate preparation for a foreign posting in order to avoid such terrors as culture shock. While the cultural divide between the United States and Britain and Ireland is, happily, a narrow one, subtle differences do exist, and you need to be aware of these before you jet off.

While every attempt has been made to ensure accuracy, information can go out of date, and I can only apologise for any inconvenience this may cause. I am, incidentally, always happy to receive suggestions and updated information from organisations which recruit for the United States, as well as from the recruited. It may be possible to include some of this material when the time comes for the book to be updated.

I wish you happy job hunting.

Roger Jones

ACKNOWLEDGEMENTS

I am grateful to a number of people and organisations who have helped me in the preparation of this book by supplying me with information, allowing me to use their facilities or offering ideas and criticism. They include the American Community School, Hillingdon; the American School in London; the British Library; Cheltenham Public Library; the Central Bureau; the Department of Social Security; Expat Network; Sarah Eykyn of BUNAC; Tommy Grant; the National Association of Temporary Services; the New York State Office in London; Frederick Pearce; Peter Rushworth; Ian Smith of Anders Glaser Wills; the US Department of Labor; the US Customs Service, London; the US Information Service, London; the US—UK Educational Commission; the Visa Branch of the US Embassy, London as well as publishers, recruitment agencies and the staff of How To Books.

1
Land of Opportunity

THE USA PAST AND PRESENT

The past

The United States has always been regarded as the land of opportunity, and over the centuries millions of Europeans have crossed the Atlantic to seek their fortunes in the New World. The Spanish were the first to settle there in what is now Florida, and were followed by the French in Maine in 1604. The English were not far behind; the settlement of Jamestown in Virginia was founded in 1607. Dutch, Swedish and German communities were also established around this time.

For two centuries or so the English and the Irish predominated. In 1780, for instance, three out of four Americans could claim English or Irish ancestry. But over the past hundred years the population has become much more diverse, with mass immigration from eastern and southern Europe, and more recently from Asia. American blacks are a special case: they were unwilling immigrants.

Money was not always the motivating factor. The Pilgrim Fathers sailed to America in order to be able to worship as they pleased; during the years of the Potato Famine tens of thousands of Irish families went there to escape starvation; from 1880 onwards there was large scale emigration of Jews escaping the pogroms of Eastern Europe; and in our own time Cubans and South East Asians have sought asylum in America in large numbers.

For every one of these unfortunates, the United States meant hope and freedom, and many were doubtless inspired by the works on the base of the statue of Liberty in New York City harbour:

> Give me your tired, your poor,
> Your huddled masses yearning to breathe free,
> The wretched refuse of your teeming shore.

Send these, the homeless tempest-tossed to me.
I lift my lamp beside the golden door.

The present

While the United States continues to open its door wide to refugees, the invitation does not extend to all comers. America, in common with most other countries, now places restrictions on immigration. The authorities are keen to protect the jobs of American citizens, and as a consequence employers are not allowed to offer jobs to outsiders ('aliens') if there is an American who can do the job just as well. So if you wish to take up employment you need to apply for a visa, and there is absolutely no guarantee that it will be granted.

Another change is that the US economy is not as buoyant as it was in the fifties and sixties, and while good opportunities undoubtedly exist you have to look harder for them and the competition is keen. Besides, if you wish to enjoy a good standard of living, Europe is as good a place as any in which to do so. We on this side of the Atlantic are no longer the poor relations of our American cousins.

Yet the United States continues to attract people from all over the world, for various reasons. Many of its industries are the leaders in their particular field and so are its academic institutions. It remains one of the world's leading economies, politically it is the most powerful country on earth and it is a trendsetter in many ways. American commercial interests span the globe and our business culture is strongly influenced by them.

For natives of the UK and Ireland there is a special benefit: it is a home from home—almost. Americans speak English—more or less—whatever George Bernard Shaw might say; American law has its roots in English law; Americans think in terms of pounds, miles, feet and inches; the food is familiar even if chips are called 'French fries'; the natives are hospitable and it is a 'swell' place to visit.

WHY WORK IN THE USA?

People hoping to work in the United States need to be clear from the start what they hope to gain from the experience. Your motives will often determine the kind of visa you apply for, and during the course of the application procedure you may well need to spell out your aims.

Here are some of the more usual reasons people give:

● To finance a stay in America. Students and young people in particular are almost invariably short of cash, so holidays or longer stays in the United States are only possible if they can find a means of financing themselves. What they do is immaterial: washing dishes, looking after children or waiting in restaurants are merely a means to an end. The important thing is to be there and to savour the country at first hand.

● To gain useful work experience. Some higher education courses require students to do a placement in a foreign country which could last from just a couple of months to over a year. Learning to work and survive in a different environment not only broadens one's outlook but could lead to excellent opportunities in the future in the international sphere.

● For career development. An increasing number of high level jobs nowadays call for people with international experience, who can work effectively in any part of the world and are equally at home in Birmingham, Bangkok or Bogota. Teachers and academics may also find that experience in a foreign country, apart from stimulating their ideas, also improves their status.

● To enjoy a better work environment. There are times when prospects at home look pretty bleak and people have an urge to look for greener pastures. In the sixties and seventies there was a considerable brain-drain from the British Isles to the United States, because R&D (research and development) facilities across the Atlantic were so much better funded. In certain areas, too, pay scales are much more generous.

● Because of family ties. If you have close relations in the United States, or you marry an American, you may have more compelling reasons than most to make your home there. You may also find that it is much easier for you to obtain the necessary documentation that will enable you to work.

● A company transfer. Some people do not specifically choose to go to the United States; they are asked to go there—to represent their company or their country, for instance, or to take control of a subsidiary firm. The move could represent a promotion and the prospect of higher earnings—in other words, you have an offer you can hardly refuse.

WHERE CAN I GO?

Clearly, people in the latter category know precisely where they are to be located. Others may be in a position to choose, and for them a brief geography lesson is perhaps in order.

One mistake people tend to make is to think of America solely in terms of New York, Los Angeles and perhaps Washington, since these are the places that have the best media coverage. In fact, the United States is a semi-continent extending over 3.6 million square miles, which means it is almost twice the size of Europe. The scenery and climate are tremendously varied; and there are vast conurbations at one end of the spectrum and sparsely populated regions at the other.

In order to gain a better understanding of the country it is convenient to divide it into regions.

New England
Connecticut (CT): 4,872 sq m (area), 3.1 million (population), Hartford (capital)
Massachusetts (MA): 7,824 sq m, 5.7 million, Boston
Maine (ME): 30,995 sq m, 1.12 million, Augusta
New Hampshire (NH): 8,993 sq m, 921,000, Concord
Rhode Island (RI): 1,055 sq m, 947,000, Providence
Vermont (VT): 9,273 sq m, 511,000, Montpelier

Arguably the most English and historic part of the United States, some areas have experienced industrial decline in recent years. People here tend to be more formal and Puritan than in other parts of the country. The climate consists of cold winters (below freezing for three to four months of the year) and mild summers with rainfall on a par with the British Isles. The major centres of the area are Boston, Hartford (important for insurance) and New Haven (home to Yale University).

The Mid Atlantic Region
District of Columbia (DC): 63 sq m, 638,000
Delaware (DE): 1,932 sq m, 594,000, Dover
Maryland (MD): 9,837, 4.2 million, Annapolis
New Jersey (NJ): 7,468, 7.4 million, Trenton
New York (NY): 47,377 sq m, 17.5 million, Albany
Pennsylvania (PA): 44,888 sq m, 11.8 million, Harrisburg
Virginia (VA): 39,704 sq m, 5.4 million, Richmond
West Virginia (WV): 24,119 sq m, 2 million, Charleston

One of the major industrial centres of America and therefore a fruitful place for job hunting. New York State is the most populous state after California, and the New York Metropolitan area is home to 18 million. Both New York City and Washington have considerable expatriate British communities—50,000 in New York; 15,000 in Washington. Some 200 British firms have a Washington base. Other important centres are Baltimore, Philadelphia and Pittsburgh. In general the summers are warmer and the winters milder than those of New England, but inland you will encounter extremes.

The South
Alabama (AL): 50,767 sq m, 3.9 million, Montgomery
Arkansas (AR): 52,078 sq m, 2.3 million, Little Rock
Florida (FL): 54,153 sq m, 9.7 million, Tallahassee
Georgia (GA): 58,056 sq m, 5.5 million, Atlanta
Kentucky (KY): 39,669 sq m, 3.7 million, Frankfort
Louisiana (LA): 44,521 sq m, 4.2 million, Baton Rouge
Mississippi (MS): 47, 233 sq m, 2.5 million, Jackson
North Carolina (NC): 48,843 sq m, 5.9 million, Raleigh
South Carolina (SC): 30,203 sq m, 3.1 million, Columbia
Tennessee (TN): 41,155 sq m, 4.6 million, Nashville

This is *Gone with the Wind* country, where the pace of life tends to be slower, the cost of living lower and the climate warmer, though there can be plenty of snow inland in winter. Florida, which has a subtropical, somewhat humid climate, has expanded enormously in recent years and is perhaps the most promising place to seek work, particularly in the hotel and leisure industry. It has a large British community of more than 100,000 living principally in Tampa and Orlando, and its own newspaper the *Florida Brit*. The main centres are Atlanta, Kansas City, Miami, Nashville, New Orleans, Raleigh and Tampa.

The Mid West
Illinois (IL): 55,645 sq m, 11.4 million, Springfield
Indiana (IN): 35,932 sq m, 5.5 million, Indianapolis
Iowa* (IA): 55,965 sq m, 2.9 million, Des Moines
Kansas* (KS): 81,778 sq m, 2.4 million, Topeka
Michigan (MI): 56,954 sq m, 9.3 million, Lansing
Minnesota* (MN): 79,548 sq m, 4 million, St Paul
Missouri (MO) 68,945 sq m, 4.9 million, Jefferson City
Nebraska* (NE): 76,644 sq m, 1.6 million, Lincoln
North Dakota* (ND): 69,300 sq m, 650,000, Bismarck
Ohio (OH): 41,004 sq m, 10.8 million, Columbus
South Dakota* (SD): 75,952 sq m, 691,000, Pierre
*Detroit car industry and Great Plains agricultural states.

Wisconsin (WI): 54,426 sq m, 4.7 million, Madison

The hub of this vast area is Chicago, the nation's third largest city, and the region contains some of the country's richest farmland as well as many important mining industrial centres. However some of the activities of the area, notably the car industry in Detroit and agriculture on the Great Plains (the states marked with an asterisk), are in decline.

Other important centres are Cincinnati, Cleveland, Detroit, Milwaukee, Minneapolis St Paul, Omaha and St Louis. The temperatures are more extreme than in the UK and on the Great Plains winter temperatures of -40 degrees Celsius are not unusual.

The Rocky Mountains
Colorado (CO): 103,595 sq m, 2.9 million, Denver
Idaho (ID): 82,412 sq m, 943,000, Boise
Montana (MT): 145,388 sq m, 787,000, Helena
Utah (UT): 82,073 sq m, 1.4 million, Salt Lake City
Wyoming (WY): 96,989 sq m, 470,000, Cheyenne

Scenically stunning but sparsely populated, this is cowboy country. There may be job opportunities in some of the larger cities and in the National Parks. Colorado with its capital, Denver, is the fastest growing state of the Union. Salt Lake City is also an important centre.

The South West
Arizona (AZ): 113,508 sq m, 2.7 million, Phoenix
New Mexico (NM): 121, 335 sq m, 1.3 million, Santa Fe
Oklahoma (OK): 68,655 sq m, 3 million, Oklahoma City
Texas (TX): 262,017 sq m, 14.2 million, Austin

The Texas oil boom has now subsided, and there are fewer job opportunities than there were. However, the economy is improving and although Americans are not exactly returning in droves, the British and other nationals are finding good opportunities here. The main centres are Austin, Dallas-Fort Worth, Houston, Oklahoma City and Phoenix. Summers in the South West can be uncomfortably hot, but air conditioning makes life bearable.

The West
Alaska (AK): 570,833 sq m, 402,000, Juneau
California (CA): 156, 299 sq m, 23.7 million, Sacramento
Nevada (NV): 109,894 sq m, 800,000, Carson City
Oregon (OR): 96,184 sq m, 2.6 million, Salem

Washington (WA): 66,511 sq m, 4.1 million, Olympia

If California were a country it would rank among the top ten economies of the world. There is a large immigrant population in southern California since this is one of the largest industrial centres in the United States and is still expanding. The population of the Los Angeles Metropolitan Area numbers 13 million, and there is a sizeable British community here (consisting not only of film stars) which supports its own community newspaper, *The British Weekly*. A monthly expatriate newspaper, *The Union Jack*, is also published in California and distributed nationwide. This is very much a home-from-home with British-style pubs and grocery shops.

Further north, in Washington State, is Seattle with its large aerospace industry. Apart from Los Angeles other important centres are Portland, San Diego, San Francisco, San Jose, Seattle, and—for gamblers and entertainers—Las Vegas. Alaska stands apart from the rest of the West; mining and oil are the mainstay of its economy and it has much of the old frontier atmosphere. It is also pretty cold in winter.

The Islands
Hawaii (HI) and various US Pacific and Caribbean territories (including Puerto Rico, Guam, American Samoa, Virgin Islands).
Hawaii (HI): 6,425 sq m, 965,000, Honolulu

One seldom associates these tropical islands with the United States. Employment opportunities here—apart from tourism—tend to be restricted.

So where should I make for?
In many cases the choice will be made for you; you go where you are sent or where you can get a good job. If the quality of life is an important consideration, the tables in Figures 2 and 3 will be of interest.

AM I ELIGIBLE TO WORK IN THE UNITED STATES?

One point you have to bear in mind throughout this book is that the United States has a well educated population and is more or less self-sufficient in skilled people. The Federal Government therefore expects employers to recruit from this pool of talent wherever possible, rather than import staff from other countries. Not that the

Quality of Life Rankings

	Education	Health Care	Cost of Living	Trans-portation	Overall Quality of Life
NEW ENGLAND					
Connecticut	14	3	2	32	4
Maine	18	17	45	17	24
Massachusetts	15	1	19	27	5
New Hampshire	32	4	33	14	17
Rhode Island	10	6	41	30	14
Vermont	9	10	49	9	19
MIDDLE ATLANTIC					
New Jersey	20	14	5	48	18
New York	26	12	35	42	31
Pennsylvania	22	13	27	25	20
EAST NORTH CENTRAL					
Illinois	33	20	9	29	23
Indiana	23	38	20	20	27
Michigan	30	27	17	33	28
Ohio	24	24	30	38	30
Wisconsin	3	8	34	23	8
WEST NORTH CENTRAL					
Iowa	4	11	37	4	3
Kansas	12	23	10	8	7
Minnesota	5	7	16	7	2
Missouri	36	19	8	40	25
Nebraska	7	16	24	12	6
North Dakota	6	2	38	3	1
South Dakota	17	26	31	1	9

Fig. 2. Quality of life rankings by region/state

	Education	Health Care	Cost of Living	Transportation	Overall Quality of Life
SOUTH ATLANTIC					
Delaware	13	28	11	37	16
Florida	49	42	6	44	44
Georgia	47	45	15	43	47
Maryland	21	18	7	46	21
North Carolina	37	46	39	36	46
South Carolina	38	49	42	45	48
Virginia	27	29	12	34	26
West Virginia	34	30	44	18	38
EAST SOUTH CENTRAL					
Alabama	45	48	13	24	43
Kentucky	41	35	23	22	39
Mississippi	48	50	29	47	50
Tennessee	46	34	4	50	45
WEST SOUTH CENTRAL					
Arkansas	42	43	26	13	40
Louisiana	50	47	36	31	49
Oklahoma	39	39	25	15	37
Texas	43	44	14	26	42
MOUNTAIN					
Arizona	31	32	32	41	41
Colorado	16	9	28	16	12
Idaho	29	36	40	11	34
Montana	8	37	47	6	22
Nevada	40	31	18	10	29
New Mexico	25	33	22	35	33
Utah	28	22	43	21	32
Wyoming	1	41	50	2	13
PACIFIC					
Alaska	2	40	46	5	11
California	44	25	1	49	35
Hawaii	35	5	21	19	15
Oregon	11	21	48	39	36
Washington	19	15	3	28	10

Education index comprises: average teacher salaries as ratio or average pay of all workers; student teachers ratio (K 12); high school graduation rate; state expenditure per student for public education (K-12), per capita higher education state expenditures as a percentage of per capita income; and literacy rates.

Health care index comprises: the number of teaching hospitals; cancer treatment units and trauma units per 100,000 population; infant death rates; percentage of non-elderly population without health insurance; and physicians, registered nurses, and dentists per 100,000 population.

Cost of living index comprises: average costs for housing, food, and utilities as a percentage of average household income; and state income and property taxes as a percentage of total personal income.

Transportation index comprises: average urban commute time; percentage of state's budget dedicated to transportation; pavement condition of roadways; traffic-related fatalities and injuries per capita; per capita state transportation expenditures; and average daily traffic volume.

Overall quality of life is weighted composite of education, health care, cost of living, and transportation indices.

Source: Grant Thornton, Manufacturing Climates Study, June 1989.

employers' choice is restricted to US citizens; nationals of other countries who have permanent resident status (and are known in bureaucratic parlance as 'resident aliens') are eligible to apply for any jobs that are going.

However, you do not have to be a resident alien in possession of an **Alien Registration Receipt Card** (sometimes called the '**green card**') in order to work in the United States. A good many foreigners work for periods ranging from a few months to several years on temporary permits. There are certain restrictions: any employer wishing to recruit will normally have to demonstrate to the State authorities that he is unable to recruit the right kind of person locally. If he fails to convince them, they may well refuse his request for labour certification without which he cannot employ a non-US resident for a particular job.

The important matter of visas is treated at length in Chapter 2. It's a good idea to work through that chapter to find out what type of visa you will need in order to work in the United States. While it is now possible to move freely across borders within the European Community in search of a job, there is no open jobs market for British people—or indeed any non-American—in the United States, except for those with residential status.

Certain kinds of people are more welcome than others. You may have outstanding ability in your field or be able to offer skills that are much in demand. In the recent past certain areas of the United States have experienced a shortage of computer experts, electronics engineers, nurses and paramedics, and this shortage has been overcome by recruitment from abroad.

Your own connections can be crucial as well. You may be able to gain permanent residence on the strength of close family relationships; or you may be transferred to the United States by your firm or organisation. Entrepreneurial skills can also gain you access to the country: America welcomes investors.

WILL AMERICA SUIT ME?

Assuming there will be no problem in getting the necessary permission to work in the United States, you still need to consider whether a job on the other side of the Atlantic will really suit you. For, while most newcomers take to the United States like ducks to water, there are some who do not. They are irritated by the exuberance of many Americans, complain about the materialism they see around them, dislike the television programmes and the extremes of climate, and long for a pint of real ale and fish and chips.

Going to live and work in a strange location inevitably calls for adaptability; you must be prepared to meet the local people on their own terms. Fortunately, the American way of life is not as different from ours as that of, say, Mexico or Yemen, but even slight differences can irritate some people. You may dislike one part of the country and feel very much at home in another. There is, after all, considerable regional variety; if you dislike the formality of the east coast, you may feel more at home on the west coast where people are more casual.

It is unwise to take everything for granted. Public transport is a case in point: in much of the country public transport systems are rudimentary or completely non-existent. The car is king, and if you cannot drive you will be at something of a disadvantage. Another difference is that there is no government funded health service except for the old and handicapped; you will need to pay for medical treatment, or better, insure yourself against illness.

Though the language may sound reasonably familiar, it is perhaps wiser to regard the United States as a foreign country with different values and different customs. Even things which sound similar may be different: an American gallon, for instance, is less than the Imperial equivalent. Driving rules are different as well, with speed limits normally lower than those in Europe. The high-speed car chases you see in films are definitely not typical of the United States.

Average Monthly Temperature and Rainfall

T, temperature in Fahrenheit; P, precipitation in inches; L, less than 0.5 inch

Station	Jan T	Jan P	Feb T	Feb P	Mar T	Mar P	Apr T	Apr P	May T	May P	June T	June P	July T	July P	Aug T	Aug P	Sept T	Sept P	Oct T	Oct P	Nov T	Nov P	Dec T	Dec P
Albany	21	2.4	23	2.3	34	3.0	47	2.9	58	3.3	67	3.3	71	3.0	69	3.3	61	3.2	51	2.9	39	3.0	26	3.0
Albuquerque, N.M.	35	0.4	39	0.4	46	0.5	55	0.4	64	0.5	75	0.5	79	1.3	76	1.5	69	0.9	57	0.9	44	0.4	36	0.5
Anchorage, Alas.	13	0.8	18	0.9	24	0.7	35	0.7	46	0.6	54	1.1	58	2.0	56	2.1	48	2.5	35	1.7	22	1.1	14	1.1
Asheville, N.C.	37	3.5	39	3.6	46	5.1	56	3.8	63	4.2	70	4.2	73	4.4	73	4.8	70	4.0	56	3.3	46	3.3	39	3.5
Atlanta, Ga.	42	4.9	45	4.4	53	5.9	62	4.4	69	4.0	76	3.4	79	4.7	78	3.4	73	3.2	62	2.5	52	3.4	45	4.2
Atlantic City, N.J.	34	3.3	35	3.2	42	3.7	51	3.1	60	2.9	68	2.9	74	3.9	74	4.5	68	2.7	58	2.8	48	3.5	38	3.5
Baltimore, Md.	33	3.0	35	3.0	43	3.7	54	3.4	63	3.4	72	3.8	77	3.9	76	4.6	69	3.5	57	3.1	46	3.1	37	3.4
Barrow, Alas.	-14	0.2	-20	0.2	-16	0.2	-2	0.2	19	0.2	33	0.4	39	0.9	38	1.0	31	0.6	14	0.6	-1	0.3	-13	0.2
Birmingham, Ala.	42	5.2	46	4.7	54	6.6	63	5.0	70	4.5	77	3.7	80	5.4	80	3.9	74	4.3	62	2.7	52	3.6	45	5.0
Bismarck, N.D.	7	0.5	15	0.5	26	0.7	43	1.5	55	2.2	64	3.0	70	2.0	69	1.7	57	1.4	46	0.8	29	0.5	15	0.5
Boise, Ida.	30	1.6	36	1.1	41	1.0	49	1.2	57	1.2	66	1.0	75	0.3	72	0.4	63	0.6	52	0.8	40	1.3	32	1.3
Boston, Mass.	30	4.0	31	3.7	38	4.1	49	3.7	59	3.5	68	2.9	74	2.7	72	3.7	65	3.4	55	3.4	45	4.2	34	4.9
Buffalo, N.Y.	24	3.0	25	2.4	33	3.0	45	3.0	56	2.9	66	2.7	71	3.0	69	4.2	62	3.4	52	2.9	40	3.6	29	3.4
Burlington, Vt.	17	1.9	18	1.7	29	2.2	43	2.8	55	3.0	65	3.6	70	3.4	67	3.9	59	3.2	48	2.8	37	2.8	23	2.4
Caribou, Me.	11	2.4	13	2.1	24	2.4	37	2.6	50	2.9	60	3.2	65	4.0	63	4.0	54	3.5	43	3.1	31	3.2	16	3.1
Charleston, S.C.	49	3.3	51	3.4	57	4.4	66	2.6	73	4.4	79	6.5	82	7.3	81	6.5	77	4.9	68	2.9	59	2.2	52	3.1
Chicago, Ill	21	1.6	26	1.3	36	2.6	49	3.7	59	3.2	69	4.1	73	3.6	72	3.5	65	3.4	54	2.3	40	2.1	28	2.1
Cleveland, Oh.	26	2.5	27	2.2	37	3.0	48	3.3	59	3.2	68	3.5	71	3.4	70	3.4	65	3.1	53	2.5	42	2.8	31	2.8
Columbus, Oh.	27	2.8	30	2.2	40	3.0	51	3.4	61	3.8	70	4.0	74	4.0	72	3.7	66	2.8	54	1.9	42	2.6	32	2.6
Dallas-Ft. Worth, Tex.	44	1.7	49	1.9	56	2.4	66	3.6	74	4.3	82	2.6	86	2.0	86	1.8	79	3.3	68	2.5	56	1.8	46	1.7
Denver, Col.	30	0.5	34	0.7	38	1.2	47	1.8	57	2.5	67	1.6	73	1.9	71	1.5	63	1.2	52	1.0	39	0.8	33	0.6
Des Moines, Ia.	19	1.0	25	1.1	35	2.2	51	3.2	62	4.0	72	4.2	76	3.2	74	4.1	65	3.1	54	2.2	39	1.5	26	1.5
Detroit, Mich.	23	1.9	26	1.7	35	2.5	47	3.2	58	2.8	68	3.4	72	3.1	71	3.2	63	2.3	52	2.1	40	2.3	29	2.5
Dodge City, Kan.	30	0.5	35	0.5	42	1.5	54	1.8	64	3.3	75	3.0	80	3.1	78	2.5	69	1.9	58	1.3	43	0.8	34	0.5
Duluth, Minn.	6	1.2	12	0.9	23	1.8	38	2.2	50	3.2	59	4.0	65	4.0	63	4.1	54	3.3	44	2.2	28	1.7	14	1.3
Eureka, Cal.	47	7.0	49	5.2	48	5.1	49	2.9	52	1.6	55	0.6	56	0.1	57	0.4	57	0.9	54	2.7	51	5.9	48	6.2
Fairbanks, Alas.	-13	0.5	-4	0.5	9	0.4	30	0.3	48	0.6	59	1.3	62	1.8	57	1.9	45	1.1	25	0.7	4	0.7	-10	0.7
Fresno, Cal.	46	2.0	51	1.9	56	1.6	60	1.0	68	0.3	75	0.1	81	L	79	L	74	0.2	65	0.4	53	1.2	45	1.6
Galveston, Tex.	54	3.0	56	2.3	62	2.1	69	2.6	76	3.3	81	3.5	83	3.8	83	4.4	80	5.8	73	2.6	63	3.2	57	3.6
Grand Junction, Col.	26	0.6	34	0.5	42	0.8	52	0.7	62	0.8	72	0.4	79	0.5	78	0.7	63	0.7	55	0.9	40	0.6	28	0.6
Gr. Rapids, Mich.	22	0.9	24	1.5	33	2.5	46	3.6	58	3.0	67	3.9	71	3.0	70	3.5	62	3.1	51	2.9	39	2.9	27	2.6
Hartford, Conn.	25	3.5	28	3.2	37	4.2	49	4.0	59	3.4	69	3.4	73	3.1	71	4.0	63	3.9	53	3.5	42	4.1	29	4.2
Helena, Mon.	18	0.7	26	0.4	32	0.7	42	1.0	53	1.7	60	2.0	68	1.0	66	1.2	56	0.8	45	0.7	31	0.5	23	0.6
Honolulu, Ha.	73	3.8	73	2.7	74	3.5	76	1.5	78	1.2	79	0.5	80	0.5	81	0.6	81	0.6	80	1.9	77	3.2	74	3.4
Houston, Tex.	51	3.2	55	3.3	61	2.7	69	4.2	75	4.7	81	4.0	83	3.3	83	3.7	78	4.9	70	3.7	60	3.4	54	3.7
Huron, S.D.	11	0.4	18	0.8	29	1.2	46	2.0	57	2.7	68	3.3	74	2.3	72	2.0	61	1.4	49	1.4	32	0.7	19	0.5
Indianapolis, Ind.	26	2.7	30	2.5	40	3.6	52	3.7	63	3.7	72	4.0	75	4.3	73	3.5	67	2.7	55	2.5	42	3.0	32	3.0
Jackson, Miss.	46	5.0	49	4.9	56	5.9	65	5.9	73	4.8	79	2.9	82	4.4	81	3.7	76	3.6	65	2.6	55	4.2	49	5.4
Jacksonville, Fla.	53	3.1	55	3.5	61	3.7	68	3.3	74	4.9	79	5.4	81	6.5	81	7.2	78	7.3	70	3.4	61	1.9	55	2.6
Juneau, Alas.	22	3.7	28	3.7	31	3.3	39	2.9	46	3.4	53	3.0	56	4.1	55	5.0	49	6.4	42	7.7	33	5.2	27	4.7

Fig. 3. Average monthly temperature and rainfall, based on a thirty-year period (National Climatic Data Center, US Department of Commerce)

City	Jan	Feb	Mar	Apr	May	Jun	Jul	Aug	Sep	Oct	Nov	Dec
Kansas City, Mo.	26 1.0	32 1.0	42 2.1	55 2.7	65 3.4	76 4.1	79 3.5	77 3.2	68 3.3	58 2.5	43 1.2	32 1.1
Knoxville, Tenn.	38 4.7	42 4.2	50 5.5	60 3.9	67 3.7	74 4.0	78 4.3	77 3.0	72 3.0	60 2.7	49 3.8	41 4.6
Lander, Wyo.	20 0.5	26 0.6	32 1.1	42 2.2	53 2.7	62 1.5	71 0.7	69 0.5	58 0.9	47 1.2	31 0.8	23 0.5
Lexington, Ky.	32 3.6	35 3.3	44 4.8	55 4.0	64 4.0	72 4.0	76 5.0	75 4.3	69 3.0	57 2.3	45 4.4	36 3.8
Little Rock, Ark.	40 3.9	44 3.8	52 4.7	62 5.4	71 5.3	79 3.7	82 3.6	81 3.1	74 4.3	63 2.8	51 4.4	43 4.2
Los Angeles, Ga.	57 3.7	59 3.0	60 1.9	62 1.2	66 0.2	69 L	74 L	75 0.1	73 0.3	63 0.2	63 1.9	58 2.0
Louisville, Ky.	33 3.4	36 3.2	44 4.3	57 4.1	65 4.2	74 3.6	78 4.1	76 3.3	70 3.6	57 2.6	48 3.5	37 3.5
Marquette, Mich.	12 2.0	14 1.9	23 2.8	37 3.6	50 3.0	60 3.9	65 3.2	63 3.3	54 3.9	44 3.3	30 2.9	18 2.4
Memphis, Tenn.	40 4.6	44 4.3	52 5.4	63 5.8	71 5.1	79 3.6	82 4.0	81 3.7	74 3.7	63 2.4	51 4.2	43 4.9
Miami, Fla.	67 2.1	68 2.1	72 1.9	75 3.1	79 6.5	81 9.2	83 6.0	83 7.0	82 8.1	77 8.1	73 2.7	69 1.9
Milwaukee, Wis.	19 1.6	23 1.3	32 2.6	45 3.4	55 2.6	65 3.6	71 3.5	69 3.1	61 2.5	51 2.3	37 2.0	25 2.0
Minneapolis, Minn.	11 0.8	18 0.9	29 1.7	46 2.1	59 3.2	68 4.1	73 3.5	71 3.6	61 2.9	50 1.9	33 1.3	19 0.9
Mobile, Ala.	51 4.6	54 4.9	60 6.5	68 5.4	75 5.5	81 5.1	82 7.7	82 6.8	78 6.6	66 2.6	59 3.7	53 5.4
Moline, Ill.	20 1.6	25 1.3	36 2.8	50 4.0	61 4.2	71 4.3	75 4.9	73 3.8	65 3.7	54 2.7	39 2.0	26 1.9
Nashville, Tenn.	37 4.5	40 4.0	49 5.6	60 4.8	68 4.6	76 3.7	79 3.8	79 3.4	72 3.7	57 3.1	49 3.5	41 4.6
Newark, N.J.	31 3.1	33 3.1	41 4.2	52 3.6	62 3.6	72 2.9	77 3.9	76 4.3	68 3.7	58 3.1	47 3.6	36 3.4
New Orleans, La.	52 5.0	55 5.2	61 4.7	69 4.5	75 5.1	80 4.6	82 6.7	82 6.0	79 5.9	69 3.0	60 4.1	55 5.3
New York, N.Y.	32 3.2	33 3.1	41 4.2	53 3.8	62 3.8	71 3.2	76 3.8	75 4.0	68 3.7	58 3.4	47 4.1	36 3.8
Nome, Alas.	9 0.8	3 0.5	7 0.6	18 0.6	36 0.8	45 1.2	51 2.2	50 3.1	42 2.3	28 1.3	16 0.9	4 0.7
Norfolk, Va.	40 3.7	41 3.3	49 3.9	58 2.9	67 3.8	76 3.5	78 5.3	78 5.3	72 4.4	61 3.4	52 2.9	44 3.2
Okla. City, Okla.	36 1.0	41 1.3	49 2.1	60 2.9	68 5.2	77 3.9	82 2.9	81 2.4	73 3.4	62 2.7	49 1.5	40 1.2
Omaha, Neb.	19 0.8	25 0.9	35 1.9	50 2.9	62 4.3	71 4.4	76 3.6	74 3.4	64 3.4	54 2.1	38 1.3	26 0.9
Pago Pago, Amer. Samoa	81 13	81 13	81 11	81 11	80 11	80 8.6	79 6.5	79 7.1	79 6.7	80 11	80 11	81 14
Philadelphia, Pa.	31 3.2	33 2.8	42 3.9	53 3.5	63 3.2	72 3.9	76 3.9	75 4.1	68 3.4	57 2.8	46 3.3	46 3.5
Phoenix, Ariz.	52 0.7	56 0.6	61 0.8	68 0.3	77 0.1	67 0.2	92 0.7	90 1.0	85 0.6	73 0.6	61 0.5	53 0.8
Pittsburgh, Pa.	27 2.9	29 2.4	39 3.6	50 3.3	60 3.5	68 3.3	71 3.8	71 3.3	64 2.8	53 2.5	42 2.3	31 2.6
Portland, Me.	22 3.8	23 3.6	32 4.0	43 3.3	57 3.3	63 2.8	68 2.8	67 2.8	59 3.3	49 3.8	38 4.7	26 4.5
Portland, Ore.	39 6.2	43 3.9	46 3.6	53 2.3	57 2.1	63 1.5	67 0.5	67 1.1	64 1.6	54 3.1	46 5.2	41 6.4
Providence, R.I.	28 4.1	29 3.7	37 4.3	48 4.0	57 3.7	67 2.8	73 3.0	71 4.4	64 3.5	53 3.8	43 4.2	32 4.5
Raleigh, N.C.	40 3.6	42 3.4	49 3.7	59 2.9	67 3.7	74 3.7	78 4.4	77 4.4	71 3.3	60 2.7	50 2.9	42 3.1
Rapid City, S.D.	21 0.4	26 0.6	33 1.0	45 2.0	56 2.6	65 3.3	73 2.1	71 1.4	61 1.0	50 0.8	35 0.5	26 0.5
Reno, Nev.	32 1.2	37 1.0	41 0.7	46 0.5	56 0.7	62 0.5	73 0.3	67 0.3	60 0.3	50 0.3	38 0.7	33 1.2
Richmond, Va.	37 3.2	39 3.1	47 3.6	58 2.9	66 3.6	74 3.6	78 5.1	77 5.0	70 3.5	59 3.7	49 3.3	40 3.4
St. Louis, Mo.	29 1.7	34 2.1	43 3.3	56 3.6	66 3.5	75 3.7	79 3.6	77 2.6	70 2.7	58 2.6	45 2.5	34 2.2
Salt Lake City, Ut.	29 1.4	34 1.3	41 1.7	49 2.2	59 1.5	68 1.0	78 0.7	75 0.9	65 0.9	52 1.1	40 1.2	30 1.4
San Antonio, Tex.	50 1.6	54 1.9	62 1.3	70 2.7	76 3.7	82 3.0	85 1.9	84 2.7	79 3.8	70 2.9	60 2.3	53 1.4
San Diego, Cal.	57 2.1	58 1.4	59 1.6	61 0.8	63 0.2	66 0.1	70 L	72 0.1	71 0.2	68 0.3	62 1.1	57 1.4
San Francisco, Cal.	49 4.7	52 3.2	53 2.6	55 1.5	58 0.3	61 0.1	62 L	63 0.1	64 0.2	61 1.1	55 2.4	49 3.6
San Juan, P.R.	77 3.0	78 2.3	78 2.3	80 3.0	79 5.6	82 4.7	82 4.9	82 5.9	82 6.0	81 5.9	80 5.6	78 4.7
Sault Ste. Marie, Mich.	13 2.2	14 1.7	24 2.0	38 2.4	50 2.9	58 3.3	64 3.0	63 3.5	55 3.9	45 2.9	33 3.2	20 2.6
Savannah, Ga.	49 3.1	52 3.2	58 3.8	66 3.2	73 4.6	79 5.7	81 7.4	81 6.7	77 5.2	67 2.3	58 1.9	51 2.8
Seattle, Wash.	39 6.0	43 4.2	44 3.6	49 2.4	55 1.4	60 1.4	65 0.7	64 1.3	60 2.0	52 3.4	45 5.6	41 6.3
Spokane, Wash.	26 2.5	32 1.6	38 1.4	46 1.1	54 1.1	62 1.2	70 0.5	68 0.7	64 1.3	48 1.1	35 2.1	29 2.5
Springfield, Mo.	32 1.6	36 2.1	45 3.4	56 4.0	65 4.3	73 4.7	78 3.6	77 2.8	60 3.8	51 3.1	45 2.9	36 2.6
Syracuse, N.Y.	23 2.6	24 2.7	33 3.1	46 3.3	57 3.2	66 3.6	71 3.4	69 3.8	62 3.3	51 3.2	41 3.5	28 3.2
Tampa, Fla.	60 2.2	61 3.0	66 3.5	72 1.8	77 3.4	81 5.3	82 8.0	82 7.6	81 6.2	74 2.3	67 1.9	61 2.1
Washington, D.C.	31 2.8	34 2.6	42 3.4	53 3.1	62 3.6	71 4.2	79 4.2	74 4.2	67 3.3	55 3.0	45 3.0	35 3.3
Wilmington, Dal.	31 3.1	33 3.0	42 3.9	52 3.4	62 3.2	71 3.5	76 4.6	75 4.0	68 3.6	56 2.9	48 3.3	36 3.5

23

Will my family like living there?

If you have a family, you need to consider the implications of a move to the United States with care. What may be an exciting challenge for you could turn out to be a mild form of torture for them.

Your spouse

This is most frequently a wife, but sometimes the wife is the main breadwinner and the accompanying spouse is male.

Problems can arise when both partners want to pursue their own careers. You need to discuss whether your spouse is prepared to give up his or her job in order to accompany you to the United States, or whether you should settle for a bachelor existence with holidays and the occasional weekend spent together.

There are also financial considerations. If your spouse gives up her/his job you are probably faced with the matter of living on one income instead of two. There is no guarantee that your spouse will be granted the type of visa that will enable him/her to work in America.

Some spouses may relish a life away from the workplace, but for others who are used to a busy existence time may hang heavy. While you may have plenty of colleagues with whom to socialise at work, your spouse has to go out and make his/her own social contacts. If they cannot drive or do not have the use of a car, this can be a problem in suburbia and in remote areas.

Fortunately, in most areas there are clubs to join and adult education classes to attend. Organisations such as the Women's

---

Starting Salaries for 1990 Graduates with Bachelors Degrees

Liberal arts	$20,244	Nursing	$27,358
Social sciences	$21,310	Civil engineering	$27,707
Business admin.	$21,845	Physics	$28,777
Geology	$24,080	Computer science	$31,389
Mathematics	$24,968	Electrical engineering	$32,107
Chemistry	$25,938	Mechanical engineering	$32,256
Accounting	$27,051	Chemical engineering	$33,380

Fig. 4. Average starting salaries for new graduates (Bureau of Labor Statistics, US Department of Labor).

Earnings by Occupation and Sex

	Median weekly earnings ($)			
	1990 Men	1990 Women	1991 Men	1991 Women
Managerial and professional specialty	717	507	741	519
Executive, administrative, and managerial	722	484	737	495
Professional specialty	712	525	744	548
Technical, sales, and administrative support	494	329	498	351
Technicians and related support	561	426	564	442
Sales occupations	506	284	499	311
Administrative support, including clerical	438	332	456	349
Service occupations	317	231	320	243
Private household	(1)	161	(1)	164
Protective service	454	369	494	436
Service, except private household and protective	273	231	279	244
Precision production, craft, and repair	487	319	488	354
Mechanics and repairers	477	476	472	541
Construction trades	486	(1)	478	(1)
Other precision production, craft, and repair	503	295	517	320
Operators, fabricators, and laborers	379	262	391	275
Machine operators, assemblers, and inspectors	391	261	403	272
Transportation and material moving occupations	426	296	421	320
Handlers, equipment cleaners, helpers, and laborers	308	249	316	269
Farming, forestry, and fishing	262	214	269	220

(1) *Data not shown where base is less than 100,000*

Fig. 5. Median usual weekly earnings of full-time wage and salary workers (Bureau of Labor Statistics, US Department of Labor)

Average Annual Pay ($)

State	1989	1990	State	1989	1990
United States	22,563	23,602	Missouri	20,900	21,716
Alabama	19,593	20,468	Montana	17,224	17,895
Alaska	29,704	29,946	Nebraska	17,690	18,577
Arizona	20,809	21,443	Nevada	21,333	22,358
Arkansas	17,418	18,204	New Hampshire	21,553	22,609
California	24,917	26,180	New Jersey	26,780	28,449
Colorado	21,940	22,908	New Mexico	18,667	19,347
Connecticut	27,500	28,995	New York	27,303	28,873
Delaware	23,268	24,423	North Carolina	19,321	20,220
District of Columbia	32,106	33,717	North Dakota	16,932	17,626
Florida	20,072	21,032	Ohio	21,986	22,843
Georgia	21,072	22,114	Oklahoma	19,533	20,288
Hawaii	21,624	23,167	Oregon	20,303	21,332
Idaho	18,146	18,991	Pennsylvania	22,313	23,457
Illinois	24,212	25,312	Rhode Island	21,128	22,388
Indiana	20,931	21,699	South Carolina	18,797	19,699
Iowa	18,420	19,224	South Dakota	15,810	16,430
Kansas	19,475	20,238	Tennessee	19,712	20,611
Kentucky	19,001	19,947	Texas	21,740	22,700
Louisiana	19,750	20,646	Utah	19,362	20,074
Maine	19,202	20,154	Vermont	19,497	20,532
Maryland	23,469	24,730	Virginia	21,882	22,750
Massachusetts	25,233	26,689	Washington	21,617	22,646
Michigan	24,767	25,376	West Virginia	19,788	20,715
Minnesota	22,155	23,126	Wisconsin	20,204	21,101
Mississippi	17,047	17,718	Wyoming	19,230	20,049

Fig. 6.   Average annual pay by State (Bureau of Labor Statistics, US Dept. of Labor)

Regional House Price Trends

City	1988	1989	1990
Akron, Oh.	$59,900	$64,500	$67,700
Albuquerque, N.M.	80,400	83,000	84,500
Anaheim/Santa Ana. Cal.	203,900	241,700	242,400
Atlanta, Ga.	NA	84,000	86,400
Baltimore, Md.	88,700	96,300	105,900
Baton Rouge, La.	64,700	63,800	64,900
Birmingham, Ala.	75,700	78,500	80,800
Boston, Mass.	181,200	181,900	174,200
Bradenton, Fla.	66,100	68,100	69,600
Buffalo, N.Y.	65,500	72,500	77,200
Charleston, S.C.	73,100	74,500	76,200
Chicago, Ill.	89,000	107,000	116,800
Cincinnati, Oh.	69,700	75,800	79,800
Cleveland, Oh.	69,200	75,200	80,600
Columbia, S.C.	69,700	73,900	77,100
Columbus, Oh.	72,600	77,900	81,600
Corpus Christi, Tex.	64,900	64,900	63,200
Dallas, Tex.	90,800	93,400	89,500
Daytona Beach, Fla.	62,600	63,400	64,100
Denver, Col.	81,800	85,500	86,400
Des Moines, Ia.	55,800	57,500	60,500
Detroit, Mich.	73,100	73,700	76,700
El Paso, Tex.	59,600	63,100	63,600
Grand Rapids, Mich.	57,900	64,200	68,300
Hartford, Conn.	167,600	165,900	157,300
Honolulu, Hi.	210,000	270,000	352,000
Houston, Tex.	61,800	66,700	70,700
Indianapolis, Ind.	66,100	71,200	74,800
Jacksonville, Fla.	67,700	69,300	72,400
Kansas City, Mo.	70,500	71,600	74,100
Knoxville, Tenn.	67,000	71,100	75,400
Las Vegas, Nev.	78,800	85,700	93,000
Little Rock, Ark.	63,900	63,700	64,800
Los Angeles, Cal.	$178,900	$214,800	$212,800
Louisville, Ky.	54,500	58,400	60,800
Madison, Wis.	72,000	76,500	82,300
Memphis, Tenn.	76,300	78,100	78,100
Miami/Hialeah, Fla.	82,900	86,900	89,300
Milwaukee, Wis.	74,500	79,600	84,400
Minneapolis/St. Paul, Minn.	85,200	87,200	88,700
Mobile, Ala.	53,000	56,700	59,100
Nashville/Davidson, Tenn.	77,600	79,900	81,800
New Haven, Conn.	169,400	163,400	153,300
New Orleans, La.	73,100	70,600	67,800
New York, N.Y.	183,800	183,200	174,900
Oklahoma City, Okla.	56,200	53,500	53,200
Omaha, Neb.	59,500	60,600	63,000
Orlando, Fla.	79,100	79,800	62,800
Philadelphia, Pa.	102,400	103,900	108,700
Phoenix, Ariz.	80,000	78,800	84,000
Pittsburgh, Pa.	63,200	65,800	70,100
Portland, Ore.	64,400	70,100	79,500
Providence, R.I.	130,600	130,200	127,900
Sacramento, Cal.	94,600	111,700	137,100
St. Louis, Mo.	78,100	76,900	75,700
Salt Lake City/Ogden, Ut.	67,700	69,400	69,400
San Antonio, Tex.	65,000	64,200	63,600
San Diego, Cal.	153,400	181,900	183,600
San Francisco, Cal.	212,900	260,600	259,300
Seattle, Wash.	94,000	115,000	142,000
Spokane, Wash.	51,100	52,400	55,500
Syracuse, N.Y.	74,600	79,300	80,700
Tampa, Fla.	65,600	71,900	71,400
Toledo, Oh.	58,400	60,800	62,800
Tulsa, Okla.	65,000	62,600	63,900
Washington, D.C.	132,500	144,400	150,200

Fig. 7. The average prices of family homes (National Association of Realtors)

Average House Prices and Mortgages

	Median-priced existing home ($)	Average mortgage rate (%)	Monthly principal and interest payment ($)	Payment as percentage of median income (%)
1981	66,400	15.12	677	36.3
1982	67,800	15.38	702	35.9
1983	70,300	12,85	616	30.1
1984	72,400	12.49	618	28.2
1985	75,500	11.74	609	26.2
1986	80,300	10.25	563	23.0
1987	85,600	9.28	565	21.9
1988	90,600	9.31	591	22.0
1989	93,100	10.11	660	23.1
1990	97,500	10.04	673	22.7
1991	99,700	9.51	671	22.3

Fig.8. Housing affordability (National Association of Realtors). The 1991 figures are for May.

Corona Society and Christians Abroad may also be able to find a contact to look after your spouse in the initial stages.

Your children
If you are planning to live in the United States for several years, or possibly for ever, you will doubtless want to take your children with you. However, if they are into their teens consideration has to be given to their education. The American education system differs fundamentally from the British system, and if crucial examinations are looming up and you want them to go on to further education in the UK, you need to consider their future carefully.

There are various options:

- enable them to continue at their present school
- put them into a UK boarding school
- enrol them in a school in the United States
- enrol them in a school in America which offers a British style curriculum.

Schools in the last category, which prepare pupils for British examinations or the International Baccalaureate, tend to be few and far between, and generally only in those centres where there is a sizeable British community (See also Chapter 5).

THE FINANCIAL AND OTHER REWARDS

Will I earn more money in the United States? Will my salary go as far as it would at home? These are the questions that are often uppermost in people's minds when they consider taking up a posting in the United States. Unfortunately, there is no simple answer.

The table of Earnings by Occupation and Sex in Figure 4 may provide some clue, though the earnings quoted relate to US residents rather than expatriates. If you are recruited in the UK for a short-term contract you may well earn more than the average for a particular job. The same will doubtless be true if you are sent to the United States by your firm when all the perks and other inducements are taken into account. Others may not be so lucky; resident aliens, for instance, may have to settle for pay rates that are closer to the local norms.

When it comes to the actual cost of living, one can only generalise. Household goods are often cheaper than in the UK and so are cars. The cost of accommodation varies considerably. New York City is expensive to live in, but probably no more so than London; and renting an apartment in Manhattan could well set you back the same amount as its equivalent in Mayfair. However, if you are living in Manhattan the chances are that your employer is paying your rent anyway.

There are, of course, cheaper areas where you can live reasonably well, just as there are in Greater London, and if you have to pay your own rent you will doubtless head for these. Boston, Los Angeles, San Francisco and Washington DC are other cities where accommodation tends to be on the expensive side, as the table in Figure 7 shows, but elsewhere housing is relatively cheap. For instance, in Houston it is possible to find a modest, three-bedroomed house for around $50,000, or an apartment to rent for $600 per month or less. (To calculate annual rents approximately, divide the figures for house prices in the table by ten.)

However, you should not count your chickens before they are hatched, since there are various obstacles to be negotiated. One of the most difficult is the immigration hurdle. The next chapter is devoted to this.

2
Getting Into the United States: The Red Tape

This book is primarily about getting a job in the United States, not about the United States immigration laws. However, an understanding of these laws is vital in order to ensure a trouble free entry into the United States. Your working intentions will determine and be determined by the type of visa you apply for.

A few myths need to be dispelled first:

- You don't need a visa in order to take up casual work in the United States.
  Wrong. If you are employed in the United States in any capacity you need a work visa; anybody without one is classified as an illegal immigrant and is breaking the law. Nonetheless, there are plenty of people who are willing to take the risk regardless of the consequences.

- In order to work in the United States you need first to obtain a 'green card'.
  Wrong. The **Alien Registration Receipt Card**, to give it its official title, is for people with permanent resident status, and not everybody wants this. Most newcomers to the United States enter on non-immigrant (temporary) visas which permit them to work and can often be extended.

- It is essential to use a lawyer to obtain a work permit.
  Wrong. United States immigration laws may be complicated, but many people and employers manage quite happily without a legal adviser. Besides, if your case is a poor one, using a lawyer is unlikely to get you the right visa anyway.

THE NEED FOR A VISA

As you saw in the first chapter, the United States no longer has an open door policy with respect to immigration. The country's population has grown enormously, so partly to protect the interests of its workforce it now imposes limits on immigrants. For instance, from 1995 onwards a maximum of 675,000 immigrants will be allowed in annually. Whether you seek temporary employment or permanent residence you have to apply for a visa before you go.

The only exceptions to the rule are citizens of certain countries (including Britain) who are making a holiday or business trip of 90 days or less, and are in possession of a return ticket. People who can claim American citizenship by reason of birth or parentage are also exempt. Anybody else needs to get an appropriate visa, whether they are involved in an exchange or a course of study, or whether they are planning to settle permanently.

Be warned. If you enter the country without an appropriate visa and take up employment, you and your employer are breaking the law. While you may manage to get away with it for a time—and quite a lot of people do—you are running a considerable risk. You will be regarded as an illegal immigrant, and if you are found out you could be deported and prohibited from entering the United States again. The longer you stay, the greater the danger of being found out.

There are ways out of the dilemma.

- You may be able to change your status to another category with the help of either an employer who requires your services, or the help of a close relation. This involved filing the appropriate form with the Immigration and Naturalisation Service. Sometimes this is a straightforward procedure that you can handle by yourself, but if it is not, it is normal practice to engage the services of a lawyer versed in immigration law.

- You can marry a United States citizen, although this will not automatically guarantee that you get a working permit.

- The Federal Government may offer an amnesty to illegal immigrants. This has happened in the past, but you cannot count on it happening in the future.

If you are hoping to enter the United States job market by the back door, you had better forget it, since any attempts to do so could count against you if you petition for a change of status in the future. Besides, immigration officials (particularly those at major ports of entry, such as New York and Los Angeles) can be very strict. If they suspect you are a job seeker posing as a tourist, they have powers to search you and your luggage. Should they find a job offer or job advertisements among your belongings, or discover that you have not enough cash to finance your visit, they could well refuse you entry.

That is why I recommend you try to get things right from the start. By wading through this chapter you should gain an insight into US immigration practices and what type of visa you should aim for.

THE 1990 IMMIGRATION LAW (IMMACT 90)

United States immigration law underwent a complete overhaul in 1990, and most of its provisions came into effect on 1st October 1991. You therefore need to make sure that any advice or information you get is completely up to date, otherwise you may find yourself setting off on completely the wrong track.

The information given below should serve as a guide, but do not regard it as the last word. If your position is a complicated one, you or any firm that wants to employ you will need to obtain advice from the nearest United States consulate (for applicants outside the United States), or the nearest Immigration and Naturalisation Department (INS) office (for applicants within the United States). Alternatively, you could refer to manuals such as Siegel and Canter's *United States Immigration Made Easy: the Insiders' Guide* or call on the services of an immigration lawyer.

If you decide to use a lawyer, the United States Embassy can supply you with a list of American immigration lawyers operating in the UK. Wherever you engage a legal adviser it is important to choose carefully, since there are some unscrupulous practitioners in the field of immigration law who charge a lot but deliver very little.

First, though, you need to decide how long you intend to be in the United States. If you do not intend to stay in the country permanently, but just for a matter of months or years, you will need a non-immigrant (temporary) visa of some kind, which in many cases can be extended.

Even if your long-term aim is permanent residence, there is no reason why you should not start off with a non-immigrant visa. For one thing, these are normally easier to obtain. There is nothing to prevent you from petitioning for adjustment of status to that of permanent resident at a later date once you are in the country.

NON-IMMIGRANT (TEMPORARY) VISAS

To determine what kind of visa you require you should ask yourself the following questions:

- Are you going purely for a holiday or for a business trip?

  You do not need a visa if your visit is for less than 90 days and you have an onward or return ticket. However, this concession is not available to nationals of all countries.

  A visa is necessary if you plan to stay longer and plan to fly or sail in a non-participating carrier—**B-1 business visitor visa, B-2 tourist visa.**

- Are you planning to undertake temporary vacation employment?

  or

  Do you want to undertake a paid traineeship (internship)?

  or

  Do you want to work as an au pair for a year?

  You will probably be eligible for exchange visitor status which is a fairly quick and straightforward process. It involves approaching a sponsoring organisation, such as BUNAC, Camp America, CIEE and certain au pair agencies, which are authorised to issue you with Form IAP-66. This enables you to obtain a category **J-1 visa.** Chapter Three deals with exchanges in detail.

- Do you plan to work in the United States on a temporary basis but do not qualify for an exchange visitor visa?

  You will need an **H-2 temporary worker visa.** However, first of all your prospective employer will need to apply to the state department of labor for labor certification and demonstrate that he has not been able to recruit a US resident for the post. In the case of non-graduates this can take time as the employer may be required to advertise the post locally first.

  If the job requires good qualifications, and you have them, you might be eligible for an **H-1B visa.**

- Are you planning to do a traineeship not covered by the exchange visitor visa?

  Your employer has to submit an application for an **H-3 industrial trainee visa** to the local office of the Immigration and Naturalisation Service (INS).

- Are you planning to study in the United States and work during the vacation?

  If you enter the United States on an **F visa** you are not normally entitled to take a job as well, though on-campus employment is permitted provided it does not displace a United States resident. If you want to undertake employment off-campus (for instance,

during the vacation), you will need to apply to the Immigration
and Naturalisation Service (INS) for permission.

● Are you involved in an approved cultural exchange programme?
  A new type of visa was introduced in IMMACT—the **Q Visa**—
  for people involved in demonstrating the customs, history and
  heritage of their home countries. The employer is responsible for
  the petitioning process. At the time of writing no programme has
  yet been approved, but it is felt that organisations such as
  Disneyworld might well come into this category.

● Are you a person considered outstanding in your particular field,
  for example as a scientist, artist or entertainer?
  You are eligible for an **H-1 visa** for which no prior labor
  certification is required.

● Do you have specialist knowledge to first degree level or beyond,
  equivalent experience, or a licence to practice?
  You are eligible to apply for a **H-1B visa** which will allow you
  to stay up to six years (with renewals). There is a quota of 65,000
  H-1B visas annually, and once the quota is used up no further
  visas can be issued until the start of the next fiscal year (which
  starts in October).
  First your prospective employer has to submit an attestation to
  the United States Department of Labor documenting the salary,
  working conditions and absence of a strike or lockout, and this
  process can take a little time. In the case of nurses and other
  professionals in great demand some of the red tape may be waived.

● Are you being sent to the United States by your company?
  You should be eligible for an **L-1 Intra Company Transferee
  visa**, provided you have worked for the company for one year
  during the three years preceding your application for a visa. The
  stay is limited to seven years for executives and managers and
  five years for individuals with specialist knowledge. There are
  usually few, if any, problems in obtaining visas for high-ranking
  executives.

● Are you seeking temporary admission to the United States to
  manage substantial trade between the United States and your own
  country?
  If so, you are eligible to apply for an **E-1 Treaty Trader visa**.
  However, you must have an executive or supervisory function or

	DO NOT WRITE IN THIS SPACE
1. SURNAMES OR FAMILY NAMES *(Exactly as in Passport)*	
2. FIRST NAME AND MIDDLE NAME *(Exactly as in Passport)*	
3. OTHER NAMES *(Maiden, Professional, Aliases)*	

4. DATE OF BIRTH			7. PASSPORT NUMBER
DAY	MONTH (letters)	YEAR	
5. PLACE OF BIRTH *(City, Province, Country)*			DATE PASSPORT ISSUED
6. NATIONALITY			DATE PASSPORT EXPIRES

8. HOME ADDRESS   *(Include apartment no., street, city, province and postal zone)*

9. NAME AND PRESENT ADDRESS OF PRESENT EMPLOYER OR SCHOOL
(Postal box number unacceptable)

10. HOME TELEPHONE NO.	11. BUSINESS TELEPHONE NO.

12. SEX ☐ Female ☐ Male	13. COLOR OF HAIR	14. COLOR OF EYES

15. COMPLEXION	16. HEIGHT	17. MARITAL STATUS
18. MARKS OF IDENTIFICATION		☐ Married ☐ Single ☐ Widowed ☐ Divorced ☐ Separated

19. NAMES AND RELATIONSHIPS OF PERSONS TRAVELING WITH YOU
(NOTE; A separate application must be made for a visa for each traveler, including children and infants.)

25. PRESENT OCCUPATION *(If retired, state past occupation)*

20. HAVE YOU EVER APPLIED FOR AN IMMIGRANT OR NONIMMIGRANT U.S. VISA BEFORE?
☐ No   ☐ Yes   Where?
☐ Visa was issued   When?
☐ Visa was refused   Type of visa?

26. AT WHAT ADDRESS WILL YOU STAY IN THE U.S.A.?

21. HAS YOUR U.S. VISA EVER BEEN CANCELED?
☐ No   ☐ Yes

27. WHAT IS THE PURPOSE OF YOUR TRIP?

22. Bearers of visitors visa may not work or study in the U.S.
DO YOU INTEND TO WORK IN THE U.S.?   ☐ No   ☐ Yes
If YES, explain

28. WHEN DO YOU INTEND TO ARRIVE IN THE U.S.A.?

29. HOW LONG DO YOU PLAN TO STAY IN U.S.A?

23. DO YOU INTEND TO STUDY IN THE U.S.? ☐ No ☐ Yes
If YES, write name and address of school as it appears on form I-20

30. DO YOU PLAN FUTURE TRIPS TO THE U.S.A. IF SO, WHEN?

24. WHO WILL FURNISH FINANCIAL SUPPORT INCLUDING TICKETS?

31. HAVE YOU EVER BEEN IN THE U.S.A.?
☐ No   ☐ Yes   When?
For how long?

NONIMMIGRANT VISA APPLICATION

COMPLETE ALL QUESTIONS ON REVERSE OF FORM

OPTIONAL FORM 156 (Rev. 6/88) PAGE 1

Fig. 9 Non-immigrant visa application

32. (a) HAS ANYONE EVER FILED AN IMMIGRANT VISA PETITION ON YOUR BEHALF?　☐ No　☐ Yes
(b) HAS LABOR CERTIFICATION FOR EMPLOYMENT IN THE UNITED STATES EVER
BEEN REQUESTED BY YOU OR ON YOUR BEHALF?　☐ No　☐ Yes
(c) HAVE YOU OR ANYONE ACTING FOR YOU EVER INDICATED TO A U.S. CONSULAR
OR IMMIGRATION EMPLOYEE A DESIRE TO IMMIGRATE TO THE U.S.?　☐ No　☐ Yes

33. ARE ANY OF THE FOLLOWING IN THE U.S.? (If YES, circle appropriate relationship and indicate what that
person is doing in the U.S., i.e. studying, working, etc.)

HUSBAND/WIFE _____　FIANCE/FIANCEE _____　BROTHER/SISTER_____

FATHER/MOTHER _____　SON/DAUGHTER _____

34. PLEASE LIST THE COUNTRIES WHERE YOU HAVE LIVED FOR MORE THAN SIX MONTHS DURING THE PAST
FIVE YEARS
　　　　　COUNTRIES　　　　　CITIES　　　　　APPROXIMATE DATES

35. IMPORTANT: ALL APPLICANTS MUST READ AND ANSWER THE FOLLOWING:

A visa may not be issued to persons who are within specific categories defined by law as inadmissible to the United
States (except when a waiver is obtained in advance). Complete information regarding these categories and whether
any may be applicable to you can be obtained from this office. Generally, they include persons:

- Afflicted with contagious diseases (e.g. tuberculosis) or who have suffered serious mental illness;

- Arrested, convicted for any offense or crime even though subject of a pardon, amnesty, or other such legal action;

- Believed to be narcotic addicts or traffickers;

- Deported from the U.S.A. within the last 5 years;

- Who have sought to obtain a visa by misrepresentation or fraud;

- Who are or have been members of certain organizations including Communist organizations and those affiliated
therewith;

- Who ordered, incited, assisted, or otherwise participated in the persecution of any person because of race, religion,
national origin, or political opinion under the control, direct or indirect, of the Nazi Government of Germany, or of the
government of any area occupied by, or allied with, the Nazi Government of Germany.

DO ANY OF THESE APPEAR TO APPLY TO YOU?

NO ☐　　　　　YES ☐

If YES, or if you have any question in this regard, personal appearance at this office is recommended. If it is not possible at
this time, attach a statement of facts in your case to this application.

36. I certify that I have read and understood all these questions set forth in this application, and the answers I have furnished
on this form are true and correct to the best of my knowledge and belief. I understand that possession of a visa does
not entitle the bearer to enter the United States of America upon arrival at a port of entry if he or she is found inadmissible.

DATE OF APPLICATION _____

APPLICANT'S SIGNATURE _____

If this application has been prepared by a travel agency or another person on your behalf, the agent should indicate
name and address of agency or person with appropriate signature of individual preparing form.

SIGNATURE OF PERSON PREPARING FORM _____

DO NOT WRITE IN THIS SPACE

HAVE YOU COMPLIED WITH THE FOLLOWING?

1. Answered ALL 35 questions completely
2. SIGNED and DATED the form
3. Affixed ONE PHOTO
4. DETACHED and RETAINED information sheet
5. Included ADDRESSED STAMPED ENVELOPE

37 mm × 37 mm
1½ inches × 1½ inches

———— PHOTO ————

Glue or staple
photo here

OPTIONAL FORM 156 (REV.6/88) PAGE 2　　　　　(This form is free of charge) be performing services that are essential to the company's operation in the United States. The company must also show that it is engaged in continuous trade of a substantial nature between the United States and a country with which the United States has a Treaty of Commerce and Navigation.

● Are you seeking temporary admission in order to develop and/or direct a substantial investment in the United States?
You are eligible to apply for **E-2 Treaty Investor** status based on the following criteria:
—investment of substantial funds
—the enterprise is up and running
—the investment is more than marginal
—you are in a position to develop and direct the enterprise.
Employees of a Treaty Investor are also eligible if they are executives, highly trained staff or essential to the operation by reason of their qualifications.
For anyone in the E category the initial period of a stay is one year, but this can be extended almost indefinitely.

Other types of visa

There are various other categories of non-immigrant visa, such as for diplomats and for the staff of international organisations, but in most cases the employer is responsible for getting the visa, and this procedure presents no real problems.

If you intend to study in the United States it is also necessary to obtain a visa, and the institution where you plan to study will provide you with the appropriate form (I-20A). However, bear in mind that a study visa does not automatically grant you the right to work on a part-time or seasonal basis. If you wish to do so, you should apply for permission to accept employment on Form I-538. This form also needs to be completed if you want to extend your stay or transfer for another academic institution.

Applying for a non-immigrant (temporary) visa

1. The first step
This will normally be to get in touch with the nearest United States consulate or INS office to find out which procedures you must go through.

● Anyone participating in an exchange must obtain **Form IAP-66** from the sponsoring organisation (eg BUNAC, CIEE).

- In many circumstances the sponsoring employer must file a **Petition to Classify a Non-Immigrant as a Temporary Worker or Trainee (Form I-129B)** check. After that you may need to provide documentation: academic diplomas and certificates, testimonials, contract or letter of appointment.
- Treaty Traders or Investors need to submit a report of their status **(Form I-126)**.

2. Approval of the application

When the application is approved the INS issues the **Notice of Approval of Non-Immigrant Visa** petition **(Form I-171C)** to the consulate that is dealing with your application.

If your application is turned down, you may appeal to the regional commissioner in control of the INS or the consulate to which you have applied.

3. Immigration procedures on arrival in the United States.

On arrival at the port of entry make sure you look reasonably presentable. Immigration officers have been known to refuse entry to people whose appearance is bohemian or unkempt, even if they are quite respectable citizens. If entry is refused unjustly, you have a right to appeal.

The length of time you are permitted to stay in the United States is entered on your **INS Arrival/Departure Record (Form I-94)**. This is an important document which will play a part in any subsequent immigration procedures and you should take good care of it.

4. Extension or change of status

Once in the United States you can apply for an adjustment of non-immigrant status (by filing **Form I-506**) or for an extension to your stay (by filing **Form I-539**). This will normally be done through the local district office of the Immigration and Naturalization Service—the addresses of which are in Appendix G.

If your application is not granted you can ask for a review—a 'motion to reopen and reconsider' in officialese.

The main types of Non-Immigrant (Temporary) Visa

B-1	Business visitor
B-2	Tourist
F-1	Foreign Student
E-1	Treaty Trader
E-2	Treaty Investor

L-1   Company transfer
H-1   Distinguished Person
H-1B   Specialist
H-2   Skilled or unskilled
H-3   Trainee
J-1   Exchange visitor
Q   Cultural programme participant

IMMIGRANT VISAS

The chances are that you will be able to skip the second half of this chapter. Immigrant visas are generally more difficult to obtain, and in any case the majority of people from the British Isles who go to work in the United States do so on non-immigrant (temporary) visas, which have already been dealt with.

However, if at some time in the future you decide to settle permanently in the United States you will need to apply for immigrant status and an Alien Registration Receipt Card (the 'green card'). (Later on you may decide to go the whole hog and become a naturalised United States citizen, but that will not be discussed in this book).

Full immigrant status can be granted on the basis of:

● family relationships
● your trade or profession (employment based preferences)
● other criteria

Family relationships
If you have close relatives living in the United States this can generally facilitate matters. During the fiscal years 1992 to 1994 the level of family sponsored immigration is set at 465,000, and this quota rises to 480,000 in 1995.

Immediate relatives
● Are you the spouse or child of a United States citizen?
● Are you the parents of United States citizens who are 21 years old or more?

In both the above cases numerical limits do not apply and you should therefore experience no difficulty in getting an immigrant visa.

Family sponsored preferences
Here you have to stand in the queue to take up places that have not been taken up by immediate relatives. The annual numerical limit is determined by subtracting the previous year's immediate relative total from the specified world-wide level of family sponsored immigrants (i.e. 465,000 or 480,000). The following questions will help you work out whether you qualify:

● Are you the unmarried son or daughter of a United States citizen? You come under **FSP 1** where there is a quota of 23,400.

● Are you the spouse or child of a permanent resident? You come under **FSP 2A** for which there is a minimum quota of 87,394.

● Are you the unmarried son or daughter of a permanent resident and over 21? You come under **FSP 2B** for which there is a minimum quota of 26,266.

● Are you the married son or daughter of a citizen? You come under **FSP 3** for which there is a quota of 23,400.

● Are you the brother or sister of a citizen aged 21 years or over? You come under **FSP 4** for which there is a quota of 65,000 a year.

● Are you the spouse or child of a legalised alien? From 1992 to 1994 there will be an annual quota of 55,000.

Employment Based Preferences
If you have no family connections in the United States you may be able to enter the country on the strength of your employment or entrepreneurial skills. Under the new Immigration Act the number of employment based immigrants has been increased substantially from 54,000 to 140,000. Work out whether you qualify by asking:

● Are you an individual with extraordinary ability in the arts, sciences, education, business or athletics?
● Are you a professor or researcher recognised internationally as outstanding in your field and with three years' experience, entering the United States for a tenured or tenure track position?

- Are you a multinational executive or manager employed with the sponsoring employer or affiliate for at least one year in the three years preceding your application for residence in or entry to the United States?

Anyone who fits the above criteria is regarded as a **Priority Worker** and falls into **Employment-Based Preference Category One** for which the annual quota is 40,000. No labour certification approval is required.

- Do you possess advanced qualifications in a professional field?
- Are you a person of exceptional ability in the arts, sciences or business?

If so, you could be considered for **Employment-Based Preference Category Two, Members of the Professions**, for which the quota is 40,000 plus any unused visas from Category One. While it is not necessary to have worked for the same company for a year before entry to the country, labor certification is required. This means that employers need to obtain a certificate from the Department of Labor demonstrating that there are not sufficient United States workers who are able, willing, qualified and available for the position in which they are seeking to recruit an alien.

- Are you a skilled worker with a minimum of two years' training or experience?
- Are you a professional with a Bachelor's degree?
- Is there a shortage of workers in your trade in the United States?

You fall into **Employment-Based Preference Category Three, Professionals, Skilled and Unskilled Workers**, for which the quota is 40,000 plus any unused visas from Categories One and Two. However, no more than 10,000 visas are available to Unskilled Workers. Labor Certification is required (see above).

- Are you a minister of religion or religious worker?
- Are you an overseas employee of the United States Government?
- Are you an employee of certain international organisations?
- Are you a current or former employee of the United States Government?

You fall into **Employment-Based Preference Category Four—Special Immigrants,** which also includes Panama Canal employees and others. The quota is 10,000, but there is a limit of 5,000 on religious workers who are eligible only during the fiscal years 1992 to 1994. Presumably after this time such workers might be eligible for Diversity Immigrant Status.

● Are you an investor in a new commercial enterprise that will create full-time employment for at least ten persons who are not members of your immediate family?

Employment Based Preference Category Five sets aside 10,000 visas for foreign investors, of which not less than 3,000 are reserved for investors in rural or high unemployment areas. The minimum investment is normally $1 million but may be lower in such areas.

Other categories of immigrant visa

Diversity Immigrants
Beginning in October 1994 a new category of visa will come into effect under which applicants from certain countries will be selected in random order. Applicants will be required to have either a high school education or at least two years' work experience in an occupation that requires two years' training or experience. Only one petition may be submitted each year and there will be a quota of 55,000.

The AA-1 Immigrant Visa Programme
During the fiscal years 1991-2, 1992-3 and 1993-4 only, 40,000 immigrant visas are available to the nationals of 34 countries 'adversely affected' by the 1965 immigration reform legislation. This includes people of British and, more especially, Irish nationality.

In 1991 the application period for the 1991-1992 fiscal year (October to September) was from noon on October 14th to noon on October 20th. Applications bearing the applicant's name, address, date and place of birth (and also those of spouse and children, if any) and nearest United States consulate had to be sent to AA-1 Program, PO Box 60000, Arlington, VA 2218-0001.

Applications on this occasion were made on a first-come-first-served basis and the system proved chaotic. It is therefore possible that in future years the procedure will be modified. If you plan to apply under this scheme you need to contact your nearest United States embassy or consulate for the latest details.

Refugees and asylum seekers
Registration for classification as a refugee requires the completion of Form I-590, and for an asylum seeker Form I-589.

Immigrant visas: application procedure

1. The first step

- For a visa under the **AA-1 Visa Programme** no special form is needed in the first instance (see above).

- For a family sponsored immigrant visa your relative should normally file a petition (Form I-130) with the local office of the Immigration and Naturalisation Service (INS) in the United States.

- For an employment based immigrant visa, Form I-140 is required. Members of the professions, professionals, skilled and unskilled workers must have their petitions filed by their prospective employers, but first the Department of Labor must certify that there are no qualified workers available for the proposed job. Priority Workers may petition on their own behalf with the INS in the United States.

- Special immigrants must file a Form I-1360 petition with an INS office.

- Investors should file a Form I-526 petition with the INS.

2. Preliminary application
In most cases the consulate will send you two forms: the **Preliminary Questionnaire for Residence (OF-169)** and the **Biographic Data for Visa Purposes Form (OF-179)**.

3. Interview
Eventually you will be called for an interview and need to submit an **Application of Immigrant Visa and Alien Registration (Form 230)**. The consular officer will inform visa applicants of the documents required to support the application (eg. passport, birth certificate, police certificates).

4. Medical Examination
You will need to undergo a medical examination conducted by a doctor designated by the consular officer, and for which a fee is payable.

5. Visa fees
A fee is payable for the visa which is not refundable.

6. Issue of a visa
Immigrant visas are issued in the chronological order in which the petitions were filed, and you should not rely on being issued with a visa very promptly. If you fall into a category which is over-subscribed there may be a waiting period of some years.

7. Arrival in the United States
On arrival the immigration authorities will stamp a temporary 'green card' stamp in your passport. Your alien registration receipt card will be sent to you in the post several months later.

Applying for immigrant status in the United States
If you decide to apply for permanent residence once you are in the country, you will normally need to contact the INS office closest to your place of residence. Applications are usually sent by post, but some offices can deal with you in person.

Note that it is not a case of 'once an immigrant always an immigrant'. If you leave the United States you could lose your immigrant status. To avoid this, you should obtain a re-entry permit if you plan to stay outside the United States for more than a year. This involves completing **Form I-130 Application for Issuance or Extension of Permit to Re-enter the United States**. If you take out citizenship, this formality is no longer necessary.

PEOPLE NOT ELIGIBLE FOR VISAS

Certain visa applicants are likely to be turned down. The main categories are:

- sufferers of communicable diseases (eg tuberculosis)
- people with a dangerous physical or mental disorder
- people who have committed serious criminal acts
- terrorists, subversives, members of a totalitarian party
- people likely to become public charges in the United States

- anyone who has used fraud or other illegal means to enter the United States.

If you have been an exchange visitor in the past you may have to live outside the United States for two years before you can apply for a visa, while physicians who plan to practise medicine must pass a qualifying exam before they can get an immigrant visa.

3
Vacation Jobs and Exchanges

This book draws a distinction between people who are interested in spending a substantial part of their careers or lives in the United States and those whose aims are short-term. Young people, for instance, want to experience the country at first hand and are prepared to undertake a variety of vacation jobs in order to finance their trip. Others, both young and old, are keen to go to America in order to develop skills in their particular fields.

While anyone wishing to undertake employment needs to obtain a visa, if you are participating in a recognised exchange programme this process is usually little more than a formality. There are a number of agencies based in Britain and Ireland which are authorised by the US Government to issue the necessary documentation (the IAP-66 form) for obtaining the **J-1 Exchange Visitor Visa**, though for some programmes different arrangements may be necessary. The most significant of these are listed towards the end of the chapter.

You must bear in mind that you may only work under the terms of the exchange programme and are not eligible to seek other employment while you are in the United States. Nor will you normally be allowed to take up employment there within two years of the exchange. On the brighter side you are automatically exempt from paying US social security and income tax, and the visa is issued free.

Unfortunately for most of these exchange programmes a limit is placed on numbers of participants and eligibility criteria are often restrictive. If you find that you do not qualify for any of the programmes mentioned in this chapter, you will have to look into the possibility of obtaining a different kind of visa, and this can take time. For an **H-2 Temporary Worker Visa** or an **H-3 Industrial Trainee Worker** the prospective employer has to obtain the necessary labor certification first, and you will be subject to social security tax.

THE OPPORTUNITIES

Working in children's camps

A great many American youngsters—some seven million—spend their summer holidays in camps run by organisations such as the YMCA, the scouting organisations, religious or philanthropic agencies as well as by private individuals. There are over 12,000 camps in all; some are fully residential and in areas of natural beauty, while others are in effect day centres providing recreational facilities during the hours of daylight.

There are broadly two types of post available.

Camp counsellors

These are camp leaders or organisers who put together a programme of activities and encourage their protegees to participate. This can be challenging work, since American youngsters can be lively and precocious, and you may well be expected to demonstrate that you have experience of dealing with children.

As the ICCP brochure points out:

'Spending a summer as a camp counsellor in an American camp may not be for everyone; it can mean long days, hard work and little privacy and spare time. Working as a camp counsellor can also mean a lot of adjustments while living in a simple and often isolated setting. Participation in ICCP is not a low-cost ticket to "see the USA" or a money-making summer job.'

Ancillary staff

These are the backroom boys and girls—the cooks, the cleaners, the people who maintain the campsite. This can turn out to be tiring work involving long hours, especially at the beginning of the camp season when there can be much to prepare. Flexibility and a capacity for hard work are essential.

The *Parents' Guide to Accredited Camps* published by the American Camping Association lists around 2,500 summer camps and includes a section on the camp job market. See also BUNAC, AIFS, Camp Counsellors USA and YMCA entries in this chapter.

Other vacation jobs in the United States

There are a number of seasonal jobs available, especially during the summer in resorts around the country. If you are still a student it may well be possible to enter the US on an Exchange Visitor visa provided you set about things the right way. The jobs do not have to

For counsellors

0700	Wake up call
0745	Flag raising
0800-0830	Breakfast
0830-0900	Clean-up
0900-1200	Activities
1200-1230	Lunch
1230-1330	Rest hour
1330-1700	Activities
1730-1830	Dinner service
1800-1830	Dinner
1900-2100	Evening activities
2100-2200	Lights out
2400-0100	Curfew—All staff back in cabins

For ancillary staff

0630	Kitchen duties begin
0730-0800	Breakfast service and auxiliary duties begin
0800-0830	Office duties begin
0830-1200	General duties
1130-1230	Lunch service duties
	(1-2 hours off midday)
1230-1700	Resume duties
1800-2030	Resume auxiliary duties
	(Evenings usually off duty)
2400-0100	Curfew—All staff back in cabins

Fig. 10. A typical Camp America Schedule.

be related to your course subjects or your intended profession, and may well pay better than jobs in summer camps.

The current *Summer Employment Directory of Jobs in the United States* will give you an idea of the types of jobs available. Many of the jobs are seasonal ones in summer resorts, notably in the hotel and catering industry. The National Park Service has openings virtually everywhere, and in states such as Colorado guiding jobs are available.

There are also behind the scenes jobs with summer theatres, in amusement and theme parks and on ranches. In the bigger conurbations temporary office work may be available. If you are particularly enterprising and lucky, you may find more unusual employment. BUNAC reports that three participants on its programmes have worked as a masseuse, an oyster digger and a private detective!

There are two ways of setting about getting a job under the exchange visitor scheme:

- You arrange your job in advance and apply to an agency such as BUNAC that can issue an **IAP-66** form. Many people do this through personal contacts in the United States or by applying to organisations mentioned in handbooks such as *Summer Employment Directory of the United States.*

- You try your luck at getting a job on arrival. However, in order to qualify for an Exchange Visitor Visa, you will need to find a private sponsor in the United States who is acceptable to the authorities. You can either contact employers direct or try an employment agency specialising in temporary work. **The National Association of Temporary Services** is the trade body for these. (See also Chapter Six.)

Au pair work
It is now possible, if you are aged between 18 and 25, to spend a year working as an au pair on an Exchange Visitor Visa. There are two main programmes:

- **Au Pair in America** administered by the American Institute for Foreign Study (AIFS)
- **Au Pair Homestay USA** organised by EIL (Experiment in International Living) Ltd.

Both schemes are recognised by the Federal Government.

For jobs in the United States you will normally be expected to have some experience of looking after children, and also to be a car driver and a non-smoker. You will be required to look after the children and undertake light household duties for around 40 hours a week. In return you receive:

- pocket money of around $100 a week
- your board and lodging
- your travel expenses
- up to six hours a week of classes in a subject of your choosing.

If you would prefer to work as an au pair just for the summer, the AIFS runs the **Family Companion** programme under which you will be expected to work for ten weeks, in return for which your air fares will be paid and you will receive board and lodging and an allowance of $300. One perk is that you may be required to accompany your host family on holiday.

A number of people enter America as tourists in order to take up positions as au pairs and nannies, but this is a risky business these days. For instance, you could be turned back by immigration officials at your port of entry; or your employers could be fined for illegally employing an alien.

An excellent reference book for would-be au pairs is *The Au Pair and Nanny's Guide* by Susan Griffith and Sharon Legg (Vacation Work).

Internships

An internship is not a prison sentence but an opportunity to gain work experience, normally in one's chosen career field. Students on vocationally based courses in Britain tend to get placements in the British Isles, but if you wish to gain international experience, why not try for a placement in the United States? Among the organisations that can facilitate such a move are **AIESEC** (business sector), the **Central Bureau** (hotel and catering sector), **IAESTE** (technical and scientific placements), the **Mountbatten Internship Programme** and **CIEE** (most sectors). If your college or employer can arrange an internship for a US national in the UK on a reciprocal basis, so much the better.

While an internship may last up to 18 months, many are much shorter, and are confined to vacations. To get an idea of the range of internships available, you should browse through a copy of the directory *Internships* (Writers' Digest). A significant proportion of internships in the directory are open to non-Americans, provided they have the necessary documentation, including federal government jobs in Washington. Some offer salaries; others do not.

Professional exchanges

These exchanges should be seen not so much as a chance to earn money as a form of professional development. Sometimes these exchanges are organised by professional organisations. Teachers and academics need to look to either the Central Bureau or the Fullbright Commission.

Post-to-post exchanges are available for teachers and lecturers with at least five years' experience. Although posts can be exchanged for a term, it is more usual for people to spend a complete academic year abroad. Under the Central Bureau scheme, teachers from the UK are seconded on full salary and receive a grant to offset the increased cost of living and travel expenses.

Other exchange programmes exist for nurses and young farmers and are arranged by their national organisations, and for youth workers with the American Youth Work Center. There are also opportunities for artists, librarians, policemen, screenwriters and others with the Fullbright Commission. If you belong to a professional organisation it would be worthwhile enquiring whether it operates any exchange scheme.

THE PRINCIPAL AGENCIES

AIESEC UK
UKIN House
26 Phipp Street
London EC2A 4NR
Tel: (071) 739 9847

An international organisation specialising in exchanges for students of business (eg accountancy, finance, marketing, business administration, computing). There are local branches throughout the UK in higher education institutions, and students apply through, or are nominated by their local branches. Normally AIESEC arranges very few placements in the United States.

American Institute for Foreign Study (UK) Ltd
37 Queen's Gate, London SW7 5HR
Tel: (071) 581 2730 (Au Pair in America)
and (071) 589 3223 (Camp America).
This organisation sponsors four exchange visitor programmes. The first step in the application involves arranging an interview with the local representative of AIFS who will forward your application to London.

Au Pair in America
This AIFS programme offers a one-year stay with a family in the USA, four days' orientation on arrival with accommodation and free air travel from London to your destination. Follow up is provided by a network of community counsellors in 130 cities throughout the USA, and if you and your host family prove incompatible you will

be able to transfer during the initial stages. You will need to pay a deposit of around £300 which is refunded on successful completion of the contract.

Camp America Family Companion Summer Programme
This offers a placement of from ten to 13 weeks as an au pair starting in early June. Some experience of baby-minding is required and possession of a driving licence is desirable. The age limit is 18 to 24. Normally you will have two weeks' paid holiday and one-and-a-half days off per week.

Camp America Camp Counsellor Programme
This programme has been in operation since 1969 and places around 7,000 people a year in over 1,000 camps. It is open to suitable people aged between 18 and 35. The commitment is for nine to ten weeks and participants must be able to start in June.

Camp America Campower Programme
This is for people who do not qualify for counsellor positions, though in this case participants have to be full-time students. Many of the jobs are kitchen jobs, but people with secretarial and technical skills are also needed as are janitors, groundsmen and nightwatchmen.

American Youth Work Center
1751 N Street NW, Suite 302
Washington, DC 20036
AYWC's Children and Youth Practical Training Exchange Program enables foreign youth workers in the early stages of their careers (usually under 30) to receive 12-18 months' practical training with American youth service agencies. You will receive similar wage and fringe benefits to American youth workers.

Whereas in the British Isles youth service is an education-based service, in the United States it involves dealing with young people with problems, including young offenders, runaways and drug addicts. Experience in social work, drug counselling, mental health as well as youth and community work would be of relevance. Over 50 placements are made annually.

Applicants in the UK or Ireland should contact the AYWC Practical Training Exchange Programme at either the Central Bureau, Seymour Mews House, Seymour Mews, London W1H 9PE or National Youth Council of Ireland, 3 Montague Street, Dublin 2.

British Universities North America Club (BUNAC)
16 Bowling Green Lane
London EC1R 0BD
Tel: (071) 251 3472.

This is a non-profit, non-political educational student club with branches on many university campuses throughout the UK. Current membership fees are £3 annually.

Since 1962 BUNAC has operated general student work exchange programmes and is recognised by the appropriate government agencies in Britain and the United States. It runs similar schemes in Canada, Australia and Jamaica, and works in conjunction with the travel bureau of:

The Union of Students in Ireland (USIT)
19 Aston Quay
Dublin 2
Tel: (Dublin) 778117.

In a normal year it handles up to 10,000 placements.

For all three of its programmes, in return for an administration fee BUNAC deals with the paperwork and arranges orientations, insurance and cheap flights to the United Sates. The programmes are:

BUNACAMP
This involves working as a camp counsellor (leader) in a children's holiday camp. To be eligible for this programme you need to be aged 19½ to 35, but not necessarily a student. You need to have experience of working with children, or medical or secretarial skills. If you are interested, you need to apply for an interview. Interviewing starts in November and carries on until early May, but it is a case of the early bird catching the worm: the sooner you apply, the better your chance of getting a placement.

Kitchen and Maintenance Programme (KAMP)
This programme also involves working at children's summer camps in an ancillary capacity, doing a variety of jobs such as cooking, laundry, cleaning, site maintenance and driving. You need to be a full-time student and a member of BUNAC, and also to attend an orientation session during the Easter vacation. You apply through BUNAC for positions listed in the KAMP directory ranking them in order of choice.

Work America
This is a more flexible programme sponsored by the Council on International Educational Exchange which enables you to take up any summer job, but quota restrictions are imposed—currently around 4,500. In order to qualify you need to demonstrate you can support yourself in one of three ways:

1. You have a definite job offer for the summer months.
2. You have a private American sponsor who could take financial responsibility for you.
3. You have an indefinite or vague offer of a job or private sponsorship backed up by substantial funds.

Many people find their jobs through the *Work America Job Directory* obtainable from BUNAC, but there is no reason why you should not make your own employment arrangements. If you can find a private sponsor, you will be able to go to the United States on spec.

Camp Counsellors USA
28A Gordon Road
West Bridgeford
Nottingham NG2 5LN.

This programme operates along similar lines to BUNACAMP and Camp America and is for people between the ages of 19 and 28 (including teachers and nurses). Applications are accepted between October and March for the coming summer. The organisation arranges orientations in Britain and in New York and provides free insurance and air fares. The minimum commitment is for nine weeks. International Headquarters is at:

698 Emerson Street
Palo Alto
CA 94301.

Central Bureau for Educational Visits and Exchanges
Seymour Mews House
Seymour Mews
London W1H 9PE
Tel: (071) 486 5101.

3 Bruntsfield Crescent
Edinburgh

EH10 4HD
Tel: (031) 447 8024.

16 Malone Road
Belfast BT9 5BN
Tel: (0232) 664418.

The Bureau's activities include:

Post-to-post exchanges for teachers and lecturers
More than a hundred British educators exchange their jobs with
American partners each year. The American side of the exchange is
handled by the **United States Information Agency** (USIA).

General Career Development Programme
This programme enables qualified professionals to work in an
American company for up to 18 months. The position contains a
training component and has to be related to a person's previous
experience. Participants are responsible for finding their own placements, and every year the Central Bureau assists on average 150
people to gain entry to the United States. For this programme the
Central Bureau also assists students from Ireland.

Hotel and Culinary Programme
This is for students and graduates of hotel and catering management
and on average 100 placements are made each year. Nine out of ten
participants arrange their own placements, but a placement service is
available.

The General Career Development Programme and the Hotel and
Culinary Programme are administered in the United States by:

The Association for Practical Training (AIPT)
Park View Building
Suite 320
1048-0 Little Patuxent Parkway
Columbia
MD 21044
Tel: (301) 997 2200.

Council on International Educational Exchange (CIEE)
33 Seymour Place
London W1H 6AT
Tel: (071) 706 3008.

CIEE is the UK affiliate of a private, non-profit organisation in the United States which promotes educational exchanges between America and other countries. It works in cooperation with organisations such as BUNAC and the Central Bureau. CIEE's Internship Programme enables students to undertake a period of work experience in the United States lasting up to a year. Students are responsible for finding their own work placements, but CIEE handles all the paperwork, offers insurance cover and can provide various support services, including an orientation day. If the proposed internship is for longer than six months, a letter must be provided from a British employer offering an internship to a qualified American during the same calendar year.

Experiment in International Living (EIL Ltd)
Otesaga
West Malvern Road
Upper Wyche
Malvern
Worcs WR14 4EN
Tel: (06845) 62577.

Norwood
1 Rosslyn
Killarney Road
Bray
Co Wicklow
Ireland
Tel: (Dublin) 829284.

This organisation operates in much the same way as AIFS (see above), except that interviews are conducted in Worcestershire (or Dublin) and there is a one-day orientation before departure, as well as a two-day orientation on arrival in the United States. If things do not work out, transfer to another family is possible during the first month. A refundable deposit is payable plus an administration charge.

The Fullbright Commission
US-UK Educational Commission
6 Porter Street
London W1M 2HR
Tel: (071) 486 10987697
Fax: (071) 224 4567.

The Commission organises a programme of educational and cultural exchanges enabling people in some 130 countries to travel to the

United States for advanced study, teaching or research. Among the awards are **Faculty Exchange Fellowships** which enable a British academic to exchange posts with an American academic for a limited period.

There are also awards for academic administrators, artists, fashion designers, film and TV practitioners, librarians, police, screenwriters —and crime writers.

International Agricultural Exchange Programme
National Federation of Young Farmer's Clubs
National Agricultural Centre
Kenilworth
Warwickshire CV8 2LG
Tel: (0203) 696584.

A work exchange programme for young people aged between 18 and 28 with at least two years' experience in agriculture.

The International Agricultural Exchange Programme, Tel: (0203) 696578, at the same address, offers exchanges of up to 14 months.

International Association for the Exchange of Students for Technical Experience (IAESTE)
Central Bureau
Seymour Mews House
Seymour Mews
London W1H 9PE
Tel: (071) 486 5101.

Founded at Imperial College London in 1948, this is a world-wide organisation represented in over 50 countries. It offers short-term, course-related work experience in three broad categories: scientific (eg in a company laboratory or research institute), professional (work designed to improve your professional capabilities) and manual (with little technical content but offering an insight into foreign work patterns and conditions).

The scheme is open to full-time students between 19 and 30 who must normally be nominated by an educational institution or sponsored by a company in the UK. IASTE welcomes reciprocal placements for incoming foreign trainees. Placements in the United States tend to be of several months' duration. The organisation works closely with AIPT in the US.

Mountbatten Internship Programme
16 Gloucester Street
Oxford OX1 2BN

Tel: (0865) 793333.

The Programme offers school leavers work experience opportunities in New York City in the year between school and college. It also organises a business internship programme for graduates with qualifications in secretarial studies, management, accountancy or business studies.

Royal College of Nursing

20 Cavendish Square

London W1M 0AB

Tel: (071) 409 3333.

The College administers a scheme known as the **ICN Programme** to enable members to gain overseas experience.

Winant-Clayton Volunteer Association

38 Newark Street

London E1 2AA

Tel: (071) 375 0547.

There are opportunities for up to 20 volunteers a year to undertake work on various community projects in New York or on the East Coast for around two months. The projects include residential and day centres for the physically and mentally handicapped, psychiatric rehabilitation centres, play schemes for inner city children and luncheon clubs for the elderly.

Volunteers receive board, lodging and pocket money during their placement, but are normally expected to pay the air fare. However, a few bursaries are available. Applications need to be submitted by early January.

John Winant, incidentally, was the US Ambassador to Britain during the Second World War who brought groups of Americans over to Britain to do voluntary social work in association with Rev 'Tubby' Clayton, the founder of Toc H.

YMCA International Camp Counsellor Programme (ICCP)

National Council of YMCAs

640 Forest Road

London E17 3DZ.

This is another programme which recruits staff for more than 400 children's summer camps. These are organised not only by the YMCA itself, but also by scouting organisations and individuals. Some camps cater for disadvantaged and handicapped people or concentrate on teaching special skills.

The age range for applicants is between 20 and 30, though camp staff usually range in age from 18-23. Camps vary in size and some may have as many as 100 staff working in different capacities. The main need is for

- **General counsellors** who live with and supervise groups of six to ten campers, care for camper health and safety, organise camp activities and assist in specific programme areas.
- **Skill specialists** who organise and teach specific activities, such as swimming, sports or crafts
- **YMAK participants**, ancillary staff involved in cooking, office work and general maintenance.

In some camps staff may perform more than one of these roles.

A placement lasts nine to ten weeks, and you will be provided with air fares, medical insurance, pocket money and support services.

Other organisations
Christian Movement for Peace
Bethnal Green United Reformed Church
Pott Street
London E2 oEF
Tel: (071) 729 1877.

International Voluntary Service
162 Upper New Walk
Leicester LE1 7QA
Tel: (0533) 549430.

United Nations Association
International Youth Service
Welsh Centre for International Affairs
Temple of Peace
Cathays Park
Cardiff CF1 3AP
Tel: (0222) 223088.

These organisations organise placements of up to one month's duration, often at international workcamps in the United States.

FURTHER READING

Working Holidays, (Central Bureau).

Summer Employment Directory of the United States, (Writer's Digest Books).

Internships, (Writer's Digest Books).

Volunteer Work, (Central Bureau).

Directory of International Internships, (Office of Overseas Study, Michigan State University, East Lansing, MI 48824, USA).

Advisory List of International Travel and Exchange Programs, (Council on Standards for International Educational Travel, 1906 Association Drive, Reston, VA 22091, USA).

4
Arranging a Job Before You Leave

Much of the rest of this book concentrates on the needs of people who are planning to work in the United States for a period of years rather than months. Chapter Six will be of more interest to people who are already in possession of a work permit, stand a good chance of getting one or qualify for permanent residence because of close family ties. If you do not fall into this category, your search starts here.

As stressed before in this book, you normally need an offer of employment before you can obtain a visa entitling you to work in the United States. Unfortunately, even if you are offered a position there, you cannot always count on a visa being forthcoming. You stand a good chance, however, if you possess good qualifications and you have skills that are in short supply in the locality of the employer.

This, though, is putting the cart before the horse. Finding a job is the initial step, so first take a look at ways and means of accomplishing it.

ADVERTISEMENTS

If you see a job advertised, it is reasonable to assume that there is a genuine vacancy to be filled. Sometimes the advertiser is the employer himself; but increasingly employers are using intermediaries (recruitment consultants and employment agencies) to find their staff.

Advertisements in British or Irish newspapers and journals
If the advertisement appears in a publication in a country outside the United States it means that the job is open to non-Americans and that the employer is reasonably confident that he can obtain the necessary authorisation for the issue of a work permit.

The majority of job advertisements tend to be placed not by the companies or organisations themselves but by intermediaries working on their behalf based in the UK or Ireland. These intermediaries will be familiar with British procedures and terminology, and you will normally need to send your application with a British style CV to an address in the British Isles.

If you have to apply to an address in the United States, you should not assume that the recipient is completely au fait with British qualifications and working practice. If you are a member of a professional association, write out your designation in full and explain what it means; the same goes for qualifications such as 'A' Level and City and Guilds. You may also need to draft an American style résumé in preference to a British style CV in order to comply with local labor laws.

Virtually every national daily or Sunday newspaper carries advertisements for jobs in America from time to time. You should also peruse professional journals for vacancies, such as *Computer Weekly* in the case of IT experts, and *Nursing Times* for nurses.

Advertisements in international job papers

The overwhelming number of advertisements in newspapers and journals tend to be for posts within the UK (or Eire, in the case of Irish publications), but there are a number of publications that concentrate on the would-be expatriate, including one which concentrates on jobs in the United States: the fortnightly *Jobtrac USA*.

Others which may include jobs in the United States are: *Overseas Jobs Express, Nexus, Careers International, Job Finder* and *Home and Away*. Their addresses are listed in Appendix D. There are also job listings which reproduce advertisements from other periodicals, but these may not be completely up to date.

Advertisements in the American Press

While some American employers may welcome applications from overseas, the majority will be looking for someone who is already resident in the country. Working on the principle that a bird in the hand is always worth two in a bush, employers will prefer to hire someone who is on the spot, not several thousand miles away.

Unless the employer is recruiting for a senior or highly specialised post, or has a number of vacancies, it will probably not be worth the time, effort and cost to set up an interview abroad and go through a lot of red tape with the Immigration and Naturalisation Service (INS). Only if the organisation cannot find the candidates it wants will its personnel department look further afield.

This is not to say that there is no point at all in looking through the adverts in US journals and magazines. These may not lead you to a specific position, but they will give you an idea of the opportunities available and the salary you could expect. Such information will come in extremely useful if you decide to try speculative approaches to find a job. But on the whole you would need to be very lucky to land a position this way.

The disadvantages

Advertisements, of course, have one major disadvantage: they often elicit a large number of applicants, the majority of whom never reach the shortlist.

In order to avoid being screened out in the early stages of the sifting process, you need to make a special effort and tailor your application to fit the specifications laid down in the advertisement, either by adapting your CV accordingly or by writing a carefully worded letter. Appendix E should give you a few ideas.

There is a school of thought that advises would-be candidates to get ahead of the competition. This means adopting a speculative approach to finding a job, seeking out vacancies before they are advertised. How does one do it?

SPECULATIVE APPLICATIONS

Recruitment consultants in the UK

The role of intermediaries in the recruitment process has already been mentioned. Firms in the United States, like those in the UK, very often delegate their recruitment. So rather than send off applications to individual firms it is more sensible to contact an agency which recruits for positions in your field for a range of companies.

You need, however, to do your homework carefully before putting pen to paper. The majority of recruitment consultants recruit only for positions within the British Isles; and those that do undertake international recruitment are more likely to recruit for the Middle East, Europe or the Far East. Even if you track down an agency that recruits for the United States, the chances are that it does not offer jobs in your particular field. Many of these international consultancies specialise in particular job sectors.

How do you find out who does what?
You get an idea by referring to *The Yearbook of Recruitment and Employment Services, The CEPEC Recruitment Guide,* or *The Executive Grapevine.* Alternatively, you can turn to Appendix B in this book which lists a select group of consultancies and agencies that recruit for the United States to a greater or lesser extent. The list is by no

means complete but includes organisations that supplied details of their current needs when this book was in progress.

Alas, circumstances change and no reference book can claim to be completely up-to-date. Employment markets tend to be volatile and recruitment requirements can change over a period of just a few months. The best plan is to peruse the advertisement columns of newspapers, international job lists and trade journals, and take note of the agencies recruiting for the United States which seem to handle your type of job. Send them your CV (British style) with a covering letter and ask them to put your details on file.

Do not necessarily expect an acknowledgement of your speculative letter; some organisations are inundated with speculative applications—often from people who have not done their homework properly and have applied to a firm that is not remotely interested in their skills. If you have selected the agency with care, you are more likely to get noticed.

Recruitment consultants in the United States

The chances of landing an appointment through a speculative approach to a recruitment consultant in the United States from abroad are slim, unless you are an exceptionally well qualified or high powered person. As Intercristo, the Christian Placement Agency explains:

'. . . Communication between the potential employer and applicant is time-consuming and cumbersome. This places the applicant at a severe disadvantage compared to candidates who are more accessible to potential employers.'

On the other hand, if you happen to be visiting America there is no harm in knocking on the doors of recruitment agencies to find out what kinds of jobs are on offer and leaving your particulars. Remember, though, that no job can be yours unless you can secure the required work visa. Note that you may have to pay a fee if the agency succeeds in placing you; more of this in Chapter Six.

Since a number of US consultancies have branches in the UK, it may be more sensible to contact these first of all to find out if there is any point in your applying to their office in, say, New York or San Francisco. If you have skills that are much in demand, the branch over here might be prepared to forward your details to their transatlantic colleagues.

Personal contacts
Have you a cousin three times removed living in Wyoming? Does
your brother-in-law have connections with a firm in Omaha? Is your
uncle on the board of a British plc with a subsidiary in Des Moines?
Does a pal of yours know a chap who runs an engineering outfit in
San Diego?

If you do not know the answers, perhaps it is time to remedy the
situation by asking around. Networking, or what used to be called
'the old boy network' continues to flourish in the 1990s. I would be
surprised if at least half the people in the UK and Ireland did not
know someone who lives in the United States, possibly a relative. If
you have no acquaintances across the Atlantic, then you should find
someone who has.

Do not expect your American contacts (once you have tracked them
down) to find you a job from out of the blue. However, they might
be able to give you an idea of the lie of the land, and suggest employers
in their immediate area that might be worth trying. They might also
be willing to keep an eye open for job openings in your particular
field.

Transfer or secondment
If you are in employment, have you explored the possibility of going
to the United States with your firm or organisation? Some multi-
nationals like to second key staff to overseas affiliates, while smaller
organisations may exchange employees for short periods with
companies abroad.

If you make it known that you are keen to work in the United
States, you may well find that opportunities do arise. Your very
keenness could be a point in your favour. You may find it surprising,
but a number of key employees do not relish the prospect of a posting
abroad, particularly if they have family commitments, and your
employer may prefer to send someone who is enthusiastic and
committed rather than a reluctant expatriate who needs various
inducements before he will budge.

If you are sent abroad by your employer you will enjoy the best of
all worlds including a generous relocation allowance, continuity of
employment and possibly an enhanced salary.

Companies in the UK
There are numerous companies and organisations which function on
both sides of the Atlantic, and if you join one of these and prove your
worth, there is a possibility that you might be posted to the United
States in the course of time.

Two categories of company are worth considering:

- British, Irish or other European companies with business interests in the United States
- American companies with subsidiaries in UK and Ireland.

The first category is more likely to offer you the opportunity of a US posting, particularly if you have prior experience or special knowledge of the country. Careful research will pay dividends; and in order to be in the right place at the right time you should watch out for companies that are aiming to expand their operations in the United States. Some British hotel companies, for instance, have acquired US hotel chains in recent years.

A good business reference library will have information on the leading firms in both the UK and the United States. You need to go and search out books such as the *Directory of US Subsidiaries of British Companies, Dun and Bradstreet's Million Dollar Directory, Dun and Bradstreet's Middle Market Directory* and *Thomas Register of American Manufacturers.* The business, trade and professional press is also required reading. (See Bibliography.)

Firms in the United States

Speculative applications from afar are unlikely to yield positive results; you may not even receive an acknowledgement. There are, of course, exceptions. If you are an acknowledged expert in your particular field or have skills that are in short supply, you could be successful in landing a position. However, do not count on it.

If you are planning a trip to America, the position is different. You can send off a copy of your résumé with a covering letter that mentions you will be passing through the city where the employer is based on such-and-such a date, and you would welcome an opportunity to visit him. While there is no guarantee that this approach will open doors, you may arouse the recipient's curiosity sufficiently to gain an invitation.

This approach could prove expensive, since your fare across the Atlantic is unlikely to be reimbursed by the people you see. However, if you target a number of companies and organisations effectively, your chances of gaining a hearing—and ultimately a position—will be enhanced.

A useful reference book for people planning direct applications is Dun's *Employment Opportunities Directory (The Career Guide)* which lists 5,000 employers and their employment needs. Unhappily, few, if any, reference libraries in this country seem to have it on their shelves and the tome is extremely expensive. There are plenty of reference books (see Bibliography) which list American companies, and you would be able to consult some of them in a large public reference library, such as:

The City of London Business Library
106 Fenchurch Street
London EC3M 5JB.

If you cannot locate the book you need, then the US Information Service Library at the US Embassy has an extensive selection of reference books. Visits are by appointment only.

'Situation wanted' advertisements

Invididuals sometimes advertise their availability in British publications that circulate in the United States (eg *The Economist*), but you could also try advertising in American newspapers and journals. Some of the main ones are listed in Appendix G and a few, but by no means all, have UK agents who can handle your advertisement.

It is difficult to judge how successful self-advertising really is. You are more likely to achieve success if you include a US address for replies, mention that you will be visiting America in the near future and indicate that you either have, or are able to obtain, the necessary permits.

Miscellaneous organisations

Leeson's Employment and Accommodation Service (LEADS) offers advice and assistance to people planning to work in the United States, including:

- lists of companies employing your particular trade or profession together with all employment bureaux and consultants in any area of your choice;
- help in assessing the prospects;
- advice on all your approaches to personnel officers and employers;
- interviews in the UK on behalf of US companies.

Expat Network operates Joblink which forwards its members' CVs to overseas employers.

WHAT ARE THE POTENTIAL PROBLEMS?

One problem you encounter when applying for a job in the United States from another country is that the process takes time. In most cases your details have to be sent across the Atlantic, and before the employer can take you on he has to obtain permission to employ you (labor certification) from the authorities. Once this comes through your nearest US consulate has to be informed, and even then some time may elapse before you are granted the appropriate visa. You may, for instance, have to be interviewed by the US consul or undergo a medical, so it could take months before you get the go-ahead. On the other hand, all the formalities might be completed in just three weeks.

Another major problem with applying for a job from the UK is that more often than not you do not get a chance to visit your prospective employer and see the working environment for yourself at first hand. Normally only senior (and well-paid) executives of some years' standing with their company are given the chance to see their workplace in advance. If you do not like what you see on arrival, it is too late to do anything about it.

This is less of a problem for people who already know the United States as a result of having visited the country or, better still, lived there. If you have not, you need to be given a thorough briefing before you commit yourself irrevocably. Do not rely on Hollywood films to give you sufficient insight into everyday American life.

Most organisations brief their staff as a matter of course or enlist the help of outside agencies, such as the Centre for International Briefing at Farnham Castle. (Others are listed in Appendix F.) If no orientation is mentioned you could contact organisations such as the Women's Corona Society—even if you are a man—or Christians Abroad, which can put you in touch with people who have returned from the US.

Even with the best of briefings you have to take certain things on trust and rely on the impressions of other people whose tastes and inclinations may diverge quite markedly from your own. What may seem like the next best thing to a holiday for some people can turn out to be a damp squib for others.

In order to avoid disappointment, you must make every effort to understand what you are letting yourself in for. Talk to people who have lived and worked in the US; make sure that you understand the differences in working practice and life style that you will encounter. Read up about the place where you will be.

The **US Travel and Tourism Administration** may have useful free information on the place you are making for, albeit with something of a tourist gloss, and the **US Information Service** (at the US Embassy) can provide an information pack. *The Economist Business Travel Guide* is worth consulting and *Inside Tracks* offers short, regularly updated destination profiles of a number of US cities including Chicago, Houston, Los Angeles, San Francisco, New Orleans and Washington DC.

YOUR CONTRACT

Before you leave the country you should be asked to sign a contract. If you are being sent abroad by your company a contract may not be deemed necessary, but you should have a memorandum which details your responsibilities and entitlements.

A contract is just as much for your benefit as that of your employer, and you should read it through carefully and query matters which are unclear. It is also sensible to ask a solicitor or an expatriate service organisation to read it through and offer their comments.

These are some of the details you need to look out for:

- the name and address of your employer
- your job title and responsibilities
- staff member you are answerable to
- the location of your employment
- your net salary and dates of payment
- the commencement date and duration of your employment
- working hours.

Some items may need to be gone into in greater detail, such as:

- Paid leave. Don't take this for granted, particularly if you are employed on contract terms. In any case, leave entitlements are far from generous—often only one or two weeks per year.

- Sick leave. Often there is no open-ended entitlement but a fixed number of days when sickness pay can be claimed. (See Chapter 7.)

- Medical insurance. Make sure this is provided and will be adequate for your needs. (See also Chapters 5 and 7.)

- Accommodation. Contract workers may get a per diem allowance to cover accommodation costs, which will be similar to those enjoyed by American employees working outside their home states. Sometimes accommodation is provided, particularly a hotel on arrival.

- Hardship allowance. This may be payable if you take up employment in Alaska.

- Married allowance. Normally contract employees would not be eligible for extra allowances if accompanied by their spouse and family. If you are being transferred to the United States by your employer such a perk is more likely to be forthcoming.

- Pension. Contract posts, particularly short-term ones, do not always have a pension provision. Some employers, however, may offer a 401K transferable pension scheme. (See also Chapter Five.)

- Termination bonus. This is not usually offered with US postings.

- Fares to and from your destination. With company transfers it is normal for fares to be paid for the employee and his dependents. If you are a contract employee, the chances are that only your fare will be paid. Only in very exceptional circumstances should you pay your own fare.

- Baggage allowance. Transferees are likely to have more generous entitlements than a contract employee.

- Premature termination of contract. There should be a clause that covers procedures in such an eventuality.

- Restrictions. There may be restrictions on your working for other organisations.

No contract will be able to deal with every eventuality, and you need to familiarise yourself with working conditions in the US before you leave. (See Chapter Seven.) Adequate preparation is, of course, vital and you should read the following chapter with care.

5
Preparations Before Departure

Any trip abroad, even just a week's holiday, involves a certain amount of preparation. If you are planning to be away for an extended period—whether months, years or forever—preparing for the move needs to be done thoroughly and systematically.

WHAT SPECIFIC ARRANGEMENTS DO I NEED TO MAKE?

This chapter is a checklist of things that you need to think about. Not all the items will be of concern to you—particularly if your stay will be a short one or you are single and unencumbered—but the longer you are planning to stay in the United States the more matters there will be to attend to. I therefore suggest you look through the list and note down what is of importance to you.

The topics covered in this chapter in alphabetical order are:

- arrival arrangements
- banking
- car
- credit and charge cards
- customs and prohibited articles
- driving licence
- doctor and dentist
- educational arrangements (for your children)
- financial advice
- your flat or house
- health
- insurance
- investment
- journals
- kin

- library
- luggage and personal effects
- moving
- National Insurance
- orientation
- passports
- pension
- personal effects
- pets
- professional advisers
- qualification certificates
- relations and friends
- redirection of mail
- rental agreements
- subscriptions
- tax
- travel
- utilities—electricity, gas, telephone, water
- visas
- voting rights.

Arrival arrangements
It is sensible to inform your prospective employer when you plan to arrive. The chances are you will be travelling to the United States by air, in which case you should state the flight number in addition to the estimated arrival time. Long haul flights are sometimes delayed.

Find out what arrangements have been made for meeting you and accommodating you on arrival; and make sure you have one or two contact telephone numbers in case arrangements go awry.

Banking
You need to inform your UK bank of your imminent change of address and discuss arrangements for the administration of your account during your absence (eg how you plan to top up your account to service regular payments).

Since the bank may not have a branch at your destination (some British and Irish banks have affiliates or representatives in the United States), you could also ask if it can recommend a bank in the locality and provide a letter of introduction. This will facilitate opening a bank account in the United States if your employer has no procedures to help you in this respect.

Even if you are planning to leave the UK for good, it is sensible to keep your account open and topped up—for the time being at least—as there may be occasions in the future when it is more convenient to make or receive payments in sterling.

You will also need to arrange for money to tide you over the first month or so in the United States. This involves purchasing foreign exchange in the form of dollars and dollar travellers cheques (other denominations are not readily accepted) and perhaps arranging for a bank transfer. Note that you will also be able to withdraw cash with a credit or charge card.

Car

In many parts of the United States public transport is fairly rudimentary, and you will find that some means of private transport is essential. There is, however, little point in shipping your car to the country—unless it happens to be a very distinguished one—since automobiles are much cheaper over there. In any case, it will probably not meet US safety, bumper and emission standards, which are very tough; modification can work out prohibitively expensive.

For more information on emission standards contact:

The US Environmental Protection Agency
Manufacturer Operations Division (EN-340F)
Investigation/Imports Section
401 M Street SW
Washington DC 20460
USA
Tel: 202 382 2504
Fax 202 245 4089

Note that in order to import a car you will need prior written approval from the EPA or a manufacturer's label affixed to the vehicle stating it meets all US emission requirements

For information on bumper and safety requirements you should get in touch with:

The US Department of Transportation,
National Highway Traffic Safety Administration
Director of the Office of Vehicle Safety Compliance (NEF-32)
400 Seventh Street SW
Washington DC 20590
USA
Tel: 202 366 5313.

As a non-resident you may import a vehicle duty-free into the United States, but duty is payable if the car is sold within a year of importation. Employees of foreign governments and international organisations on assignment in the United States may be exempt from the compliance regulations; and the same is true for non-residents who import the car for one year and then export it.

If you are going to America for a number of years it will make sense to sell your vehicle and rely on car hire for visits to the UK. Do not forget to inform the Driver Vehicle Licensing Office and your insurance company when the car is sold and claim a refund on your insurance if appropriate.

If your stay in the United States is for a shortish period, you could put your vehicle in storage or entrust it to a friend or relation. Whatever you do, make sure you inform your insurance company of your plans.

The US Customs Service publishes a useful leaflet entitled *Importing A Car* which is obtainable either from:

The US Customs Service
Department of the Treasury
Washington
DC 20229
USA
or the Customs Attaché of the US Embassy.

Credit and charge cards

Before you leave, you ought to inform your card company of your new address for statements. You should also ask if it has a list of banks that accept your particular card in the United States. Credit and charge cards are used widely in America, and are a most convenient method of payment and obtaining cash. If you need to hire a car, for instance, the deposit is often waived if you produce a credit or charge card.

In view of the widespread use of these cards in the United States, you might find yourself at a disadvantage if you do not own one. It is therefore worth looking into the possibility of obtaining either type of card, ideally by approaching a bank or building society that does not charge for their issue.

If your credit limit is fairly low, this might be a good time to have it raised, to enable you to cope with the extra expenses you will incur in settling in. Note that you will continue to be billed in sterling.

Ultimately you may well decide to open a credit card account in the United States which will bill you in dollars. However, as in the UK, it may take a little time before the account is operational.

Customs and prohibited articles

You will normally be allowed to import personal and household effects free of duty. One litre of alcohol may be brought in duty free provided this does not conflict with the laws of the state in which you arrive. Two hundred cigarettes or the equivalent can also be imported free of duty. The leaflet *US Customs Hints*, available from the Customs Attaché of the US Embassy, offers further information.

Restrictions are imposed on the import of firearms, narcotics and certain foodstuffs, notably meat. For further information on the import of foodstuffs contact:

The Import/Export and Emergency Planning Staff,
US Department of Agriculture
APHIS
VS 6505
Belcrest Road
Hyattsville
MD 20782
USA.

The Customs Attaché at the US Embassy may also be able to advise.

During your flight or voyage to the United States you will be given a customs declaration (Form 6059B) to fill in, which is designed to expedite customs clearance on arrival. Failure to declare a prohibited item can lead to an on the spot fine.

Driving licence

You could acquire an International Driving Licence from the AA or RAC but it is really not necessary to do so, since you will be able to drive on your own licence for a year. When the year is up you will need to take a US driving test.

The ability to drive is a great asset in the United States since public transport is not available everywhere. If you do not drive already, sooner or later you will probably need to learn, simply in order to survive. Although US driving tests are reckoned to be easier than UK ones, you may prefer to pass your test in more familiar home surroundings.

The rules of the road in the United States differ in some respects from the British Highway Code, and you should take steps to familiarise yourself with them.

Doctor and dentist

Visit your dentist before you leave and ask him to make sure your teeth are in good shape, since dental care in the United States can be extremely expensive and is not always covered by medical insurance.

A visit to your doctor is also in order to tell him of your plans and perhaps have a check-up. You may in any case have to have a medical examination prior to confirmation of your appointment or in order to satisfy immigration requirements. If you have a particular medical condition that requires you to take prescription drugs, you should ask the doctor for a letter that you can take to a medical practitioner in the United States. You may also need to show the letter to customs officials at your port of entry.

If you are likely to be out of the country for a lengthy period of time you should surrender your NHS card to the local Family Practitioner Committee, or hand it to the immigration officer at your point of departure.

Educational arrangements
If your children are of secondary school age, you need to decide whether they are likely to re-enter the British educational system later in their lives. If so, they really need to be enrolled at a school which adheres to the British system or prepares them for the **International Baccalaureate** (IB)—a highly regarded qualification which is recognised by all universities.

There are various options:

- A boarding school in Britain. Private sector schools can be costly, unless your employer can be persuaded to meet most or part of the bill, but a number of local authorities also run schools for children whose parents are abroad, and you could discuss the problem with your local education authority. Further information is available from Dean Associates, the Independent Schools Information Service (ISIS), Gabbitas, Truman & Thring, and SFIA.

- A school offering a British style or IB curriculum in the USA, such as:

Anglo-American School
18 West 89 Street
New York
NY 10024.

Armand Hammer United World College of the American West
PO Box 248

Montezuma
NM 87731.

United Nations International School
24-50 East River Drive
New York
NY 10010.

Washington International School
3100 Macomb Street NW
Washington
DC 20008.

There are also French schools in Los Angeles, San Francisco and Houston. If you wish to enrol your children in one of the above mentioned schools, do not leave it until the last moment, otherwise you will find there are no places available.

- A correspondence course. Mercer's College provides a complete tuition service by correspondence for children living abroad with their parents up to the age of 18, while the Worldwide Educational Service offers an educational programme for the under-13s which enables parents with no teaching experience to educate their children.

Bear in mind that the residential status of your children could be crucial when the authorities in the UK come to deciding whether they are to be treated as British students or foreign students with respect to fees and grants. It would be wise to explore the financial implications of moving your children to the United States if they are approaching college age.

If, on the other hand, you are likely to be living in the United States indefinitely, there is everything to be said for enrolling your child(ren) in an American school. If you opt for **public (i.e. state) education** (which is free), you can find out about local schools by contacting the Department of Education of the state in which you will be living (addresses in Appendix G) or the School Board of the district where you plan to reside. Alternatively, you may decide to opt for a **parochial school** (run by a religious denomination) or a **private (independent) school**. *The Handbook of Private Schools* (Porter Sargent Publishers, 11 Beacon Street, Boston, MA 02108) can provide details of the latter.

Ultimately your offspring may well want to attend a college in the United States, though this can prove an expensive business since grants are not as readily available as they are in the UK. For more information on higher education I suggest one of the following:

- *Lovejoy's College Guide*, C.E. Lovejoy (Simon & Schuster). 0-671-41234-5.
- *Comparative Guide to American Colleges*, J. Cass and M. Birnbaum (Harper & Row). 0-06-096022-1.
- *Profiles of American Colleges*, (Barron's Educational Series). 0-8120-4742-7.
- *Study in the USA*, (Study in the USA Inc, 119 S Main St, Suite 220, Seattle, WA 98104).

Financial advice

If you are planning to be in the United States for some time it will pay you to find a reputable adviser who can help you understand the tax and other financial implications of the move and give you advice on such matters as insurance, pensions, etc. Your bank may be able to offer advice through one of its specialist branches, or you could turn to one of the specialist advisers that advertise in expatriate journals. Some of these are included under Useful Addresses (Appendix F).

Your flat or house in the UK

If you own a house or flat there are various options open to you, depending on how long you will be away.

Leave the accommodation empty

This is fine provided you live in a part of the country that is reasonably secure, your absence is likely to be short and there is no risk of squatters moving in. However, your insurance company may increase the premium, and if you have a mortgage, your bank or building society might have qualms. In any case, both organisations should be informed.

Ask someone to look after it for you

This is quite a sensible option provided the person lives quite close. If you are unable to find a neighbour, friend or relative who will take on the responsibility, you could contact an organisation that offers houseminding services, such as Animal Aunts or Homesitters Ltd. People participating on exchange programmes often allow their exchange partners use of the house.

Let it
This is a way of paying for the upkeep of the property and helps pay off the mortgage, if you have one, but you need to check first whether the lender approves. It is always best if you can find a tenant whom you know and trust, as not every tenant turns out to be reliable. Failing that, you can either advertise for a tenant yourself or appoint a letting agent to do the work for you. A good agent will

- advertise for tenants
- interview prospective tenants
- take up references
- draw up a leasing agreement and serve relevant notices
- draw up inventories
- visit properties and attend to any complaints or queries
- collect rent
- serve notice to quit and attend court
- attend to building repairs and any major building work
- account to clients by way of statements and payment of rents
- pay water rates and other charges
- negotiate rent increases
- deal with insurance claims.

If you plan to return during your vacations, contact the accommodation office of local colleges and universities to see if they have staff or students who need to rent accommodation during term time only.

Sell it
This is a sensible option if you are planning to stay in the US for several years, but you will need to set the process in train some time before you leave. In recent years houses have taken ages to sell.

There is no need to deal with such matters here, since there are several excellent books on buying and selling houses and flats, eg: *Which Way to Buy, Sell and Move House* (Consumers' Association).

You may well decide to use some of the proceeds to finance the purchase of property in the US. Initially you should find a safe and profitable haven for your cash.

And if your accommodation is rented
Make sure that you give your landlord plenty of notice.

Health
There are no special vaccinations that you need to have before going

to the United States, since you are unlikely to encounter any particular health hazards there. However, in view of the costs of health care in America it makes sense to ensure you are in the best of health before you go. Visits to your doctor and dentist have already been suggested; it would also be a good idea to go to the optician for an eye test or for a spare pair of spectacles.

The Department of Health produces two useful booklets: *Before You Go* (SA40) and *While You're Away* (SA41). See also the note on medical insurance.

Insurance

Medical and accident insurance
The United States does not have the equivalent of the British National Health Service, and what government health provision there is tends to be limited to only a small sector of the population, particularly the destitute and the elderly.

It is therefore up to the individual to ensure that he is properly insured against illness. Many employers assume this responsibility, and if you are fortunate you may well find that medical insurance is one of the perks of the job. If this is not the case, you will need to make your own arrangements, though this could work out expensive.

None of the medical expenses you incur in the United States can be refunded by the NHS, but you will continue to be eligible for free treatment in Britain when you return or when visiting, provided you have not taken up permanent residence in the United States.

There are a number of insurance companies and brokers in the UK that will insure you for a short visit to America, including BUPA, Citihealth, Exeter HAS and PPP. Not all will be prepared to do so for the longer term, and you may find it is easier to insure yourself with an American insurer, such as Blue Cross, when you arrive.

The Health Insurance Association of America will be able to answer any queries. The organisation produces a number of useful leaflets, such as *What You Should Know About Health Insurance* and *How to Use Private Health Insurance with Medicare.*

When looking at a health plan, whether it is to be provided by your employer or financed by yourself, it is vital to make sure you have adequate cover. Here are a few of the questions you need to ask.

● What percentage of the cost of treatment do I have to pay, if any?
● What kinds of treatment are excluded? (eg dental, psychiatric)
● How soon do benefits start?

- Am I covered for existing medical conditions?
- Does the policy cover prescription drugs?
- Is there a ceiling on the amount I can claim each year?

Life insurance
You need to notify your insurance company of your impending move. This might be a good time to review your needs.

Insurance of personal effects
This is a matter that you should look into. If you employ removers they should be able to advise you; otherwise you may be able to arrange an insurance package which includes medical, accident, loss and damage provisions.

Investment
If you have any investments, you need to inform the organisations concerned (eg unit trust managers, the Premium Bond office, your stockbroker) of your change of address. You may also wish to appoint someone to look after them in your absence (eg your bank or solicitor).

This may be a timely moment, if you are planning to be away an appreciable length of time, to review your investment strategy in the light of your new circumstances, in order to make your investments as tax efficient as possible. Bear in mind that if you become a permanent US resident, the Inland Revenue Service will tax you on your total worldwide income.

In the past many expatriates have found it profitable to move their investments into an offshore haven such as the Channel Islands or the Isle of Man, but you could run into legal difficulties if you try to do this with any US earnings. So you would be wise to take advice from a financial expert who is au fait with expatriate financial matters.

Journals and newspapers
If you subscribe to journals you need to weigh up whether to continue your subscription or not. If not, you need to cancel; if you wish to continue, you should notify the publisher of your change of address.

If you are going to a part of the United States where British publications are hard to come by, you might consider taking out a subscription to a publication such as *The Guardian Weekly* or *The Economist* in order to keep abreast of developments in the UK and elsewhere. Only a minority of US newspapers provide extensive coverage of international news. There are, incidentally, some British newspapers in the United States: the *British Weekly* serves the British community in California, the *Florida Brit* circulates in Florida, while the monthly *Union Jack* has a national circulation. (See under California, Appendix G.)

Another way of keeping in touch is to listen in to the BBC World Service, in which case you may wish to take out a subscription to its monthly programme bulletin *London Calling*. The BBC also produces a fortnightly video compilation of news and other BBC TV programmes, and is planning to extend its satellite TV coverage in due course. (See Appendix F.)

There are a number of journals which cater especially for expatriates to which you might consider, eg: *Expatxtra, Home & Away, Resident Abroad* (See Appendix D for details.)

Kin (next of)

Make sure that your employers and professional advisers know the name and address of your next of kin in case of accidents. Details of your next of kin should also be noted in your diary and passport.

Library

Your local public library will probably have some useful books on the United States, and you should endeavour to read or, at least, browse through some of them before you go, in order to familiarise yourself with the prospect before you. The **Centre for International Briefing** has an excellent library, geared to expatriate needs, which can be used for a fee.

Do not forget to return any library books you have borrowed otherwise you could incur a steep fine in the future.

Luggage and personal effects

If you are only planning to be in America for a matter of months, the best plan is to travel light. If you are planning to be there for some years you will want to take a lot of your possessions with you, if at all possible. However, due to cost constraints you will not be able to take everything, so you need to work out what you really need and what you can do without.

For instance, if you are going to be in furnished accommodation there is clearly no need to take much furniture with you, except perhaps for a few choice items. It can either stay in your home or, if you are selling the house, you could put it in storage. Bulky electrical goods are best left behind since they are relatively cheap in the United States. Besides, the current US is different (110V 60Hz against 240V 50Hz in the UK), the TV transmission system is different, and you would need transformers and adaptors for two-pin sockets.

Household items (such as cutlery, sheets, blankets, kitchen utensils) are quite sensible items to take along; curtains are not, since you won't know the size of your windows. Books are weighty items, and you will need to think twice about shipping out your whole library, unless it happens to be very valuable.

There is little point in indulging in a shopping spree before you leave, since items are often available more cheaply in the United States. Instead save your cash until you arrive and discover exactly what you need.

Airlines are more generous these days than they used to be with regard to accompanied luggage, with dimensions a more important consideration than weight. Check whether your employer is prepared to pay for a modest amount of extra accompanied luggage, and whether there are allowances for items sent by sea or unaccompanied air freight.

Moving

If you have a large number of items to ship, the best plan is to enlist the aid of an experienced and reputable international removal contractor and leave him to do the packing, make all the transport arrangements and sort out the paperwork. Normally, if your employer is paying for the move, he will expect you to get a number of quotes before giving the go-ahead.

There are a number of removal firms that can handle international removals, a few of which are listed in Appendix F. If no firm near you is mentioned contact the British Association of Removers (Overseas Group) or the Institute of Freight Forwarders Ltd.

National Insurance

There is a **Social Security Agreement** between the UK and the United States to ensure that you do not have liability for contributions in both countries at the same time.

If you work in America for a UK employer for not more than five years you will remain insured under the UK National Insurance scheme and normal Class I contributions will be paid. Contributions will not be payable to the US scheme. Self employed people ordinarily resident in the UK also remain insured in the UK when working in the United States.

On the other hand, if you go to America to work for a US or other non-UK employer you may have to contribute to the US social security scheme. It is sensible to contact the US authorities on arrival to find out about your obligations.

You should let your local social security office know of your date of departure and address in the UK. Further information is available from:

Department of Social Security
Overseas Branch
Newcastle upon Tyne NE98 1YX.
For information on the US social security scheme contact:

Federal Benefits Unit
United States Embassy
24 Grosvenor Square
London W1A 2LQ.
The relevant authorities in the United States are:

Social Security Administration Office of International Policy
PO Box 17741
Baltimore
MD 21235 (contribution enquiries).

Social Security Administration Office of International Policy
PO Box 17049
Baltimore
MD 21303 (other enquiries).

Orientation

In order to get off to a good start it is vital to be briefed thoroughly not only about the job, but also about living conditions. There are subtle differences between the way of life in the United States and life on this side of the Atlantic which could catch you unawares, so you need to be aware of these differences and prepare for them.

A number of organisations conduct their own orientation programmes; others use the expertise of briefing centres, such as the Centre for International Briefing at Farnham Castle and Employment Conditions Abroad. Christians Abroad and Focus Information Services may also be able to help, as can the Women's Corona Society, which also publishes a useful series of booklets entitled *Notes for Newcomers*. Finally, Howell & Associates offer courses designed by the Institute for Training in Intercultural Management.

There are a number of useful books you could consult, such as *How to Live and Work in America, Living in the USA, Long Stays in America* and *Coping with America*. (See Bibliography). However, a person-to-person briefing is infinitely preferable, since you have the opportunity to ask your own questions.

Passports

One year Visitor's Passports are not valid for the USA and you will need to obtain a full passport from a passport office; you can get a passport application form from your Post Office. If your passport is about to expire, you would be wise to renew it.

UK Passport Office addresses
Clive House
70 Petty France
London SW1H 9HD
Tel: (071) 213 3434. (For residents of Greater London).

Olympia House
Upper Dock Street
Newport
Gwent NP1 1XA
Tel: (0633) 56292. (For Wales and the West of England).

55 Westfield Road
Peterborough PE3 6TG
Tel: (0733) 895555. (For the Midlands and Eastern England).

5th Floor
India Buildings
Water Street
Liverpool L2 0QZ
Tel: (051) 237 3010. (For the North of England).

Pension

If you are taking up a contract appointment, the chances are that you will not be covered by any pension scheme, and it would be worth your while to explore the possibility of contributing to a personal pension scheme. If you are already working for a company based in the UK or Ireland, you need to clarify whether the company pension scheme covers postings abroad. The Society of Pensions Consultants or Company Pensions Information Centre, both in London, may be able to advise or put you in touch with someone who can.

Pets

It is normally possible to take your pets with you to the United States, but you need to be aware of certain restrictions, such as quarantine periods in certain states. The leaflet *Pets, Wildlife, US Customs* gives full details of the restrictions.

However, you ought to consider whether your pet will necessarily relish the change. Your local branch of the RSPCA or Cats Protection League, or the ISPA (International Society for the Protection of Animals) should be able to advise you on this and on the transport of animals abroad.

If you are off on a short term assignment it may be more convenient to find your pet a home with friends or relations during your absence; or you could enlist the aid of a pet-minding service, such as Animal Aunts. (See Useful Addresses.)

Professional advisers

It is important to inform professional advisers, such as solicitors and accountants, of your new address. In addition, you may have to make arrangements with at least one of them for the day to day management of your affairs while you are away. By granting him power of attorney, for instance, he will be able to sign documents on your behalf. If you have not yet made a will, this could be a good time to do so.

On the other hand, you may feel you are quite able to handle your affairs yourself from the other side of the Atlantic.

Qualification certificates

It is advisable to take all your diplomas and certificates—and those of your dependents—with you, as prospective employers and the authorities may need to inspect them. Photocopies alone may not suffice.

Redirection of mail

While you may make a Herculean effort to inform all and sundry of your move, you will inevitably miss out someone or some organisation, such as a long-lost aunt in Australia who decides to get in touch after 20 years. You therefore need to arrange to have your mail redirected. If you have tenants, you may be able to prevail on them to do the honours; or the Post Office will redirect your mail—for a fee. Forms are available at any Post Office.

Rental agreements

If you have rental agreements remember to cancel them in good time. If buying on credit or hire purchase, you should inform the company in question of your movements.

Subscriptions

Subscriptions to associations should either be cancelled or the organisation concerned be informed of your new address. See also under Journals.

Tax

You need to inform both the Inland Revenue and the Treasurer of your local district or borough council so that they can assess your liability to income tax and local taxes (i.e. council charge, community charge or rates). You might even get a rebate! If you are self-employed and subject to VAT, you will have to tell the local VAT inspector as well.

The Inland Revenue produces a number of booklets that will guide you, including IR 25 which sets out the rules governing the taxation of income from overseas. As a rule of thumb, if the Inland Revenue regards you as non-resident in the UK for tax purposes you will not be liable to UK income tax, though you may well have to pay it to the United States authorities. You should not, however, have to pay income tax twice over since there is a double taxation agreement between the UK and the United States. US taxation is dealt with in the next chapter but you can obtain advance information from the Inland Revenue Service c/o the US Embassy.

There are a number of expatriate tax advisers (some of them listed in Appendix F) and if your tax affairs are complicated you may wish to seek advice in order to minimise tax liability both in the UK and United States. Books such as the *Allied Dunbar Expatriate Tax Guide* and *Working Abroad* are also worth dipping into.

Travel arrangements

It is normal for your employer to pay your fares, and if not, you should enquire why not. Expect to travel by air rather than on the QE2, and if you are on contract do not rely on getting free air travel for your dependents. Allow yourself plenty of time to get to the airport.

Utilities—electricity, gas, telephone, water

Inform the respective companies of the date of your departure and arrange for the payment of outstanding bills and disconnection, if appropriate. Also cancel milk and newspaper deliveries.

Visas

The different visa categories are explained in Chapter 2. If you have any doubts, the Visa Department of the US Embassy should be able to put you wise. If your position is a complicated one you may need to seek help from a lawyer specialising in US immigration law. The Embassy can supply you with a list of these.

Voting rights
British people who live abroad now have the right to vote in elections, thanks to the **Representation of the People Act 1989**, and you can receive information on this from the Electoral Registration Officer of the district in which you reside.

If you wish to receive election literature you should inform the offices of the different political parties in the constituency in which you reside, since this is the place where you have your vote. On arrival in the United States you need to contact the nearest British Consulate for the appropriate voting registration forms and an explanatory leaflet.

6
Looking for a Job on Arrival

Making contact with potential employers who are thousands of miles away is not an easy matter. Conducting your job search from within the United States itself can work out more satisfactory. You then have a chance to see what conditions are like, assess job prospects and employers, and understand what you are letting yourself in for.

However—and I cannot stress this point too much—in order to be able to work in the United States you need to be in possession of the appropriate kind of visa. If you are not, before you take up a position you must seek to regularise your status with the Immigration and Naturalisation Service. (The local offices are listed in Appendix G.) This is no mere formality, and there is no guarantee that you will be granted the necessary permission.

If you possess an Alien Registration Receipt Card (the 'green card') there is no problem. This document indicates that you have been granted permanent residence, and allows you to get a job anywhere without restriction. In most other situations, the employer will have to obtain permission to employ you, and since it can take months to get the necessary go-ahead, many firms will think twice before taking you on. The subject of visas has been dealt with in Chapter Two.

This chapter is aimed mainly at people who have the necessary permission to work in the United States. However, it will also be of interest to anyone who decides to visit America for a holiday or business trip and carry out a job reconnaissance at the same time. You may be fortunate enough to come across an employer who offers you a job on the spot, but it is just as valuable to glean information about the jobs market that will be useful to you in the future.

As in the UK there is no one golden way of finding a job, and you will achieve success sooner if you try a variety of approaches. Where you base yourself is also crucial. Generally speaking, you need to position yourself in an area where there are plenty of opportunities in your particular field. This will normally mean in or near a large and expanding commercial or industrial centre. In this respect

California, New York and parts of Texas are better bets than Wyoming or South Dakota.

SHOULD I APPROACH AN EMPLOYER DIRECT?

The direct approach can be very productive, especially if you research the jobs market thoroughly beforehand. You need to identify employers who could make use of your expertise, and in particular ones that appear to be expanding and taking on extra staff. Among the useful sources of information are:

● Commercial and professional directories (see Bibliography). Dun's *Employment Opportunities Directory* is particularly useful because it gives details of the recruitment practices and requirements of different companies.

● Reports and articles in newspapers and journals, on radio and TV, particularly the business news.

● Professional associations, careers counsellors, friends and acquaintances.

You then need to see if you can identify individuals within the organisation who might be interested in your expertise and have the authority to recruit personnel. In small outfits this could well turn out to be the managing director himself. Otherwise, contact the personnel officer, who in larger firms is likely to have the title Vice President of Human Resources.

This step involves one of the following procedures:

A personal visit
If the organisation is in the locality where you are staying, you could call in and ask about current and future recruitment needs. If things look promising, see if you can make an appointment with the relevant person and leave a copy of your résumé (American style CV). If the firm is a small one you may be lucky enough to see someone straight away, but normally you will have to make an appointment for a later date.

Be prepared to ask questions about the organisation itself and how a person with your experience and qualifications would fit in. Before leaving, see if you can pick up brochures about the organisation. Such information could prove useful at some future meeting.

A letter
On the whole speculative letters are less effective than personal visits, but unless you are prepared to spend an enormous amount on your job hunting it is not feasible to visit organisations throughout the United States purely 'on spec'. Distances are greater than you think: for instance, Istanbul is much closer to London than Los Angeles is to Boston.

If the organisation is within a few hundred miles of your base, you could increase the effectiveness of your application by indicating that you will be in the vicinity during the course of the next few weeks and asking for an appointment. For positions further afield you should consider targeting a number of employers in just a few, well chosen states. Then, if some interest is shown, you can back the application up with a visit in which you kill several birds with one stone.

In the case of more distant employers you need to stress your mobility and willingness to relocate. Your initial base in the United States, after all, is (or should be) essentially a temporary one.

(For a sample of a speculative application letter turn to Appendix E.)

A telephone call
If you have a confident telephone manner, you could try canvassing for job leads by telephone. In this way you can cover a lot of ground in a short period of time. John Truitt's book *Telesearch: Direct Dial the Best Job of Your Life* describes this technique in some detail.

Do not expect every phone call to result in a job interview. Some organisations may dislike this type of approach and will ask you to apply in writing; others will give you details of their needs and send you an application form; others will state that they have no recruitment plans. But if you do get an encouraging reaction, be prepared to describe briefly your skills and job objectives.

You may achieve greater success if you adopt a more subtle approach. Instead of asking for a job, why not mention that you are visiting the area and would like to have a look at the company or organisation? Americans are usually very welcoming to foreign visitors and might be flattered by your interest. You may not land a job as a result of your enquiry, but you will doubtless pick up useful information and possibly some job leads.

PRIVATE RECRUITMENT AGENCIES

As in the UK there are many recruitment organisations that find staff for their clients, some of which are household names on this side of the Atlantic, too. The main difference is that firms operating in the United States have the right to charge job seekers a fee—normally a percentage of the first month's or year's salary—if they achieve a placement. Not all do so, and generally speaking the more reputable agencies don't. In some states there are laws that place a limit on how much an agency can charge.

Just as in the UK, too, there are agencies which cover the whole range of jobs and others that specialise in certain sectors. Catering for the top of the market are the executive search firms (sometimes known as 'headhunters') which recruit for high level positions. The vacancies they handle are not always advertised, and the firms approach candidates they deem suitable for the positions. There is no harm at all in sending your résumé to a consultancy with a good track record in your particular field and asking to be put on their files.

There is often an overlap between executive search firms and those that deal with jobs at middle management and other levels. Some firms operate under one roof, using a number of different names according to job level and specialisation.

One very good way of finding an employment agency is by personal recommendation. There are, alas, cowboy outfits that are more intent on earning a fast buck than on making satisfactory placements, and these are to be avoided. Otherwise you can find the names by looking through the job advertisement columns of newspapers and journals or in telephone directories (*Yellow Pages*). In some directories employment agencies are classified according to their specialisation.

Many recruitment consultancies belong to one of the following organisations that publish directories of their members: Association of Executive Search Consultants, National Association of Executive Recruiters, National Association of Personnel Consultants and the National Association of Corporate and Professional Recruiters. (Addresses: see Appendix G).

Temporary help agencies

There are some 3,500 national, regional and independent companies operating in this field, including some names familiar in UK high streets (eg Manpower). Normally such companies recruit their own employees and assign them to clients for limited periods as needed.

The breakdown of jobs in the industry is as follows:

63 per cent office/clerical positions
15 per cent industrial work; eg assembly line workers and janitors
11 per cent technical and professional jobs; eg engineers,

accountants, lawyers, computer programmers, draughtsmen, managers

10 per cent medical; eg nurses, therapists, nursing orderlies, lab technicians

(Source: National Association of Temporary Services)

Temporary employment is a growth area, and according to *Contemporary Times* (Spring 1991) the technical and medical sectors are growing faster than the others and this trend is expected to continue. It is particularly attractive to people in search of flexible working hours, additional income or a way back into the job market. In some cases a temporary job can lead to a permanent engagement.

This is probably only an option for people in possession of a 'green card', since non-immigrant visas are not normally issued to people engaged by a temporary help agency. If you are a student with permission to work or have exchange visitor status (see Chapter Three) you might well contact such a firm in your quest for vacation employment.

The National Association of Temporary Services is the national trade organisation for the temporary help industry and publishes a directory of its members.

NEWSPAPER ADVERTISEMENTS

In the United States there is no national press as we know it. Virtually all newspapers serve a particular locality, and even a national newspaper such as the *Wall Street Journal* appears in regional editions.

This means that when looking for a job you will need to look in the newspapers published in the region where you plan to work. If you are living in New York and want to work in San Francisco, there is little point in looking through the classified ads of the *New York Times*. You need to get hold of a San Francisco paper.

In Appendix D and Appendix G the names and addresses of the leading newspapers are listed state by state. If you are living outside the state concerned you may have to arrange for copies to be sent to you. Find out which are the best days for job advertisements; the Sunday editions are usually a good bet.

Professional and trade journals normally have national distribution, and would therefore inclue job advertisements for all areas in the United States. *The National Business Employment Weekly*—a weekly supplement of the *Wall Street Journal*—and other more specialised job listings are also worth looking at. (See Appendix D.)

As you saw in Chapter Four, the trouble with job advertisements is that they normally generate a lot of replies. You are probably up against stiff competition and therefore need to prepare your application as expertly as possible. (See Appendix E for ideas on how to do this). Furthermore, it is no use replying to just one or two job ads; you need to reply to several in order to increase your chances of success.

PUBLIC SECTOR AND OTHER EMPLOYMENT SERVICES

The state employment service, sometimes called **Job Service**, operates in conjunction with the US Department of Labor Employment Service and has some 2000 local offices. It bears a resemblance to Job Centres in the UK, does not charge a placement fee, and recruits for both white collar and blue collar positions, though not usually for senior and middle ranking ones.

Most states have computerised job banks which provide daily listings of job openings in the area of public and private sector vacancies. In addition there is a network of **Federal Job Information Centers** throughout the country. The addresses of the departments handling the employment service are listed state by state in Appendix G.

There are various other non-commercial recruitment organisations operated by voluntary organisations. **Intercristo,** for instance, is a Christian placement network which finds personnel for Christian organisations within the United States. For the older job seeker there are **40 + Clubs.**

College placement offices are another source of information about jobs, more specifically for graduates. Of course, their main preoccupation is finding jobs for their own graduates, but if you are lucky, you may find a placement officer who can spend a little time with you. For addresses you should consult the *Directory of Career Planning & Placement Officers* obtainable from:

College Placement Council Inc.
Box 2263
Bethelehem
PA 18001
USA.

NETWORKING

Making use of one's contacts is one of the most succesful methods of landing a job in the United States—for US residents, at least—but as a newcomer you may feel at a disadvantage. You arrive knowing virtually nobody and need time to build up a network of contacts in a strange land.

How can you overcome this difficulty? The best solution is to begin to develop your network before your departure for the New World. You should have plenty of contacts at home—relatives, business colleagues, people you socialise with, professional contacts, etc.—so why not ask them to suggest people who you might look up on your visit?

Do not overlook the services of organisations to which you belong— your trade union, professional association, local church, the local Rotary Club, for instance. Many such associations have counterparts in the United States, and some of the professional ones are listed in the appropriate job sector of Appendix A. Find out the names and addresses of local representatives in the area(s) where you will be staying and either get a letter of introduction or drop them a line to announce your visit. Chambers of Commerce in the United States are also worth approaching.

WHAT ARE THE PROS AND CONS OF JOB HUNTING FROM A US BASE?

There are obvious advantages to conducting your job search within the United States. You have a chance to meet potential employers and their staff face to face and to see working conditions in different companies at first hand. You also have access to much more information on job opportunities in the form of press advertisements, reference books, job guides and advisers.

On the other hand, if you do not have residential status (and most visitors to the United States do not) you may find companies reluctant to employ you, even if you possess exceptionally good qualifications and experience. This could be because there are plenty of skilled people in the area and so there is no need to call on expertise from abroad. However, a more plausible reason is that the employer (like most American employers) has no experience of recruiting 'aliens' and is therefore unfamiliar with the procedures for obtaining a work visa.

To overcome this reluctance the onus is on you to explain the immigration rules: how the employer must apply to the State Department of Labor for labor certification and that when this comes through you will need to contact the Immigration and Naturalisation Service (INS). The American Council on International Personnel may also be able to advise. (For addresses, please see Appendix G.)

While immigration attorneys can be used, they are not always necessary if the employer has good grounds for offering you the job.

Visits 'on spec' cost money, of course, and there is no guarantee that in the end you will find a job. As I write, certain regions of the United States are experiencing a tough recession so jobs are few and far between. You therefore need to make sure that you have adequate financial support to proceed with your job search, since you will not qualify for government handouts if you have never worked in America before.

Another consideration is that if you are recruited outside the United States, you will normally get extra perks, notably free travel to your post and back together with some help in moving your belongings. There is also a better chance that you will be dealing with people who know the ropes about work visas for aliens and are able to make all the necessary arrangements speedily.

A final point: make sure that you sign a contract, which sets out the terms and conditions of your employment in detail. Then, in the event of a dispute between your employer and yourself you have some form of legal protection.

7
Working Conditions and Financial Obligations

One golden rule for a person planning to work overseas is: take nothing for granted. This applies just as much to the United States as it does to some country in the Third World; for while superficially things may look the same as they do back home, they seldom are.

This is certainly true with respect to the world of work. US employment laws and working practices may be different from those you are used to. Contracts, for instance, are less likely to be open-ended; in fact, many people are on short-term contracts and new agreements have to be negotiated every two or three years. Moreover, American employers are in a position to terminate a job at any time without justification.

In some respects employees in the United States receive less protection than workers in Europe. That is not to say that America has no labor laws; in fact, there is plenty of legislation both at the federal and state levels, some of it extremely detailed. It is designed to prevent unfair employment practices and discrimination, and to regulate the health and safety of employees.

Your best protection, however, is the contract that you sign. It should spell out the terms and conditions of your employment clearly, so that if your employer should renege on any parts of the agreement you can take him to court. As Americans are somewhat litigious by nature, legal disputes with employers are not uncommon.

YOUR CONTRACT

At the end of Chapter Four you saw what conditions you should look for in a contract signed in the UK or Ireland.

What should I look for in a USA contract?
A contract signed in the United States should include:
- the name and address of your employer
- your job title and responsibilities

- the staff member you are answerable to
- the location of your employment
- your net salary and dates of payment
- the commencement date and duration of your employment
- the working hours.

Statutory benefits
In addition to pay there are three benefits that the employer is required to provide by law:

Social security payment
He has to make a contribution to your Social Security account (the equivalent to National Insurance in the UK) with the Federal Government.

Unemployment compensation
Your employer must pay into the Government insurance programme that pays unemployment benefit to employees who lost their jobs. The employee does not have to contribute to the scheme.

Workmen's Compensation
The employer also has to bear the full cost of contributions to this scheme which provides benefits to employees injured or disabled at work.

Discretionary benefits
The other benefits are discretionary (i.e. employers are not required by law to provide them, though most of them offer at least some). When negotiating your contract you need to pay attention to these points.

Vacation
Vacation entitlements are modest by European standards: seldom more than two weeks per annum except for senior employees, while a new employee might only get one week off.

In addition there are various public holidays: New Year's Day, Memorial Day (last Monday in May), Independence Day (July 4), Labor Day (first Monday in September, Thanksgiving (fourth Thursday in November) and Christmas Day. Note that the idea of a lengthy break at Christmas is unusual.

Sick leave
Employees are allowed to take a specific number of days each year

for sickness or compassionate leave—typically six days in all. Note that visits to the dentist or doctor during the working day may be deducted from your sick leave entitlement.

Life insurance
Many employers offer low-cost or free life insurance, normally based on the employee's salary.

Medical insurance
Traditionally businesses have provided health care insurance for their staff, but as the cost of health care rockets some have started to cut back on benefits. When negotiating your contract you should make sure that the provision offered will be adequate for your needs. (See below.)

Pension plans
As in the UK there are company pension plans, some of them funded entirely by the employer, others requiring contributions from both employer and employee. If you are working on a short-term contract, you may be ineligible for such a scheme.

Other benefits
These would include profit sharing schemes (normally restricted to long-term employees), training allowances, social and sports facilities, counselling, low-cost loans. Company cars and luncheon vouchers are not very common.

MEDICAL MATTERS

In the United States there is no government funded health service catering for everybody on the lines of the National Health Service in the UK. The **Medicare** programme, which accounts for 15 per cent of Federal Government spending, is limited to the over-65s and long term disabled.

Medical costs in America are high and are rising fast. In 1990 health care spending came to $680 billion—12.4 per cent of GNP; the UK percentage is less than half that. Even a routine visit to the dentist can set you back a tidy sum. That is why you ought to make sure that you and any dependents you have in the United States have adequate medical insurance cover.

Fortunately, many employers have company medical plans for their staff, and around 90 per cent of employees with private health insurance are covered by such plans. However, a number of these plans cover only a proportion of the expenses incurred (normally between 70 and 90 per cent), and may exclude dental care. So you may need to explore the possibility of topping up your employer's scheme with an individual policy.

Sickness benefit is provided by:

- the Federal Government in the case of disabilities that are total and permanent
- certain states for short periods of illness or disability
- private insurance plans in other states. These are often funded by employers.

The Health Insurance Association of America publishes some useful consumer guides, including *The Consumer's Guide to Health Insurance, The Consumer's Guide to Medicare Supplement Insurance* and *The Consumer's Guide to Disability Insurance.*

WORKING PRACTICES

The working day is normally from 8am to 4.30pm in factories, 8.30am to 5pm for offices and the 40-hour week tends to be the norm. Americans tend to be sticklers for timekeeping, and you will be expected to arrive punctually and not slide off before the end of the working day. It is quite normal even for executives to clock in.

Employees are expected to pull their weight, and if you want to succeed in your job you must be prepared to work long hours; firms are quite ready to dismiss backsliders with no reasons given. There is no specific federal government regulation regarding termination of employment, but the normal practice is to give two weeks' notice or severance pay. If you are laid off you may be able to collect unemployment insurance, but not for an open-ended period as in the UK.

By contrast, equal opportunity legislation tends to work in the employee's favour. The Equal Employment Opportunity Commission of the Federal Department of Labor prohibits discrimination on the basis of race, religion, colour, sex, national origin, handicap, age and virtually everything else. Americans are much more prone to taking employers to court than employees on this side of the Atlantic.

Many states have additional laws designed to counter discrimination in employment, sexual harassment and smoking in public places, and one needs to be aware of these. State laws can affect the way you apply for a job: in some states you should not enclose a photograph with your application. One clearly has to be circumspect in one's relationships towards subordinates of the opposite sex, while chain smokers are in danger of being ostracised.

Working practices often reflect the values of the society in which they operate. In the United States individualism, enterprise and financial success are highly regarded, especially in the urban areas. While British people share many of these attitudes, people from other cultures may find the American way of work perplexing because their societies have a different system of values.

If you come into this category, Geert Hofstede's *Cultures Consequences* is required reading. The Institute for Training in Intercultural Management in the Hague offers courses in understanding and working with other nationalities, as does its UK affiliate, Howell & Associates. Other organisations involved in preparing people for working in the United States are: the Centre for International Briefing, Employment Conditions Abroad and Moran Stahl & Boyer.

TAXATION

'In this world nothing can be said to be certain, except death and taxes', wrote Benjamin Franklin over 200 years ago. In the United States the tax system, like death, has the habit of catching up with you in the end, so you need to be aware of some of its features.

Federal Income Tax

If you take up employment in America, you are liable to be taxed unless you fall into one of the exempt categories, such as diplomats, students and exchange visitors.

Many Americans live in awe of the Internal Revenue Service (the US equivalent of the Inland Revenue) whose tentacles seem to be everywhere. Departing aliens, for instance, may not be permitted to leave the country unless they can produce a certificate of compliance (sometimes known as the sailing permit or departure permit) at the port of departure.

To obtain this certificate, if you have earnings in the United States you must first file Form 1040C to the IRS office in your district; if you have received no income from US sources you need to submit Form 2063. Mercifully, tourists, students and the staff of foreign governments and international organisations are exempt.

The ins and outs of US taxation are long and complex, and beyond the scope of this book. You can, though, get various guides free of charge from the Inland Revenue Service itself. The relevant ones are *US Tax Guide for Aliens* and *Your Federal Income Tax* (which is at least three times as long as this book!).

The first thing the IRS will want to establish is whether you are a non-resident alien or resident alien for tax purposes. Green card holders are automatically regarded as residents by the IRS, and people on non-immigrant visas who have been present in the United States for a substantial part of the year also fall into this category. The chart in Figure 12 will help you decide. Complications occur in the case of people who commute between the UK and America, and if you have been both a non-resident alien and a resident alien during the course of one tax year.

The US tax year coincides with the calendar year. If you are a non-resident alien in the eyes of the IRS, and engaged in a trade or business, you will need to apply for a **taxpayer identification number** at the local office of the Social Security Administration and file your income tax return on Form 1040NR. Resident aliens file Form 1040EZ, 1040A or 1040 and must apply for a taxpayer identification number too, as soon as they start earning income subject to US tax.

A US income tax form is a complex document, since there are several allowances you may be able to claim (including certain medical and dental expenses). Many Americans employ a certified public accountant (CPA) to complete their tax return for them—at a cost of a few hundred dollars—but if you work diligently through the tax guides mentioned above you should be able to do it yourself.

For employees a system similar to Pay as You Earn operates in the United States, though it is not obligatory. You must let your employer know whether you are a resident or non-resident alien and agree with him how much tax you expect to pay so that the correct amount of tax can be withheld. If you are resident alien you need to let him have a **Certificate of Alien Claiming Residence in the United States** (Form 1078).

When you come to fill in your tax form at the end of the tax year, you may find you are due for a refund or additional payment if there is a discrepancy between what has been withheld and what you should have paid on your tax form. Note that there are deadlines for the submission.

State and local taxes

Most of the states also levy taxes on individuals (though until now Texas has been an exception). This takes the form of income tax, and the rates can vary considerably from state to state. To find out what proportion of your income you have to pay, you should contact the tax department of the state in which you intend to live and work.

(Addresses in Appendix G.) The table in Figure 10 will also give some indication.

You may also need to pay local taxes to the city or county in which you live, and these often take the form of a sales tax or a property tax. Residents of Metropolitan Atlanta, for instance, pay:

- state income tax
- property taxes (rates)
- a sales and use tax (currently 4 per cent).

Social Security

The federal government also deducts social security tax, which is similar to our National Insurance and goes towards your pension and Medicare. However, bear in mind that Medicare benefits are only available to certain groups. Because of reciprocal agreements between the United States and other countries, including the UK, as a non-resident alien you may well be able to pay UK National Insurance contributions instead. You may also have to contribute to a disability insurance scheme in certain states.

Start here to determine your status for year X

Were you a lawful permanent resident of the United States
(had a 'green card') at any time during year X?

YES   NO

Were you physically present in the United States on at least 31
days during year X?

YES   NO ⟶

Were you physically present in the United States on at least
183 days during the three-year period up to the end of year X
counting all days of presence in year X, one third of the days of
presence in the preceding year and one sixth of the days of
presence in the year before that?

YES   NO ⟶

Do you still meet the 183 day test of the preceding question if
you disregard days for which you were an exempt individual
(student, teacher, diplomat, etc.) or were unable to leave the
US because of a medical condition that arose while you were in
the US?

YES   NO ⟶

Were you physically present in the United States on at least
183 days during year X?

YES   NO

Can you show that for year X you have a tax home in a foreign
country and have a closer connection to that country than to
the United States?

NO   YES ⟶

You are a resident alien   You are a non-resident
for US tax purposes.   alien for US tax purposes.

(Source: US Tax Guide for Aliens)

Fig. 11.   Determining your tax status

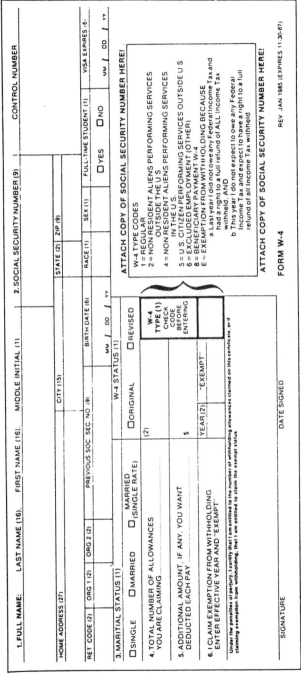

Fig. 12. Employer's tax deduction card

EMPLOYEE'S PAY STATEMENT

C.G. NICKERSON SUPPLY CO.
4567 MELROSE
MIAMI, FL. 33199

HOURS		WAGES				DEDUCTIONS				
REGULAR	OVERTIME	REGULAR	OVERTIME	OTHER	GROSS PAY	FICA	WITHHOLDING TAX	HEALTH INSURANCE	CREDIT UNION	NET PAY

Fig. 13. Example of an employee's pay statement showing basic and overtime pay, tax and other deductions

(a) State individual tax collections per $1000 of personal income (1988–89)

Rank	State	Amount	Rank	State	Amount
1	Oregon	$ 41.90	27	Kansas	$ 21.47
2	Hawaii	41.74	28	Missouri	21.25
3	New York	40.04	29	West Virginia	21.23
4	Delaware	36.66	30	Alabama	20.17
5	Massachusetts	34.97	31	Utah	20.12
6	Minnesota	34.77	32	Nebraska	20.03
7	Wisconsin	34.18	33	New Mexico	18.56
8	North Carolina	32.65	34	Arizona	17.49
9	Maine	31.38	35	Illinois	17.20
10	California	29.48	36	New Jersey	17.06
11	Maryland	29.48	37	Pennsylvania	15.70
12	Virginia	29.22	38	Mississippi	13.78
13	Georgia	28.23	39	Louisiana	12.49
14	Iowa	28.22	40	North Dakota	12.33
15	South Carolina	27.82	41	Connecticut	6.05
16	Idaho	27.30	42	New Hampshire	1.72
17	Montana	25.65	43	Tennessee	1.41
18	Rhode Island	25.13	44	Alaska	.03
19	Vermont	25.01		Florida	0
20	Michigan	24.78		Nevada	0
21	Indiana	23.45		South Dakota	0
22	Colorado	23.42		Texas	0
23	Arkansas	23.30		Washington	0
24	Kentucky	23.27		Wyoming	0
25	Ohio	22.59			
26	Oklahoma	21.59		U.S. Average	24.69

(b) Percentage of personal income remaining after state and local taxes (1988–89)

Rank	State	Amount	Rank	State	Amount
1	New Hampshire	92.1	27	Maryland	89.5
2	Tennessee	91.1	28	California	89.5
3	Missouri	91.0	29	Rhode Island	89.4
4	Alabama	90.9	30	South Carolina	89.4
5	Arkansas	90.8	31	West Virginia	89.3
6	Florida	90.7	32	Washington	89.2
7	Nevada	90.7	33	Delaware	89.1
8	South Dakota	90.3	34	Nebraska	89.1
9	Virginia	90.3	35	North Dakota	89.1
10	Illinois	90.1	36	Montana	88.9
11	Indiana	90.0	37	Louisiana	88.9
12	Texas	90.0	38	Oregon	88.7
13	Pennsylvania	90.0	39	Vermont	88.7
14	Mississippi	89.9	40	Iowa	88.7
15	Kentucky	89.9	41	Michigan	88.6
16	Connecticut	89.9	42	Arizona	88.4
17	Colorado	89.8	43	New Mexico	88.2
18	New Jersey	89.8	44	Maine	88.0
19	Georgia	89.8	45	Minnesota	87.8
20	Idaho	89.8	46	Wisconsin	87.7
21	North Carolina	89.7	47	Hawaii	86.9
22	Ohio	89.7	48	Wyoming	86.1
23	Kansas	89.6	49	New Mexico	88.2
24	Massachusetts	89.6	50	Alaska	81.9
25	Oklahoma	89.6			
26	Utah	89.5		U.S. Average	89.2

Fig. 14 Two charts showing the range of state and local taxes throughout the country

Form **1040** Department of the Treasury—Internal Revenue Service

U.S. Individual Income Tax Return **1990**

For the year Jan.–Dec. 31, 1990 or other tax year beginning _____, 1990, ending _____, 19___

Label (See Instructions on page 8.)

Use IRS label. Otherwise, please print or type.

Your first name and initial: Sam R. Last name: Brown

If a joint return, spouse's first name and initial _____ Last name _____

Home address (number and street). (If you have a P.O. box, see page 9.) 2617 Pewter Place   Apt. no.

City, town or post office, state, and ZIP code. (If you have a foreign address, see page 9.) Anytown, VA 23000

Your social security number: 000 00 0000
Spouse's social security number: _____

For Privacy Act and Paperwork Reduction Act Notice, see Instructions.

Presidential Election Campaign (See page 9.)

Do you want $1 to go to this fund? Yes [ ] No [ ]

If joint return, does your spouse want $1 to go to this fund? Yes [ ] No [ ]

Note: Checking "Yes" will not change your tax or reduce your refund.

Filing Status

Check only one box.

1 [✓] Single. (See page 10 to find out if you can file as head of household.)
2 [ ] Married filing joint return (even if only one had income)
3 [ ] Married filing separate return. Enter spouse's social security no. above and full name here. ▶
4 [ ] Head of household (with qualifying person). (See page 10.) If the qualifying person is your child but not your dependent, enter this child's name here. ▶
5 [ ] Qualifying widow(er) with dependent child (year spouse died ▶ 19___). (See page 10.)

Exemptions (See Instructions on page 10.)

6a [✓] Yourself. If your parent (or someone else) can claim you as a dependent on his or her tax return, do not check box 6a. But be sure to check the box on line 33b on page 2
b [ ] Spouse
c Dependents:

(1) Name (first, initial, and last name)	(2) Check if under age 2	(3) If age 2 or older, dependent's social security number	(4) Dependent's relationship to you	(5) No. of months lived in your home in 1990

No. of boxes checked on 6a and 6b _____

No. of your children on 6c who:
• lived with you _____
• didn't live with you due to divorce or separation (see page 11) _____

No. of other dependents on 6c _____

If more than 6 dependents, see Instructions on page 11.

Fig. 15. USA income tax form: Dual Status Return

d If your child didn't live with you but is claimed as your dependent under a pre-1985 agreement, check here ▶ ☐

e Total number of exemptions claimed

			Add numbers entered on lines above ▶	

Income

Attach Copy B of your Forms W-2, W-2G, and W-2P here.

If you do not have a W-2, see page 8.

			Amount	
7	Wages, salaries, tips, etc. (attach Form(s) W-2)	7	88,300 00	
8a	Taxable interest income (also attach Schedule B if over $400)	8a	395 00	
b	Tax-exempt interest income (see page 13). DON'T include on line 8a	8b		
9	Dividend income (also attach Schedule B if over $400)	9	120 00	
10	Taxable refunds of state and local income taxes, if any, from worksheet on page 14	10		
11	Alimony received	11		
12	Business income or (loss) (attach Schedule C)	12		
13	Capital gain or (loss) (attach Schedule D)	13		
14	Capital gain distributions not reported on line 13 (see page 14)	14		
15	Other gains or (losses) (attach Form 4797)	15		
16a	Total IRA distributions . 16a	16b Taxable amount (see page 14)	16b		
17a	Total pensions and annuities 17a	17b Taxable amount (see page 14)	17b		
18	Rents, royalties, partnerships, estates, trusts, etc. (attach Schedule E)	18		
19	Farm income or (loss) (attach Schedule F)	19		
20	Unemployment compensation (insurance) (see page 16)	20		
21a	Social security benefits 21a	21b Taxable amount (see page 16)	21b		
22	Other income (list type and amount—see page 16)	22		
23	Add the amounts shown in the far right column for lines 7 through 22 This is your total income ▶	23	28,815 00	

Adjustments to Income

(See Instructions on page 17.)

24a	Your IRA deduction, from applicable worksheet on page 17 or 18 24a			
b	Spouse's IRA deduction, from applicable worksheet on page 17 or 18 24b			
25	One-half of self-employment tax (see page 18) 25			
26	Self-employed health insurance deduction, from worksheet on page 18 26			
27	Keogh retirement plan and self-employed SEP deduction 27			
28	Penalty on early withdrawal of savings 28			
29	Alimony paid Recipient's SSN ▶ 29			
30	Add lines 24a through 29 These are your total adjustments	30	-0-	

Adjusted Gross Income

31	Subtract line 30 from line 23 This is your adjusted gross income. If this amount is less than $20,264 and a child lived with you, see page 23 to find out if you can claim the "Earned Income Credit" on line 57	31	28,815 00	

Tax Computation	32	Amount from line 31 (adjusted gross income)	32	28,815 00
	33a	Check if: ☐ You were 65 or older ☐ Blind; ☐ Spouse was 65 or older ☐ Blind Add the number of boxes checked above and enter the total here ▸ 33a		
If you want IRS to figure your tax, see Instructions on page 19.	b	If your parent (or someone else) can claim you as a dependent, check here ▸ 33b ☐		
	c	If you are married filing a separate return and your spouse itemizes deductions, or you are a dual-status alien, see page 19 and check here ▸ 33c ☑		
	34	Enter the larger of: { • Your standard deduction (from the chart (or worksheet) on page 20 that applies to you). OR • Your itemized deductions (from Schedule A, line 27). If you itemize, attach Schedule A and check here. ▸ ☑ }	34	9,322 00
	35	Subtract line 34 from line 32	35	19,493 00
	36	Multiply $2,050 by the total number of exemptions claimed on line 6e	36	2,050 00
	37	Taxable income. Subtract line 36 from line 35. (If line 36 is more than line 35, enter -0-.)	37	17,443 00
Tax from Table $2,814. Tax from Form 1040NR $3,3...	38	Enter tax. Check if from: a ☑ Tax Table, b ☐ Tax Rate Schedules, or c ☐ Form 8615 (see page 21) (If any is from Form(s) 8814, enter that amount here ▸ d ☐)	38	2,650 00
	39	Additional taxes (see page 21). Check if from: a ☐ Form 4970 b ☐ Form 4972	39	
	40	Add lines 38 and 39 ▸	40	2,650 00
Credits	41	Credit for child and dependent care expenses (attach Form 2441)	41	
	42	Credit for the elderly or the disabled (attach Schedule R)	42	
(See Instructions on page 21.)	43	Foreign tax credit (attach Form 1116)	43	
	44	General business credit. Check if from: a ☐ Form 3800 or b ☐ Form (specify) _____	44	
	45	Credit for prior year minimum tax (attach Form 8801)	45	
	46	Add lines 41 through 45	46	-0-
	47	Subtract line 46 from line 40. (If line 46 is more than line 40, enter -0-.) ▸	47	2,650 00
Other Taxes	48	Self-employment tax (attach Schedule SE)	48	
	49	Alternative minimum tax (attach Form 6251)	49	
	50	Recapture taxes (see page 22). Check if from: a ☐ Form 4255 b ☐ Form 8611	50	
	51	Social security tax on tip income not reported to employer (attach Form 4137)	51	

Dual Status Return (*continued*)

52	Tax on an IRA or a qualified retirement plan (attach Form 5329)	52	
53	Advance earned income credit payments from Form W-2	53	
54	Add lines 47 through 53. This is your total tax ▶	54	2,650 00

Payments

Attach Forms W-2, W-2G, and W-2P to front.

55	Federal income tax withheld (If any is from Form(s) 1099, check ▶ ☐ *INCludeS $36 from Form 1040NR*	55	2,736 00
56	1990 estimated tax payments and amount applied from 1989 return	56	
57	Earned income credit (see page 23)	57	
58	Amount paid with Form 4868 (extension request)	58	
59	Excess social security tax and RRTA tax withheld (see page 24)	59	
60	Credit for Federal tax on fuels (attach Form 4136)	60	
61	Regulated investment company credit (attach Form 2439)	61	
62	Add lines 55 through 61. These are your total payments ▶	62	2,736 00

Refund or Amount You Owe

63	If line 62 is more than line 54, enter amount OVERPAID	63	86 00
64	Amount of line 63 to be REFUNDED TO YOU ▶	64	86 00
65	Amount of line 63 to be APPLIED TO YOUR 1991 ESTIMATED TAX ▶	65	
66	If line 54 is more than line 62, enter AMOUNT YOU OWE. Attach check or money order for full amount payable to "Internal Revenue Service." Write your name, address, social security number, daytime phone number, and "1990 Form 1040" on it.	66	
67	Estimated tax penalty (see page 25)	67	

Sign Here

Keep a copy of this return for your records.

Under penalties of perjury, I declare that I have examined this return and accompanying schedules and statements, and to the best of my knowledge and belief, they are true, correct, and complete. Declaration of preparer (other than taxpayer) is based on all information of which preparer has any knowledge.

▶ Your signature *Sam R. Brown*	Date *3-16-91*	Your occupation *R's*
▶ Spouse's signature (if joint return. BOTH must sign)▶	Date	Spouse's occupation *Specialist*

Paid Preparer's Use Only

Preparer's signature ▶	Date	Check if self employed ☐	Preparer's social security no.
Firm's name (or yours if self employed) and address ▶		E.I No	
		ZIP code	

SCHEDULES A&B
(Form 1040)

Department of the Treasury
Internal Revenue Service

Schedule A—Itemized Deductions

(Schedule B is on back)

▶ Attach to Form 1040. ▶ See Instructions for Schedules A and B (Form 1040).

OMB No. 1545-0074

1990

Attachment
Sequence No. 07

Name(s) shown on Form 1040   Sam R. Brown

Your social security number   00:00:0000

Medical and Dental Expenses	Caution: *Do not include expenses reimbursed or paid by others.*		
	1 Medical and dental expenses. (See page 27 of the Instructions.)	1	
	2 Enter amount from Form 1040, line 32 │ 2 │		
	3 Multiply the amount on line 2 by 7.5% (.075). Enter the result	3	
	4 Subtract line 3 from line 1. Enter the result. If less than zero, enter -0-	▲ 4	
Taxes You Paid	5 State and local income taxes	5	662 00
	6 Real estate taxes	6	
(See Instructions on page 27.)	7 Other taxes. (List—include personal property taxes.) ▶	7	
	8 Add the amounts on lines 5 through 7. Enter the total	▲ 8	662 00
Interest You Paid	9a Deductible home mortgage interest paid to financial institutions and reported to you on Form 1098. Report deductible points on line 10	9a	
(See Instructions on page 27.)	b Other deductible home mortgage interest. (If paid to an individual, show that person's name and address.) ▶		
	....		
	....	9b	
	10 Deductible points. (See Instructions for special rules.)	10	
	11 Deductible investment interest (attach Form 4952 if required). (See page 28.)	11	
	12a Personal interest you paid. (See page 28.) │ 12a │		
	b Multiply the amount on line 12a by 10% (.10). Enter the result	12b	
	13 Add the amounts on lines 9a through 11, and 12b. Enter the total	▲ 13	

Dual Status Return (*continued*)

Gifts to Charity (See Instructions on page 29.)	Caution: *If you made a charitable contribution and received a benefit in return, see page 29 of the Instructions.*			
	14	Contributions by cash or check	14	360 00
	15	Other than cash or check. (You MUST attach Form 8283 if over $500.)	15	
	16	Carryover from prior year	16	
	17	Add the amounts on lines 14 through 16. Enter the total ▶	17	360 00
Casualty and Theft Losses	18	Casualty or theft loss(es) (attach Form 4684). (See page 29 of the Instructions.) ▶	18	
Moving Expenses	19	Moving expenses (attach Form 3903 or 3903F). (See page 30 of the Instructions.) ▶	19	8,300 00
Job Expenses and Most Other Miscellaneous Deductions (See Instructions on page 30 for expenses to deduct here.)	20	Unreimbursed employee expenses—job travel, union dues, job education, etc. (You MUST attach Form 2106 if required. See Instructions.) ▶	20	
	21	Other expenses (investment, tax preparation, safe deposit box, etc.). List type and amount ▶	21	
	22	Add the amounts on lines 20 and 21. Enter the total	22	
	23	Enter amount from Form 1040, line 32.	23	
	24	Multiply the amount on line 23 by 2% (.02). Enter the result.	24	
	25	Subtract line 24 from line 22. Enter the result. If less than zero, enter -0-. ▶	25	
Other Miscellaneous Deductions	26	Other (from list on page 30 of Instructions). List type and amount ▶	26	
Total Itemized Deductions	27	Add the amounts on lines 4, 8, 13, 17, 18, 19, 25, and 26. Enter the total here. Then enter on Form 1040, line 34, the LARGER of this total or your standard deduction from page 20 of the Instructions . . . . . . ▶	27	9,322 00

For Paperwork Reduction Act Notice, see Form 1040 Instructions.

Form **1040NR**	U.S. Nonresident Alien Income Tax Return	OMB No. 1545-0089
Department of the Treasury Internal Revenue Service	For the year January 1–December 31, 1990, or other tax year beginning _____, 1990 and ending _____, 19___	**1990**

Please print or type

Your first name and initial	Last name	Identifying or social security number
Sam R.	Brown	000-00-0000

Present home address (number, street, and apt. no., or rural route) (If a P.O box, see page 4 of Instructions.)
2617 Pewter Place

Check if: ☑ Individual ☐ Fiduciary

City, town or post office, province/state, and ZIP code
Anytown, VA 33000

For Paperwork Reduction Act Notice, see page 1 of Instructions.

Country ▶ U.S.A.

Of what country were you a citizen or national during the tax year? ▶ United Kingdom

Give address outside the U.S. to which you want any refund check mailed (if same as above, write "Same"). N/A

Give address in the country where you are a permanent resident (if same as above, write "Same"). SAME

Filing Status and Exemptions for Individuals (See pages 4 and 5 of the Instructions.)

Filing status (Check only one box.)

1 ☐ Single resident of Canada or Mexico, or a U.S. National
2 ☐ Other single nonresident alien.
3 ☐ Married resident of Canada or Mexico, or a U.S. National
4 ☐ Married resident of Japan or the Republic of Korea (South)
5 ☐ Other married nonresident alien
6 ☐ Qualifying widow(er) with dependent child (year spouse died ▶ 19___). (See page 5 of Inst.)

If your spouse is filing a return, you cannot take an exemption for him or her.

		Yourself	Spouse
7a		▨	▨
7b		▨	▨

Caution: *If your parent (or someone else) can claim you as a dependent on his or her tax return, do not check box 7a. But be sure to check the box below line 34 on page 2.*

7c Dependents: (1) Name (first, initial, and last name)	(2) Check if under age 2	(3) If age 2 or older, dependent's social security number	(4) Dependent's relationship to you	(5) No. of months lived in your home in 1990

No. of boxes checked on 7a and 7b ▲ ____

No. of your children on 7c who:
• lived with you ▲ ____
•• didn't live with you due to divorce or separation ▲ ____

Copy B of your Forms W-2, W-2G, and W-2P here

Dual Status Statement

Attach

Attach check or money order on top of any Forms W-2, W-2G, etc.

* Applies only to residents of Canada, Mexico, Japan, the Republic of Korea, and U.S. Nationals. (See page 5 of Instructions.)
** Applies only to residents of Canada, Mexico, and U.S. Nationals. (See page 5 of Instructions.)

No. of other dependents on 7c ►

d If your child didn't live with you but is claimed as your dependent under a pre-1985 agreement, check here ► ☐

e Total number of exemptions claimed ·

Add numbers entered on lines above ►

Income Effectively Connected With U.S. Trade/Business	8 Wages, salaries, tips, etc. (attach Form(s) W-2)	8	6,500 00
	9a Taxable interest income	9a	
	b Tax-exempt interest income (see page 6). DO NOT include on line 9a ⬜9b⬜		
	10 Dividend income	10	
	11 Taxable refunds of state and local income taxes (see page 6 of instructions)	11	
	12 Scholarship and fellowship grants (attach explanation—see page 6 of Instructions)	12	
	13 Business income or (loss) (attach Schedule C (Form 1040)) .	13	
	14 Capital gain or (loss) (attach Schedule D (Form 1040)) .	14	
	15 Capital gain distributions not reported on line 14 (see page 7 of Instructions) .	15	
	16 Other gains or (losses) (attach Form 4797) .	16	
	17a Total IRA distributions . 17a 17b Taxable amount (see page 7)	17b	
	18a Total pensions and annuities . 18a 18b Taxable amount (see page 7)	18b	
	19 Rents, royalties, partnerships, estates, trusts, etc. (attach Schedule E (Form 1040))	19	
	20 Farm income or (loss) (attach Schedule F (Form 1040)) .	20	
	21 Unemployment compensation (insurance) (see page 8 of Instructions)	21	
	22 Other income (list type and amount—see page 8 of Instructions)	22	
	23 Add lines 8, 9a, 10–16, 17b, 18b–22. This is your total effectively connected income ►	23	6,500 00
Adjustments	24 IRA deduction (see page 9 of Instructions) . . 24		
	25 Self-employed health insurance deduction, from worksheet on page 9 . 25		
	26 Keogh retirement plan and self-employed SEP deduction . . 26		
	27 Penalty on early withdrawal of savings . . . 27		
	28 Scholarship and fellowship grants excluded . . 28		
	29 Add lines 24 through 28 (see Instructions). These are your total adjustments ►	29	0
	30 Subtract line 29 from line 23. Enter here and on line 31. This is your adjusted gross income ►	30	

115

Tax Computation

31	Amount from line 30 (adjusted gross income)	31	
32	Enter itemized deductions (from page 3, Schedule A, line 10)	32	245 00
33	Subtract line 32 from line 31. Enter the result (if less than zero, enter zero)	33	
34	Exemptions (see pages 4, 5, and 9 of Instructions)	34	
	Caution: If your parent (or someone else) can claim you as a dependent, check here ▶ ☐		
35	Taxable income. Subtract line 34 from line 33. Enter the result (if less than zero, enter zero)	35	
36	Enter tax. Check if from: ☐ Tax Table, ☐ Tax Rate Schedules, or ☐ Form 8615 (see page 9)	36	
37	Additional taxes (see page 10). Check if from: ☐ Form 4970 ☐ Form 4972	37	
38	Add lines 36 and 37 ▶	38	

Credits

39	Credit for child and dependent care expenses (attach Form 2441)	39		
40	Foreign tax credit (attach Form 1116)	40		
41	General business credit. Check if from: ☐ Form 3800 or ☐ Form (specify)	41		
42	Credit for prior year minimum tax (attach Form 8801)	42		
43	Add lines 39 through 42	43		
44	Subtract line 43 from line 38. Enter the result (if less than zero, enter zero) ▶	44		

Other Taxes

45	Alternative minimum tax (attach Form 6251)	45	
46	Recapture taxes (see page 10 of Instructions). Check if from: ☐ Form 4255 ☐ Form 8611	46	
47	Tax on income not effectively connected with a U.S. trade or business (from page 4, line 81)	47	36 00
48	Social security tax on tip income not reported to employer (attach Form 4137)	48	
49	Tax on an IRA or a qualified retirement plan (attach Form 5329)	49	
50	Transportation tax (see page 11 of Instructions)	50	
51	Add lines 44 through 50. This is your total tax ▶	51	

52	Federal income tax withheld (if any is from Form(s) 1099, check ▶ ☐)	52	345 00
53	1990 estimated tax payments and amount applied from 1989 return	53	
54	Earned income credit (see page 11 of Instructions)	54	
55	Amount paid with Form 4868 (extension request)	55	
56	Excess social security tax and RRTA tax withheld (see pages 11 and 12 of Instructions)	56	

Dual Status Statement (*continued*)

Payments

57	Credit for Federal tax on fuels (attach Form 4136)	57
58	Regulated investment company credit (attach Form 2439)	58
59	Credit for amount paid with Form 1040C	59
60	U.S. tax withheld at source:	
	a From page 4, line 78	60a 36 00
	b By partnerships under Section 1446 (from Form(s) 8805 or 1042S)	60b
61	U.S. tax withheld on dispositions of U.S. real property interests:	
	a From Form(s) 8288-A	61a
	b From Form(s) 1042S	61b
62	Add lines 52 through 61b. These are your total payments ▲	62

Refund or Amount You Owe

63	If line 62 is larger than line 51, enter amount OVERPAID ▲	63
64	Amount of line 63 to be REFUNDED TO YOU ▲	64
65	Amount of line 63 to be APPLIED TO YOUR 1991 ESTIMATED TAX ▶	65
66	If line 51 is larger than line 62, enter AMOUNT YOU OWE. Attach check or money order for full amount payable to "Internal Revenue Service." Write your name, address, identifying or social security number, and "1990 Form 1040NR" on it. ▲	66 381 00
67	Estimated tax penalty (see page 12)	67

Please Sign Here

Under penalties of perjury, I declare that I have examined this return and accompanying schedules and statements, and to the best of my knowledge and belief, they are true, correct, and complete. Declaration of preparer (other than taxpayer) is based on all information of which preparer has any knowledge.

▲ Your signature	Date	Your occupation in the United States

Paid Preparer's Use Only

Preparer's signature ▲	Date	Check if self-employed ☐	Preparer's social security no
Firm's name (or yours if self-employed) and address ▲		E.I. No	
		ZIP code	

117

Schedule A—Itemized Deductions (See pages 13 and 14 of the Instructions.)

State and Local Income Taxes

1a State income taxes	1a	245.00
b Local income taxes	1b	
2 Add the amounts on lines 1a and 1b. Enter the total ▲	2	245.00

Gifts to U.S. Charities

Caution: *If you made a charitable contribution and received a benefit in return, see page 13 of the Instructions.*

3a Contributions by cash or check	3a	
b Other than cash or check. (You MUST attach Form 8283 if over $500.)	3b	
c Carryover from prior year	3c	
4 Add the amounts on lines 3a through 3c. Enter the total ▲	4	
5 Casualty or theft loss(es) (attach Form 4684) ▲	5	
6 Moving expenses (attach Form 3903) ▲	6	

Job Expenses and Most Other Miscellaneous Deductions (See Instructions on pages 13 and 14 for expenses to deduct here.)

7a Unreimbursed employee expenses—job travel, union dues, job education, etc. (You MUST attach Form 2106 if required. See Instructions.) ▶ . . . . | **7a**

b Other expenses (investment, tax preparation, etc.). List type and amount ▶ . . . .

. . . .

. . . . | **7b**

c Add the amounts on lines 7a and 7b. Enter the total . . . . . | **7c**

d Enter the amount from Form 1040NR, line 31 | **7d**

e Multiply the amount on line 7d by 2% (.02). Enter the result. . . . . | **7e**

8 Subtract line 7e from line 7c. Enter the result (if less than zero, enter zero). . . . . ▲ | **8**

Other Miscellaneous Deductions

9 Other (certain expenses of disabled employees, estate tax on income of decedent, etc.). List type and amount ▶ . . . .

. . . .

. . . .

. . . . ▲ | **9**

10 Total itemized deductions. Add the amounts on lines 2, 4, 5, 6, 8, and 9. Enter the total here and on Form 1040NR, line 32 . . . . ▶ | **10** | 245 00

Tax on Income Not Effectively
(Please attach Forms 1042S,

Nature of Income		U.S. tax withheld at source	
68 Dividends paid by:			
a U.S. corporations	68a	36	00
b Foreign corporations	68b		
69 Interest:			
a Mortgage.	69a		
b Paid by foreign corporations.	69b		
c Other	69c		
70 Industrial royalties (patents, trademarks, etc.)	70		
71 Motion picture or T.V. copyright royalties	71		
72 Other royalties (copyrights, recording, publishing, etc.) .	72		
73 Real property income and natural resources royalties. .	73		
74 Pensions and annuities	74		
75 Social security benefits	75		
76 Gains (include capital gain from line 83 below) . . .	76		
77 Other (specify) ▶..			
....	77		
78 Total U.S. tax withheld at source. Enter here and on Form 1040NR, line 60a. . . . . ▶	78	36	00

79 Add the amounts on lines 68a through 77 in columns (a)–(d) . . . . | 79 |

80 Multiply the amount on line 79 by rate of tax at top of each column . | 80 |

81 Add amounts on line 80, columns (a)–(d). This is your tax on income not effectively connected with a

Capital Gains and

Enter only the capital gains and losses from property sales or exchanges that are from sources within the U.S. and not effectively connected with a U.S. business. Do not include a gain or loss on disposing of a U.S. real property interest. Report these gains and losses on Schedule D (Form 1040).	(a) Kind of property and description (if necessary, attach statement of descriptive details not shown below)	(b) Date acquired (mo., day, yr.)
Report property sales or exchanges that are effectively connected with a U.S. business on Schedule D (Form 1040), Form 4797, or both.	82 Add amounts in columns (f) and (g)	
	83 Capital gain. Combine columns (f) and (g) of line 82. Enter the n	

Dual Status Statement (*continued*)

Connected With a U.S. Trade or Business
SSA-1042S, RRB-1042S, 1001, or similar form.)

Enter amount of income under the appropriate rate of tax (see pages 14 and 15 of Instructions)

(a) 10%	(b) 15%	(c) 30 %	(d) Other (specify) .... %	.... %
	240 00			
	240 00			
	36 00			

U.S. trade or business. Enter here and on Form 1040NR, line 47 . . ▶ | 81 | 36 00

Losses From Sales or Exchanges of Property

(c) Date sold (mo., day, yr.)	(d) Sales price	(e) Cost or other basis	(f) LOSS If column (e) is more than (d), subtract (d) from (e)	(g) GAIN If column (d) is more than (e), subtract (e) from (d)
		82 (	)	

et gain here and on line 76 above (if zero or less, enter zero) . . . . ▶ | 83 |

Other Information *(If an item does not apply to you, enter "N/A.")*

A What country issued your passport? United Kingdom

B Were you ever a U.S. citizen? ☐ Yes ☒ No

C Give the purpose of your visit to the U.S. Temporary Assignment

D Type of entry visa and visa number. H-1 Visa No. 654321 and type of current visa. Permanent

E Did you give up your permanent residence as an immigrant in the U.S. this year? ☐ Yes ☒ No

F Dates you entered and left the U.S. during the year. (Residents of Canada or Mexico entering and leaving the U.S. at frequent intervals, give name of country only.)
Entered - March 18, 1990.
Departed - May 25, 1990.
Entered - September 10, 1990.

J To which Internal Revenue office did you pay any amounts claimed on Form 1040NR, lines 53, 55, and 59?
N/A.

K Have you excluded any gross income other than foreign source income not effectively connected with a U.S. trade or business? ☒ Yes ☐ No

If "Yes," attach a statement showing the amount, nature, and source of the excluded income. Also give the reason it was excluded.

(Do not include amounts shown in item L.)

L If you claimed the benefits of a U.S. income tax treaty with a foreign country, please give the following information. Also see page 15 of the instructions.
Country United Kingdom

Kind and amount of income exempt from or subject to a reduced rate of tax. (Do not enter exempt income on page 1 of Form 1040NR.) Also identify the applicable tax treaty article: For 1990 Dividend Income of $240 received 4-3-90 and 7-3-90 taxed at 15% under Article 10.

For 1989 N/A

G Give number of days (including vacation and non-work days) you were in the U.S. during: 1988 .O. . . 1989 .O. . . and 1990 18.2 .

H If you are a resident of Canada, Mexico, Japan, or the Republic of Korea, or a U.S. National, did your spouse contribute to the support of any child claimed on Form 1040NR, line 7c?   ☐ Yes ☒ No

If "Yes," state amount $ . . . .

If you were a resident of Japan or the Republic of Korea for any part of the tax year, enter your total foreign source income not effectively connected with a U.S. trade or business in the space below. This information is needed so that the exemption for your spouse and dependents residing in the United States (if applicable) may be allowed in accordance with Article 4 of the income tax treaties between the U.S. and Japan or the U.S. and the Republic of Korea.

Total foreign source income not effectively connected with a U.S. trade or business $. N/A. . . . .

I Did you file a U.S. income tax return for any year before 1990?   ☐ Yes ☒ No

If "Yes," give the latest year and form number: . . . .

To which Internal Revenue Service Center was it sent? . . . . .

Were you subject to tax in that country on any of the income you claim is entitled to the treaty benefits? . . . . .   ☒ Yes ☐ No

Did you have a permanent establishment or fixed base (as defined by the tax treaty) in the U.S. at any time during 1990? .   ☐ Yes ☒ No

M If you file this return to report community income, give your spouse's name, address, and social security number. Also show the address of the Internal Revenue Service Center where his or her return was filed

. . . . . N/A . . . . . .

N If you file this return for a trust, does the trust have a U.S. business? . . . .   ☐ Yes ☐ No

If "Yes," give name and address

. . . . . N/A . . . . . .

8
Working for Yourself

So far in this book you have looked at ways of finding an employer in the United States—an exercise which will prove none too easy in the economic climate of the early nineties. This chapter looks at another option worth consideration: working for yourself.

Self-employment is admittedly not an easy option, but for anyone who has experience of running his own business, setting up in the United States will not be so very different. Immigrants from all over the world have done this: and the many ethnic shops, restaurants and factories you find in the country prove that success often favours the bold.

If you have a million dollars to invest, it should be fairly easy to get an immigrant visa under the new immigration legislation. The less wealthy, however, will have to be content with a non-immigrant (temporary) E visa. In the normal course of events this can be extended, and you may eventually be in a position to apply for permanent resident status, if you so wish. (See Chapter Two.)

WHAT'S MY FIRST STEP?

How does one set up on one's own account in the United States? There are basically four approaches you could consider:

- buy a business
- open a branch of your UK business in the United States
- set up a joint venture with an American company
- set up your own business from scratch.

Before you take the plunge it is vital to do some market research. To do this properly will involve one or more visits to the United States to find out the lie of the land.

If you are thinking of **acquiring a business** you need to ask around to see if the asking price is reasonable and the business has a bright future. This is not a time for throwing caution to the wind, and you should bear in mind that even some leading companies based in the UK have made disastrous acquisitions in America over the past decade.

A **branch office** is an excellent plan for anyone seeking to distribute or service his company's products in the United States. However, there is plenty of scope for the small businessman outside manufacturing; for example, as an international recruitment consultant, estate agent, relocation expert or business consultant servicing clients on both sides of the Atlantic.

A **joint venture** is also worth considering, not least because of the benefit in terms of market experience and local know-how an American partner can offer. However, you will need to proceed with caution and consider a number of possible partners before coming to any decision.

Starting from scratch is a risky activity, and you need to be confident of the viability of your project before embarking on it. New businesses wherever they are started tend to have a high casualty rate, with only a small proportion surviving until their fifth birthday.

UK sources of advice and assistance
Anyone planning to start a business in their own country requires advice and assistance. If you are planning to start a business—however large or small—in a foreign country your need is even greater.

If you are a UK citizen there are a number of British organisations you can call on:

- Department of Trade and Industry, British Overseas Trade Board. Exports to North America Branch, which publishes the *UK Businessman's Guide to American Law, Business Practices and Taxation.*

- British Trade and Investment Office, British Consulate General, New York, which publishes a booklet entitled *Setting Up Your Own Business in the USA* and can provide a list of recommended lawyers.

- Other British missions in the United States—the Commercial Office of the Embassy in Washington and the various Consulates-General.

- The British-American Chamber of Commerce, in London, New

York and California, and the British-Florida Chamber of Commerce.

US sources of advice and assistance

There are also plenty of organisations in the United States that may be able to provide you with advice. The larger you are, and the more likely you are to employ US residents and contribute to the US economy, the greater the range of financial incentives available to you.

The Department of Commerce

The International Trade Administration publishes *Investment in the USA*. The Industrial Development Section publishes the *Site Selection Handbook*, which has details of the financial assistance, tax incentives and special services for industrial development. The Bureau of Economic Analysis produces the *Survey of Current Business* and other publications. The Commercial Attaché at the US Embassy may be able to provide you with the information you need.

The state governments

Generally speaking, the individual states of the Union have a very positive attitude to foreigners wishing to set up in business, even if the business is relatively small. Different states compete with one another to attract newcomers, often offering tax and other incentives, and many produce detailed brochures on the advantages they offer to investors. Their economic development departments (listed in Appendix G) should be able to offer you advice. Many of them have offices in Europe and a few, notably California and New York, are represented in London.

Local chambers of commerce and trade or professional associations

City and state chambers of commerce are a useful source of local business intelligence, and should be able to suggest useful professional contacts. (Chambers of commerce are listed in Appendix G; a number of trade and professional associations appear in Appendix A.)

US Small Business Administration

Although created to assist US residents set up their own businesses, the Administration produces a wide range of publications and videos of interest to any small scale entrepreneur, which cover all elements of business from financial management to marketing and crime prevention. In addition, Small Business Development Centers provide training, counselling and research; Small Business Institutes provide free management studies; SCORE (Service Corps of Retired Executives) provides free training and one-to-one counselling; and specialised financing is available. While you as a newcomer may not be eligible for all of these benefits, there is no harm in asking about them.

Other sources of advice
These include banks, lawyers, accountants and business consultants; in the larger centres you may find the affiliates of UK or Irish firms. There are also several excellent handbooks on starting businesses.

MATTERS FOR CONSIDERATION

American law can be baffling to a newcomer, and if you are setting up in business you will have to take care not to put a foot wrong. It is therefore advisable to engage the services of a reputable lawyer who can not only deal with the legal requirements of your business, but also ensure that you do not fall foul of the Immigration and Naturalisation Service.

As in the UK there are basically three types of business organisation:

- the sole proprietor
- the partnership
- the corporation

It is up to you and your adviser to decide which of the three is most suitable for you. There are, incidentally, four other types of companies—the limited partnership, the statutory partnership association, the unincorporated associations and the business trust, but these are rarely used these days.

All entities doing business in the United States are subject to laws enacted at three levels of government—federal, state and local. While there may be considerable similarity between the laws, there are also significant differences. If you are planning to employ people, you need to be conversant with the labor regulations of the state in which you operate.

The economic development office of the state may help to steer you through some of the red tape. Its officials can advise you about any licences you need to operate your business and of the regulations that apply to your activities. The relevant chamber of commerce or local branch of the Small Business Administration should also be able to help.

From the city, town or county in which you intend to operate you may well have to obtain a business licence and make sure that you are not contravening planning laws, building codes and other regulations. You will also have to register with the state tax office and the federal Inland Revenue Service, which can provide you with a *Going Into Business* Tax Kit.

If you start to employ people, the IRS will provide you with an employer's identification number, and you will need to contact the state labor department and various arms of the federal Department of Labor, notably:

● The Occupational Safety and Health Administration, which sets standards for health and safety at work;

● Unemployment Insurance Service, which levies a contribution from employers to provide dole to the unemployed;

● Employment Standards Administration, which regulates working hours, the employment of minors, minimum wages, etc.

WHAT BUSINESS?

The details mentioned above should indicate that people starting up on their own in the United States, as indeed anywhere, need to have their wits about them. Americans are not averse to driving hard bargains, and make no allowances for enterprises that are just finding their feet. All the more reason for doing a thorough investigation into the market in advance.

Many people prefer to make use of their professional skills, and this is very sensible. If you are qualified in some branch of the health care field, for instance, you could set up your own practice, though care needs to be taken to choose the right locality. Bear in mind that you will need to make sure your qualifications are recognised, and you may be required to take an examination.

Computer consultants and electronic systems designers should also be able to make a good living. There could also be scope for self-employed plumbers, electricians and gardeners, particularly in such states as Florida where there are large numbers of elderly people and a booming construction industry. However, you will need to make out a good case for yourself in order to get the necessary work visa.

You may find there is no real demand for the skills you deployed back home, in which case you will need to investigate alternatives. You could look into the possibility of buying a small business, such as a shop, a rest home or a restaurant. There is something of a vogue for British style pubs in California and Florida, and if you see yourself in the role of 'mine host' this could be an option for you.

You should however guard against jumping on a bandwagon, since such vehicles have a nasty habit of coming to an abrupt halt. Ideally, you need to be in a sector with good prospects for expansion. The final chapter will attempt to suggest which sectors these are.

9
Looking Ahead

Most of this book has concentrated on the here and now, but if you have long-term aspirations you have to look ahead. In the words of John Galsworthy: 'If you do not think about the future you cannot have one.'

This chapter looks into the future. It speculates about future job prospects in the United States, and in particular, the most promising job sectors and areas for employment. If, however, you are interested in exploring other options—returning home or perhaps moving on to some other country—these questions are also dealt with briefly.

WHAT ARE THE FUTURE JOB PROSPECTS?

At the time of going to press the United States is experiencing a recession, and this has a dampening effect on the jobs market. However, recessions do not affect every region equally, nor do they last forever. One of these days the US economy will experience an upturn, and this will mean more job opportunities.

This does not necessarily mean more of the same. Certain industries will require fewer staff, either because they are in decline or because of increases in productivity; the automobile and textile industries are cases in point. Others will require more staff, because they are expanding. The outstanding examples here are the health care and home care sectors.

Clearly it makes sense to look for jobs where there is going to be a growth in demand. Fortunately we have some useful forecasts to go by; every two years the Bureau of Labor Statistics of the US Department of Labor produces employment projections for each occupation. The latest projections to hand relate to the period 1990–2005.

Figure 16 shows the occupations that are expected to grow the fastest, with home health aides topping the bill and many other health care occupations in hot pursuit. Computer personnel and legal assistants are also going to be much in demand, also human services workers (social workers), travel industry personnel and correction officers (prison officers)—a sign that crime is likely to increase as well.

Other occupations which are likely to undergo expansion by 40 per cent or more are: pre-school and special school teachers, entertainment sector personnel, securities and financial sales workers, private detectives, gardeners and groundsmen. Prospects also look good for accountants, lawyers, opticians, cameramen and manicurists!

By contrast numerous manufacturing occupations are likely to decline, especially in the textile, electronics and plastics industries, as a result of automation. Fewer bookkeepers, accounting and auditing clerks will be needed in offices, and the number of typists is likely to fall as well. Telecommunications is also going to lose jobs. However, these are not sectors where much recruitment was done from abroad anyway.

To return to the expanding occupational sectors, while many of the extra jobs mentioned will be taken up by Americans, not all of them will be. Reviewing data showing the mathematical proficiency of pupils in the twelfth grade, an American labor expert notes that 'a very small pool of young people today appear educationally prepared for many of the occupations projected to grow most rapidly in the 1990–2005 period.'[1]

THE MOST PROMISING AREAS

Americans are much more mobile than Europeans, and far more prepared to move to where the action is. Consequently during the seventies and eighties there was a migration from the north and east of the country to the booming Sunbelt region stretching from southern California to Virginia. The Rocky Mountain states also experienced growth during this period, while the Great Plains experienced decline.

It is difficult to predict whether these trends will continue. Many Americans headed back north when the Texan oil industry went through a lean time in the eighties, and did not move back when the economy bounced back. Now a significant section of the workforce in places like Houston is of foreign origin; the ten-gallon hat image has bitten the dust.

[1]Ronald Kutscher in his article *New BLS Projections: Findings and Implications* (Monthly Labor Review, November 1991).

Occupation	Employment		Numerical change	Percent change
	1990	2005		
Salesperson, retail	3,619	4,506	+887	+24.5
Registered nurses	1,727	2,494	+767	+44.4
Cashiers	2,633	3,318	+685	+26.0
General office clerks	2,737	3,407	+670	+24.5
Truckdrivers, light and heavy	2,362	2,979	+617	+26.1
General managers and top executives	3,086	3,684	+598	+19.4
Janitors and cleaners, including maids and housekeeping cleaners	3,007	3,562	+555	+18.5
Nursing aides, orderlies, and attendants	1,274	1,826	+552	+43.4
Food counter, fountain, and related workers	1,607	2,158	+550	+34.2
Waiters and waitresses	1,747	2,196	+449	+25.7
Teachers, secondary school	1,280	1,717	+437	+34.2
Receptionists and information clerks	900	1,322	+422	+46.9
Systems analysts and computer scientists	463	829	+366	+78.9
Food preparation workers	1,156	1,521	+365	+31.6
Child care workers	725	1,078	+353	+48.8
Gardeners and groundskeepers, except farm	874	1,222	+348	+39.8
Accountants and auditors	985	1,325	+340	+34.5
Computer programmers	565	882	+317	+56.1
Teachers, elementary	1,362	1,675	+313	+23.0
Guards	883	1,181	+298	+33.7
Teachers aides and educational assistants	808	1,086	+278	+34.4
Licensed practical nurses	644	913	+269	+41.9
Clerical supervisors and managers	1,218	1,481	+263	+21.6
Home health aides	287	550	+263	+91.7
Cooks, restaurant	615	872	+257	+41.8
Maintenance repairers, general utility	1,128	1,379	+251	+22.2
Secretaries, except legal and medical	3,064	3,312	+248	+8.1
Cooks, short order and fast food	743	989	+246	+33.0
Stock clerks, sales floor	1,242	1,451	+209	+16.8
Lawyers	587	793	+206	+35.1

Fig. 16. Fastest growing occupations projected for the period 1990 to 2005

Occupation	Employment		Numerical change	Percent change
	1990	2005		
Farmers	1,074	850	-224	-20.9
Bookkeeping, accounting, and auditing clerks	2,276	2,143	-133	-5.8
Child care workers, private household	314	190	-124	-39.5
Sewing machine operators, garment	585	469	-116	-19.8
Electrical and electronic assemblers	232	128	-105	-45.1
Typists and word processors	972	869	-103	-10.6
Cleaners and servants, private household	411	310	-101	-24.5
Farm workers	837	745	-92	-11.0
Electrical and electronic equipment assemblers, precision	171	90	-81	-47.5
Textile draw-out and winding machine operators and tenders	199	138	-61	-30.6
Switchboard operators	246	189	-57	-23.2
Machine forming operators and tenders, metal and plastic	174	131	-43	-24.5
Machine tool cutting operators and tenders, metal and plastic	145	104	-42	-28.6
Telephone and cable TV line installers and repairers	133	92	-40	-30.4
Central office and PBX installers and repairers	80	46	-34	-42.5
Central office operators	53	22	-31	-59.2
Statistical clerks	85	54	-31	-36.1
Packaging and filling machine operators and tenders	324	297	-27	-8.3
Station installers and repairers, telephone	47	21	-26	-55.0
Bank tellers	517	492	-25	-4.8
Lathe and turning machine tool setters and set-up operators, metal and plastic	80	61	-20	-24.4
Grinders and polishers, hand	84	65	-19	-22.5
Electromechanical equipment assemblers, precision	49	31	-18	-36.5
Grinding machine setters and set-up operators, metal and plastic	72	54	-18	-25.1
Service station attendants	246	229	-17	-7.1
Directory assistance operators	26	11	-16	-59.4
Butchers and meatcutters	234	220	-14	-5.9
Chemical equipment controllers, operators, and tenders	75	61	-14	-19.1
Drilling and boring machine tool setters and set-up operators, metal and plastic	52	39	-13	-25.6
Meter readers, utilities	50	37	-12	-24.8

Fig. 17. Fastest declining occupations projected for the period
1990 to 2005

As far as one can predict, the need for oil is going to continue, so 'the oil patch', as it is sometimes known, will continue to prosper, apart from a few blips now and then. Although the computer industry is currently in the doldrums, one would expect the high-tech industries that have sprung up in the region to have a bright future, too. Defence related industries, however, look less secure.

One should not disregard the Atlantic seaboard. Though part of the North East is depressed there are several centres of high-tech excellence with a promising future in the area—Long Island, Boston and parts of Connecticut, Vermont and New Hampshire. New York City has always been the leading centre for finance, publishing, fashion and entertainment, and is likely to remain so into the distant future.

RETURNING HOME TO AN ESTABLISHED POSITION

If you are on the permanent staff of a company you can expect a transfer home sooner or later. This can be a relief to some; but more often than not it will be a wrench, particularly if you have come to enjoy the American life style.

'Reentry', as the return home is sometimes described, is not always a smooth process, and you will need to call on your capacity for adaptation once more. The International Committee of the Institute of Personnel Management offers sound advice:

- Take time to wind down properly.
- Assess and review the change in yourself and those at home.
- Gradually re-establish relations with friends, relatives and professional contacts.
- Plan long- and short-term goals along with strategies for achieving them.
- Accept that you will probably suffer some reverse culture shock, particularly of an organisational, financial and psychological nature.

MOVING ON

If you are on a contract, you may have the option of renewing it; but on the other hand you may well feel it is time to get up and go. Americans believe that if you want to get on you move on rather than stay with the same company for years on end.

There are five main options to consider:

Get another job in the United States

You are well placed to find yourself a better position with another employer. This is easy if you are a resident alien with a 'green card'; but if you are on a temporary visa your new employer will have to be informed and told about the business of obtaining labor certification. This can of course take time, so you need to plan ahead.

Start your own business in the United States

It is relatively easy to buy a small business or to set up your own, but if you are not a permanent resident you will need to obtain the appropriate visa. See also Chapter 8.

Find a job back home

If you are on an exchange visitor visa you will be expected to return home, as your stay in America has been in the nature of an educational visit designed to develop your career in your own country rather than in the United States.

People who have been overseas for a number of years often need time to readjust, and would be wise to take note of the IPM advice to permanent employees given above. It is also advisable to set about the process of finding yourself a job in the UK well before your departure. Keep your eye on the job columns in UK publications and send off speculative applications.

Seek an overseas posting elsewhere

It is a good idea to approach contacts who know you first of all. Your present employer, for instance, may have operations overseas, and if you have been recruited through an agency, they may have other overseas postings that might be suitable.

The United States is a good place for overseas job hunting, particularly for South America and the Pacific Rim. American companies often recruit non-Americans for overseas assignments, partly because they are more adaptable but also because there are usually fewer visa problems. There are a number of manuals that will set you off in the right direction, such as A Lieber's *How To Get the Job You Want Overseas*. *How To Get a Job Abroad* or *How to Teach Abroad* (if you are a teacher) also contain useful advice (How To Books).

Sign up for a study course

The international jobs market is a very competitive place, and if you want to stay in it you need to keep abreast of modern developments in your field. If you do not, you will soon cease to be an attractive

proposition to employers. No company is going to employ a has-been
—especially a foreign has-been—when they can pick someone more
recently qualified who may well be cheaper to employ.

You may be lucky enough to be with an employer who offers
training facilities, though if you are employed on contract terms the
chances are that you will not benefit from them. Otherwise, why not
look into the possibility of home study courses, part-time tuition at
night school, or consider taking a sabbatical?

If you plan to stay in the United States, take a look at handbooks
such as the *NHSC Directory of Home Study Schools*, the *Handbook
of Trade and Technical Careers and Training* or one of the guides to
higher education mentioned in the Educational Arrangements section
in Chapter Five.

GETTING ADVICE

At some stage in your career you may decide that you need advice,
particularly if you are contemplating changing direction.

Where can I find advice in the USA?

In the United States you will find a range of facilities at your disposal.

College career services
Most colleges, universities and community colleges have career
counselling centres offering workshops, individual counselling and
other programmes, and you should be able to use these services even
if you are not following a course at the institution.

Libraries
Many public libraries have career information centres which bring
together a wide range of materials relating to careers and job finding.
Some of them also provide courses or lectures on career choice.

Adult education centres
Some of these provide career guidance in the form of courses,
seminars or individual counselling sessions.

Voluntary organisations
A number of voluntary organisations exist to help job seekers, often
those from minority groups. One of these—Catalyst—is devoted to
women's career development and produces a range of useful pam-
phlets and books, including *Where Can You Start?* and *What to Do
with the Rest of Your Life?*

Employers
A number of the larger firms now have career development officers, usually within the personnel and training departments, who can help you plan ahead. They also bring in outplacement agencies to counsel staff who are made redundant.

Private careers counsellors
The International Association of Counseling Services produces a *Directory of Counseling Services*, and Richard N Bolles's *What Color is your Parachute* also lists selected job counselors. Catalyst also produces a guide: *The Catalyst National Network of Career Resource Centers.* You might also contact the National Employment Counselors Association.

If you return to the UK and require some form of counselling, the British Association of Counselling can suggest qualified people you can turn to or you might approach the careers service of a local education authority. *How To Get The Job You Really Want*, Roger Jones, also offers some useful pointers.

THE KEY TO SUCCESS

Hopefully by this stage no reader has any illusions that finding a job in America is an easy task, especially for a non-American. No job is going to come looking for you; instead you need to put in considerable effort to search out suitable opportunities, more so than if you are seeking a job in your own country.

Persistence, however, is not sufficient; you also need to be well informed. An expatriate jobs magazine boasts, 'The *Nexus* commitment is research, research and more research,' and this is precisely the attitude you need to adopt if you are serious about working in the United States.

The remainder of this book is devoted to helping you with your research into job opportunities. Follow up the various leads, offer a good account of yourself, and one day you may well surmount the odds and attain your objective: a worthwhile and interesting job in the USA. Good luck!

Appendix A

JOB SECTORS

Accountancy

One plan is to join a large international accountancy firm such as Arthur Andersen and see if it is possible to transfer to the US or join a British company with important interests in the US. Opportunities arise from time to time for recently qualified ACAs in mainstream auditing.

Certified public accountants (CPAs) need a licence and are regulated by the accountancy board of the state in which they practise. This could entail taking a four-part exam prepared by the American Institute of Certified Public Accountants. Registered public accountants offers a certificate in management accounting and the Institute of Internal Auditors also offers a certificate.

To find out more about the requirements you should contact either your own professional institute in the UK, the accountancy board of the state where you wish to work, or one of the American professional associations.

Useful addresses
American Institute of Certified Public Accountants, 1211 Avenue of the Americas, New York, NY 10036.
National Association of Accountants, 10 Paragon Drive, Montvale, NJ 07645.
National Society of Public Accountants, 1010 N Fairfax Street, Alexandria, VA 22314.
Institute of Internal Auditors, 249 Maitland Ave, Altamonte Springs, FL 32701-4201.

Recruitment consultants
Beament Leslie Thomas, Harrison & Willis.

Advertising, public relations and marketing

A very competitive but expanding business, and you might do best to try one of the British firms operating in this area.

Useful addresses and publications

Public Relations Society of America Inc, 33 Irving Place, New York, NY 10003.

American Association of Advertising Agencies, 666 Third Ave, New York, NY 10017.

American Advertising Federation, 1400 K Street, Suite 1000, Washington DC 20005.

American Marketing Association, 250 S Wacker Drive, Chicago, IL 60606. Publishes *The Green Book, Directory of Market Research Companies.*

Market Research Association, 111 E Wacker Drive, Suite 600, Chicago, IL 60601.

Public Relations News, 27 E 80th St, New York, NY 10021-0333.

Public Relations Career Directory, R.W. Fry, ed (Career Press Inc).

PR Reporter, PO Box 600, Exeter, NJ 03833.

Handbook of Advertising & Marketing Services, Executive Communications Inc, 919 Third Ave, 9th Floor, New York, NY 10022-3903.

Bradford's Directory of Market Research & Management Consultants, PO Box 276, Fairfax, VA 22030-0276.

Standard Directory of Advertising Agencies, National Register Publishing, 11500 W Olympic Blvd, Suite 355, Los Angeles, CA 90064-1527.

Major employers

Among the leading companies in this field are:

Interpublic Group of Companies, 1271 Avenue of the Americas, New York, NY 10020.

JWT Group, 466 Lexingon Ave, New York, NY 10017.

A C Nielson & Co, Nielson Plaza, Northbrook, IL 60062.

Recruitment consultants

DGH, DM, Knight Chapman.

Aerospace

In the past there has been a strong demand for aerospace engineers, though with the anticipated decline in defence spending, opportunities are likely to decline. The main manufacturing areas are California, Texas and Washington State.

Useful addresses

American Institute of Aeronautics and Astronautics, The Aerospace Center, 370 L'Enfant Promenade SW, Washington, DC 20024.

Major employers
Boeing Company Inc, PO Box 3703, Seattle, WA 98124.
General Dynamics Corp, Pierre LaClede Center, St Louis, MO 63105.
General Electric Company, 3135 Easton Turnpike, Fairfield, CT 06431.
Lockheed Corp, Box 551, Burbank, CA 91520.
McDonnell Douglas, PO Box 516, St Louis, MO 63166.
Northrop Corp, 1800 Century Park East, Los Angeles, CA 90067.
Rockwell International Corp, 600 Grant Street, Pittsburg, PA 15219.
United Technologies Group, United Technologies Building, Hartford, CT 06101.

Recruitment
Moxon Dolphin Kerby.

Agriculture

Generally speaking there are few opportunities in this field, unless you fancy becoming a cowboy and the low pay that comes with it. Pay is better if you perform as a rodeo cowboy, but the profession is competitive and the work exhausting. If you have cash to spare, you could consider buying a ranch or farm, but prospects in this sector are none too bright.

Useful addresses
National Cattlemen's Association, PO Box 3480, 5420 S Quebec St, Englewood, CPO 80155.
Dude Ranchers' Association, Box 4711, Laporte, CO 80535.
Professional Rodeo Cowboys' Association, 101 Prorodeo Drive, Colorado Springs, CO 80901.
American Farm Bureau Federation, 225 Touky Ave, Park Ridge, IL 60008.
American Society for Agricultural Science, 701 North Saint Asaph St, Alexandria, VA 22314.

Architecture

To practise architecture in the US you need to be registered with the National Architectural Accrediting Board in most states or work under a registered architect. Landscape architects tend to be concentrated in the sunbelt states.

Useful addresses
American Institute of Architects, 1735 New York Avenue NW, Washington, DC 20006.
American Society of Landscape Architects, 4401 Connecticut Avenue, Washington, DC 20008.

Banking and finance
Opportunities when they occur would tend to be for experienced people in very specialist fields, eg Eurobonds. There are a number of British financial institutions with branches in the US, and you could always apply for a transfer.

Useful addresses and publications
American Bankers' Association, 1120 Connecticut Ave, NW, Washington, DC 20036.
American Financial Services Association, 4th Floor, 1101 14th Street NW, Washington, DC 20005.
American Bank Directory, McFadden Business Publications, 6195 Crooked Creek Road, Norcross, GA 30092-3105.
US Savings and Loans Directory, (Rand McNally).
Insurance and Financial Services Careers, Wallace Witners, PO Box 40169, 1509 Madison Ave, Memphis, TN 38174.

Recruitment consultants
Kennedy Stephens, NPA.

Construction
Nine out of ten construction managers work in the contract construction industry and the same applies to most of the other specialists in this sphere. Perhaps the best plan is to subscribe to one of the American construction magazines to find out where the main areas of activity are. In the past decade the sunbelt states, especially Florida, have seen a great deal of construction activity, but one cannot say whether this will continue. If you have worked on contract for an American construction firm in the past—in the Middle East, for instance—you could ask for suggestions.

Useful addresses
American Society of Civil Engineers, 345 E 47th St, New York, NY 10017.
Associated General Contractors of America, 1957 E St, NW, Washington, DC 20006.
Associated Builders & Contractors, 729 15th Street NW, Washington, DC 20005.
American Society of Cost Engineers, 308 Monongahela Building, Morgantown, WV 26505.
American Society of Professional Estimators, 6911 Richmond Highway, Suite 230, Alexandria, VA 22306.
Construction Management Association of America, Suite 640, 12355 Sunrise Valley Drive, Reston, VA 22091.
United Brotherhood of Carpenters and Joiners of America, 101 Constitution Avenue NW, Washington, DC 20001.

Recruitment
Morson.

Creative
The jobs outlook for artists and designers is good, and a few people go to the US to operate on a freelance basis. This is, however, a competitive field and there could be visa problems.

Useful addresses
American Society of Interior Designers, 1430 Broadway, New York, NY 10018.
American Institute of Graphic Artists, 1059 Third Avenue, New York, NY 10021.
Graphic Artists Guild, 30 E 20th St, Room 405, New York, NY 10003.
Industrial Designers Society of America, 1142 E Walker Road, Great Falls, VA 22066.
Professional Photographers of America Inc, 1090 Executive Way, Des Plains, IL 60018.

Electronics
This is a field which employs a large number of foreign engineers, usually on contract, and jobs advertisements appear from time to time in the British press. A number of these jobs are in defence related industries, so in the future there could be a slight decline in opportunities in this sector.

For further information:
Institute of Electrical and Electronics Engineers, 1828 L Street NW, Suite 1202, Washington, DC 20036.

Major employers
Advanced Micro Devices Inc, 901 Thompson Place, Sunnyvale, CA 94086.
Amp Inc, 470 Friendship Road, Harrisburg, PA 17105.
CTS Corp, 905 NW Boulevard, Elkhart, IN 46514.
E G & G Inc, 45 William Street, Wellesley, MA 02181.
Emerson Electric Co, 8000 W Florissant Avenue, St Louis, MO 63136.
Motorola, 1313 E Algonquin Road, Schaumburg, IL 60196.
Perkin-Elmer Corp, Main Avenue, Norwalk, CT 06856.
RCA Corp, 30 Rockefeller Plaza, New York, NY 10020.
Square D, Executive Plaza, Palatine, IL 60069.
Tektronix, PO Box 500, Beaverton, OR 97077.
Westinghouse Corp, Westinghouse Building, Gateway Centre, Pittsburgh, PA 15222.

Recruitment consultants
Anders Glaser Wills, Beechwood, Morson, Moxon Dolphin Kerby, Randall
 Massey.

Engineering

In recent years there has been a decline in the number of graduates
in engineering in the US, and to make good this shortfall there should
be good opportunities for foreign engineers. If your work affects life,
health or property you will need to register with the state in which
you operate. Salaries in industry start at around $30,000 and can reach
$90,000 at senior management level.

Useful addresses and publications
National Society for Professional Engineers, 2029 K St, NW, Washington,
 DC 20006.
Society of Women Engineers, 345 E 47th St, New York, NY 10017.
American Institute of Chemical Engineers, 345 E 47th St, New York, NY
 10017.
American Society of Civil Engineers, 345 E 47th St, New York, NY 10017.
American Society of Mechanical Engineers, 345 E 47th St, New York, NY
 10017.
Peterson's Engineering, Science and Computer Jobs, 202 Carnegie Center,
 Box 2123, Princeton, NJ 08543.
JETS Guidance, 1420 King Street, Alexandria, VA 22314. Central distribu-
 tion point for information on engineering careers in the US.
Peterson's Engineering, Science and Computer Jobs, 202 Carnegie Center, Box
 2123, Princeton, NJ 08543.

Recruitment agencies
Anders Glaser Wills, Beechwood, Morson, Moxon Dolphin Kerby, Randall
 Massey, Wrightson Wood.

Entertainment and performing arts

As in the UK this is an overcrowded profession, with the overwhelming majority of its practitioners 'resting' at a given moment.
While Robert Redford may get a fabulous salary, most people live
very modestly and have to supplement their earnings. Also, unless
you happen to be very distinguished yourself or a member of a very
distinguished company, you may well find difficulty in obtaining the
necessary work visa.

Many of the dance companies are centred on New York. If you
want to be a film extra you will have to register with Central Casting
. . . and unless you have some very unusual features there is a long
waiting list.

Useful contacts and publications
Actors' Equity Association, 165 W 46th Street, New York, NY 10036.
American Federation of Musicians, 1500 Broadway, Suite 600, New York, NY 10036.
American Dance Guild, 33 W 21st Street, 3rd Floor, New York, NY 10010. Publishes *Jobs Express Registry*.
American Guild of Musical Artists, 1727 Broadway, New York, NY 10019.
Art Search—National Employment Service Bulletin for the Performing Arts, Theatre Communications Group Inc, 355 Lexington Ave, New York, NY 10017.
Theatre Careers—A Comprehensive Guide to Non-Acting Careers, J.W. Greenburg (Holt Rinehart Winston).

Environment, forestry and nature conservation
Since the majority of jobs are with the federal or state governments, these are the organisations you need to approach. This is a particularly good sector for vacation employment.

Useful addresses and publications
American Forestry Association, PO Box 2000, Washington, DC 20013.
US Department of Agriculture, Forest Service, PO Box 96090, Washington, DC 20090-6090.
US Department of Agriculture, Soil Conservation Service, PO Box 2890, Washington DC 20013.
US Fish and Wildlife Service, Department of the Interior, Washington, DC 20250.
Bureau of Land Management, Department of the Interior, Washington, DC 20240.
Society for Range Management, 1839 York Street, Denver, CO 80206.
Environmental Opportunities, PO Box 670, Walpole, NH 03608.
A Complete Guide to Environmental Careers, CEIP, 68 Harrison Ave, Boston, MA 0211.
Conservation Directory, US National Wildlife Federation, 1412 16th Street NW, Washington, DC 20036.

Health care
(See also under **Medical** and **Nursing**)
An ageing population and advances in medical technology means that this sector is likely to grow rapidly, especially the home health care sector. However, it is not sure whether the US will produce enough qualified people to cope with the demand, in which case there will be plenty of opportunities for foreigners.

It is worth bearing in mind that in order to practise your profession, whether on a self-employed basis or in a hospital, you will normally have to be licensed by the state in which you are active. This may involve taking an exam and having approved qualifications. Osteopathy, incidentally, is particularly widespread in the sunbelt states.

A number of British and Irish employment consultants recruit for the United States and are acquainted with the rules and regulations. Otherwise you should contact the appropriate body in the US for further details.

Useful addresses

American Chiropractors' Association, 1701 Clarendon Boulevard, Arlington, VA 22209.

American College of Healthcare Executives, 840 North Lake Shore Drive, Chicago, IL 60611.

American Dental Association, 211 E Chicago Ave, Chicago, IL 60611.

American Dental Hygienists' Association, 444 N Michigan Ave, Suite 3400, Chicago, IL 60611.

American Medical Technologists, 710 Higgins Rd, Park Ridge, IL 60068.

American Medical Record Association, John Hancock Center, Suite 1850, 875 N Michigan Ave, Chicago, IL 60611.

American Occupational Therapy Association, 1383 Piccard Drive, Rockville, MD 20850.

American Optometric Association, 243 North Lindberg Boulevard, St Louis, MO 63141.

American Osteopathic Association, 142 E Ontario Street, Chicago, IL 60611.

American Podiatric (footcare) Medical Association, 9312 Old Georgetown Road, Bethesda, MD 20814-1621.

American Psychological Association, 1200 17th Street NW, Washington, DC 20036.

American Association of State Psychology Boards, PO Box 4389, Montgomery, AL 36103.

American Physical Therapy Association, 1111 N Fairfax Street, Alexandria, VA 22314.

Opticians' Association of America, 10341 Democracy Lane, PO Box 10110, Fairfax, VA 22030.

National Health Council, Health Careers Program, 70 W 40th St, New York, NY 10019.

International Chiropractors' Association, 1910 L St, NW, Suite 800, Washington, DC 20036.

Private Care Association, 801 Princeton Ave SW, Suite 426, Birmingham, AL 35211. Placement service for carers for the elderly.

Major employers

American Medical International, 414 N Camden Drive, Beverly Hills, CA 90201.

Charter Medical Corporation, 577 Mulberry Street, PO Box 209, Macon, GA 31298.

Hospital Corporation of America, 1 Park Plaza, Nashville, TN 37203.

Humana Inc, PO Box 1438, Louisville, KY 40201.
Manor Care Inc, 10750 Columbia Pike, Silver Springs, MD 20901.
National Medical Enterprises, 11620 Wilshire Boulevard, Los Angeles, CA 90025.

Job listings
Jobmart, Association of Homes for the Ageing, 1129 20h Street NW, Suite 200, Washington, DC 20036.
Employment in National Institutes of Health, Clinical Center, National Institute of Health, Bethesda, MD 20892.

Recruitment consultants
Angel, BNA, Grafton, Knight Chapman, Medic, Miller Brand, Nurse America, O'Grady Peyton, USA Careers.

Hotels and catering
The industry is a useful source of vacation jobs, particularly in the main holiday areas where jobs as waiters and barmen are fairly easy to come by, especially if you arrive early in the season. If you are a student, see the BUNAC entry in Chapter Three. This is a sector which is easy to get into and employs a large number of foreigners, many of them illegal immigrants.

More senior posts are difficult to come by because of visa restrictions, unless you happen to be a senior executive with a British owned international hotel chain. However, there are no such restrictions on jobs on US based luxury cruises which are handled by VIP Luxury Cruise Management Division.

This is also a sector which is ideal for the entrepreneur with cash to invest or a friendly backer.

Useful addresses and publications
American Hotel and Motel Association, 1201 New York Avenue NW, Washington, DC 20005.
National Institute for the Foodservice Industry, 20 N Wacker Drive, Suite 2620, Chicago, IL 60606.
Official Guide to Food Service and Hospitality Management Careers, International Publishing Co of America, 665 La Villa Drive, Miami Springs, FL 33166.

Major employers
Brock Hotels Corp, 4441 West Airport Freeway, Irving, TX 75062.
Holiday Inns Inc, 3742 Lamar Avenue, Memphis, TN 38195.
Marriott Corp, 1 Marriott Drive, Washington, DC 20058.

Recruitment consultants
Profile, VIP.

Information technology

Another fruitful area for jobs which offers very good prospects. Computer positions in the US are advertised regularly in computer journals and there are a number of recruitment consultants handling these jobs in the UK.

Useful addresses and publications
American Federation of Information Processing Societies, 1815 N Lynn St, Arlington, VA 22209.
Association for Systems Management, 24587 Bagley Road, Cleveland, OH 44138.
Peterson's Engineering, Science and Computer Jobs, 202 Carnegie Center, Box 2123, Princeton, NJ 08543.

Major employers
Automatic Data Processing, 1 ADP Boulevard, Roseland, NJ 07068.
Burroughs Corp, Burroughs Place, Detroit, MI 48232.
Computer Sciences Corporation, 650 N Sepulveda Boulevard, El Segundo, CA 90245.
Control Data Corp, 8100 34th Avenue S, Minneapolis, MN 55440.
Data General Corp, 4400 Computer Drive, Westboro, MA 01580.
Electronic Data Systems Corp, 7171 Forest Lane, Dallas, TX 75230.
Hewlett Packard Co, 3000 Hanover Street, Palo Alto, CA 94304.
Honeywell Inc, Honeywell Plaza, Minneapolis, MN 55408.
IBM, Old Orchard Road, Armonk, NY 10504.
Intel Corp, 3065 Bowers Avenue, Santa Clara, CA 95051.
Wang Laboratories Inc, 1 Industrial Avenue, Lowell, MA 01851.

Recruitment consultants
Beechwood, Computer People, DGH, Hunterskil, James Baker, MDA, Randall Massey, Track International.

Insurance

The headquarters of the main American insurance companies are based in Boston, Chicago, Hartford, New York and Philadelphia. However, several British insurance companies operate in the US and it might be easier to try for a transfer.

Useful addresses and publications
Alliance of American Insurers, 20 N Wacker Drive, Chicago, IL 60606.
Insurance Information Institute, 110 William St, New York, NY 10038.
Society of Actuaries, 475 N Martindale Road, Schaumburg, IL 60173.

Society of Chartered Property and Casualty Underwriters, Kahler Hall, CB/9, 720 Providence Road, Malvern, PA 19355.
Insurance and Financial Services Careers (Wallace Witners), PO Box 40169, 1509 Madison Ave, Memphis, TN 38174.

Major employers
Aetna Life & Casualty Co, 151 Farmington Avenue, Hartford, CT 06156.
American International Group, 70 Pine Street, New York, NY 10270.
Cigna Corp, 1 Logan Square, Philadelphia, PA 19103.
Marsh & McLennan (insurance broking), 1221 Avenue of the Americas, New York, NY 10020.

Recruitment consultants
Insurance Personnel Selection.

Law

This is a sector which is likely to experience expansion in coming years, and this is particularly true for legal assistants (paralegals). American law is similar to British Common Law, so there should be few problems; however the Americans make no distinction between barristers and solicitors. To practise as a lawyer you may need to take the Multistate Bar Examination (MBE) and perhaps a written ethics examination as well. To obtain information about the requirements you should contact the Clerk to the Supreme Court of the state in which you will be practising or the State Board of Bar Examiners.

Useful addresses
American Bar Association, 750 North Lake Short Drive, Chicago, IL 60611. Publishes *Regulation of Foreign Lawyers* which deals with the jurisdictions in a number of states.
National Association of Legal Assistants Inc, 3005 E Skelly Drive, Suite 120, Tulsa, OK 74105.
National Federation of Paralegal Associations, Box 1410, Ben Franklin Station, Washington, DC 20044. Publishes information on job prospects in particular areas.
National Employment Listing Service for the Criminal Justice System and Social Services, Criminal Justice Center, Sam Houston State University, Huntsville, TX 77341.
FBI, US Dept of Justice, Washington, DC 20535.

Recruitment consultants
Quarry Dougall.

Librarianship and information science
Opportunities tend to be few and far between, unless you have specialist skills that are in demand.

Useful addresses
American Library Association, 50 E Huron St, Chicago, IL 60611.
American Society for Information Science, 1424 16th Street, Washington, DC 20036.

Management
The best idea would probably be to ask your organisation for a transfer to the US. However, management and management consultancy posts are advertised from time to time in the British press. Prospects for management analysts look particularly good.

Useful addresses and publications
Administrative Management Society, 4622 Street Road, Trevose, PA 19147.
American Management Association, 135 W 50th St, New York, NY 10019.
American Society for Personnel Administration, 30 Park Drive, Berea, OH 44017.
Institute of Management Consultants, 230 Park Avenue, Suite 544, New York, NY 10169.
National Association of Purchasing Management, PO Box 22160, Tempe, AZ 85285.
National Contract Management Association, 1912 Woordford Road, Vienna, VA 22182.
National Management Association, 2210 Ann Arbor Boulevard, Dayton, OH 45439.
Peterson's Business and Management Jobs, 202 Carnegie Center, Box 2123, Princeton, NJ 08543.
VGM's Handbook of Business and Management Careers, C.T. Norback, ed (VGM Career Books).

Recruitment consultants
Beament Leslie Thomas, DM.

Medicine
At one time doctors encountered few barriers to entering and practising in the US, but since 1977 they have needed to apply for labor certification (unless they are eminent in their field) and pass a visa qualifying examination. It is possible to do non-clinical work on a B2 visa provided it is non-remunerative, and on a J-1 visa provided it is related to your training programme.

The North East has the highest doctor-patient ratio, so your chances will be increased if you head for areas where the ratio is lower, eg the southern states. The Dept of Health and Human Resources can provide a list of areas where medical practitioners are in short supply.

Working as a doctor in the US can be extremely remunerative. However, medical insurance companies are now seeking to keep costs down by shifting to managed care health programmes that rely to a greater extent on medical assistants. The era of fat fees for consultations could be drawing to a close.

Useful addresses
American Medical Association, 535 Dearborn St, Chicago, IL 60610.

Mining
There are few signs of expansion in this sector and jobs are probably few and far between.

Useful addresses
Society of Mining Engineers of AIME, PO Box 625002, Littleton, Co 80127-5002.
Minerals, Metals & Materials Society, 420 Commonwealth Drive, Warrendale, PA 15086.
Geological Society of America, PO Box 9140, 3300 Penrose Place, Boulder, CO 80301.

Recruitment consultants
British Mining Consultants.

Miscellaneous trades
There could be opportunities as a self-employed person provided you can get a visa. A number of trades are heavily unionised and you may have to join a union in order to get a good job.

Useful addresses
Automotive Service Industry Association, 444 N Michigan Ave, Chicago, IL 60611.
International Brotherhood of Electrical Workers, 1125 15th St, NW, Suite 1201, Washington, DC 20005.
National Association of Plumbing-Heating-Cooling Contractors, 1016 20 St, NW, Washington, DC 20036.
National Machine Tool Builders Association, 7901 Westpark Drive McLean, VA 22102.

National Association of Television and Electronic Services of America, 5930
    S Pulaski St, Chicago, IL 60629.
The American Welding Society, 2501 N W 7th St, Miami, Fl 33125.

Nursing
(See also **Health Care**)
There are excellent opportunities for nurses in the USA since
health care is an expanding sector. However, before you can practise
in the US, in nearly every state except Arkansas you need to pass a
licensing examination. This can either be a state board exam or the
CGFNS examination which is held three times a year at various
locations around the world, including London.

There are four nursing grades:

- Licensed Practical Nurse. An LPN works under the supervision
  of doctor or registered nurse in hospitals, private homes, surgeries
  and clinics.
- Registered Nurse. The next step up the ladder. Two-thirds of
  RNs work in hospitals, and the rest working in nursing homes,
  community clinics, private clinics and industry.
- Certified Nurse-Midwife. A CNM is a registered nurse with
  additional training.
- Nurse Practitioner. The highest grade of all. This is a registered
  nurse with additional training who is licensed to perform routine
  medical procedures.

Useful addresses
American College of Nurse-Midwives, 1012 14th St NW, Washington, DC
    20005.
American Nurses' Association, 2420 Pershing Road, Kansas City, MO 64108.
National Federation of Licensed Practical Nurses, PO Box 1088, Raleigh,
    NC 27619.
National League for Nursing, 350 Hudson Street, New York, NY 10014.
American Hospital Associates, Division of Nursing, 840 North Lake Shore
    Drive, Chicago, IL 60611.
Commission on Graduates of Foreign Nursing Schools (CGFNS), 3624
    Market Street, Philadelphia, PA 19104.
National Association for Healthcare Recruitment, Box 5769, Akron OH
    44372.

Recruitment consultants
Angel, BNA, Grafton, Medic, Miller Brand, O'Grady Peyton, Nurse
    America.

Personnel and training

There are good prospects in this area, particularly in the employment agency sector, but a foreigner would need to become fully versed in US employment legislation in order to obtain a management post. There are advantages in becoming a certified personnel consultant.

Useful addresses
National Association of Personnel Consultants, 3133 Mount Vernon Avenue, Alexandria, VA 22305.
American Society for Personnel Administration, 606 N Washington Street, Alexandria, VA 22314.
American Society for Training and Development, 1630 Duke Street, PO Box 1443, Alexandria, VA 22313.

Petroleum (oil and gas) engineering

There are a number of foreigners working in this sector, and job advertisements appear from time to time in the British press. Texas, Oklahoma, Louisiana, California and Alaska are the main areas for this industry.

Useful address
Society of Petroleum Engineers, PO Box 833836, Richardson, TX 75083-3836.

Major employers
Atlantic Richfield, 515 South Flower Street, Los Angeles, CA 90071.
Chevron, 225 Bush Street, San Francisco, CA 94104.
Exxon Corp, 1251 Avenue of the Americas, New York, NY 10020.
Gulf Oil Corp, PO Box 1166, Pittsburgh, PA 15230.
Halliburton Co, 2600 Southland Center, Dallas, TX 75201.
Occidental Petroleum Corp, 10889 Wilshire Boulevard, Los Angeles, CA 90024.
Phillips Petroleum Co, Adams Building, Bartlesville, OK 74004.
Texaco, 2000 Westchester Avenue, White Plains, NY 10650.
Unocal, 461 South Boylston Street, Los Angeles, CA 90017.

Recruitment consultants
Anders Glaser Wills.

Pharmaceuticals

If you wish to practise as a pharmacist all states require that you be licensed. For this you will need a qualification from an accredited pharmacy college (some states accept foreign study programmes), to pass a state board exam, to demonstrate good character and serve an internship under the supervision of a licensed pharmacist.

Useful addresses
American Pharmaceutical Association, 2215 Constitution Ave, NW, Washington, Dc 20037.
National Association of Boards of Pharmacy, 1300 Higgins Road, Suite 103, Park Ridge, IL 60068.

Major employers
Abbott Laboratories, Abbott Park, North Chicago, IL 60064.
American Home Products Corp, 685 Third Avenue, New York, NY 10017.
Dupont de Nemours & Co, 1007 Market Street, Wilmington, DE 193898.
Bristol-Myers Co, 345 Park Avenue, New York, NY 10154.
Lilly & Co, 307 East McCarty Street, Indianapolis, IN 46285.
Merck & Co, PO Box 2000, Rahway, NJ 07065.
Sterling Drug Inc, 90 Park Avenue, New York, NY 10016.
Upjohn Co, 7000 Portage Road, Kalamazoo, MI 49001.
Warner Lambert Co, 201 Tabor Road, Morris Plains, NJ 07950.

Recruitment consultant
Knight Chapman.

Printing
There would appear to be few opportunities in this sector for foreigners.

Useful address
Printing Industries of America Inc, 1730 N Lynn St, Arlington, VA 22209.

Property
Estate agents (called real estate agents in the US) are required to pass a state licensing exam. There could be opportunities in serving the needs of the growing British communities in California and Florida.

Useful addresses
Building Owners and Managers Institute, 1521 Ritchie Highway, Arnold, MD 21012.
International Association of Corporate Real Estate Executives, Suite 8, 471 Spencer Drive South, West Palm Beach, FL 33409.
National Association of Realtors, 439 N Michigan Ave, Chicago, IL 60611.
National Property Management Association, Suite 105, 16418 W Sixth Street, Boulder, CO 80401.

Public sector jobs
(See also **Teaching, Social Work**)

The widest range of jobs is found in the public sector at the federal, state or local level, though some of these jobs will be open only to US citizens. The US Office of Personnel Management has a network of Federal Job Centers involved in recruitment in cities throughout the country and the states have a similar system. If you are in the US, this should be the first place to head for.

Alternatively, you could write to the department of the Federal Government, state, county or municipality which is likely to be interested in your qualifications. A few addresses are listed in Appendix G, but if the one you need is not, contact the US Information Service at your nearest US Embassy. Most USIS libraries have a range of directories relating to the public service, including those listed in this section.

Useful addresses and publications
Federal Job Information Center, US Office of Personnel Management, 1900 East Street NW, Washington, DC 20415.
National Employment Listing Service for the Criminal Justice System and Social Services, Criminal Justice Center, Sam Houston State University, Huntsville, TX 77341.
National Association of the Counties, 440 First Street NW, Washington, DC 20001.
International City Management Association, 1120 G Street NW, Washington, DC 20005. Publish *The Municipal Yearbook*.
International Association of Fire Fighters, 1750 New York Ave, NW, Washington, DC 20006.
National Federation of Federal Employees, 1016 16th Street NW, Washington, Dc 20036.
American Federation of Government Employees, 80 F Street NW, Washington, DC 20001.
Fraternal Order of Police, 2100 Gardiner Lane, Louisville, KY 40205.
Federal Employment Bulletin, PO Box 11715, Washington, DC 20008. Fortnightly bulletin.
How to Get a Federal Job—A Guide to Finding and Applying for a Job with the US Government Anywhere in the US, K. Kraus (Facts on File).
Federal Career Opportunities, Federal Research Services, Inc, 370 Maple Ave W, PO Box 1059, Vienna, VA 22180.
National Directory of State Agencies, (Cambridge Information Group).
Book of the States, Council of State Governments, Iron Works Pike, Lexington, KY 40578.

Publishing and the media
This is a competitive field, but opportunities are expected to grow as

more local newspapers are established. A number of British publishing companies, such as Reed International, are active in the US, and if you are on the staff of one of these you could look into the possibility of a transfer.

Useful addresses and publications
National Association of Broadcasters, 1771 N St, NW, Washington, DC 20036.
Newspaper Guild, 8611 Second Street NW, Silver Springs, MD 20910.
Editor and Publisher Market Guide and *Editor and Publisher International Yearbook*, 11 W 19th St, New York, NY 10011- 4202.
National Directory of Magazines, Oxbridge Communications, 150 Fifth Ave, Suite 301, New York, NY 10011-4311.
Ulrich's International Periodicals Directory, R. R. Bowker.
Literary Market Place, R. R. Bowker.

Major employers
American Broadcasting Companies Inc, 1330 Avenue of the Americas, New York, NY 10019.
Dun & Bradstreet Corp, 299 Park Avenue, New York, NY 10171.
Gannett Co, Lincoln Tower, Rochester, NY 14604.
Grolier Inc, Sherman Turnpike, Danbury, CT 06816.
Harte-Hanks Communications, 40 NE Loop 410, San Antonio, TX 78216.
Knight Ridder Newspapers Inc, 1 Herald Plaza, Miami, Fl 33101.
New York Times, 229 W 43rd Street, New York, NY 10036.
Taft Broadcasting Co, 1718 Young Street, Cincinnati, OH 45210.
Time Inc, Time & Life Building, New York, NY 10020.

Religion
Ministers of religion come into a special visa category, which could mean it is easier for them to enter the US than a layman. Most of the American religious denominations have their counterparts in the British Isles, and if you are interested in working in the US it is likely that you will make arrangements through your own religious organisation. The Roman Catholic Church is currently experiencing a shortage of priests and is particularly anxious to increase its numbers and there is a shortage of rabbis away from the main urban areas.

As religion is not taught in public sector schools, the only openings for teachers of religious instruction are in church and private schools and colleges.

Reference
Yearbook of American and Canadian Churches, Abingdon Press.

Scientific work

The United States possesses excellent facilities for scientific research in industry, in academic institutions and the public sector, and these have attracted scientists from all over the world.

Useful addresses and publications
American Chemical Society, 1155 16th St, NW, Washington, DC 20036.
American Institute of Physics, 335 E 45th St, New York, NY 10017.
American Mathematical Society, PO Box 6248, Providence, RI 02940.
American Institute of Biological Sciences, 730 11th Street NW, Washington, DC 20001-4584.
American Society of Biological Chemists, 9650 Rockville Pike, Bethesda, MD 20014.
American Statistical Association, 1429 Duke Street, Alexandria, VA 22314.
Society for Industrial and Applied Mathematics, 1405 Architects Building, 117 S 17th St, Philadelphia, PA 19103.
Jobs Bulletin, Association for Women in Science, 2401 Virginia Avenue NW, Suite 303, Washington, DC 20037.
VGM's Handbook of Scientific and Technical Careers: C.T. Norback, ed (VGM Career Books).

Secretarial work

There is always a need for good secretaries, though there could be problems in gaining labor certification unless the prospective employer is able to make out a good case. If you have residential status there are plenty of employment agencies offering both temporary or permanent employment.

Useful addresses
Professional Secretaries International, 2440 Pershing Road, Suite G10, Kansas City, MO 64108.
National Association of Legal Secretaries, 3005 E Skelly Drive, Tulsa, OK 74105.
Office and Professional Employees International Union, 265 W 14th Street, New York, NY 10011.

Social services
(See also **Public Sector**)

Two-fifths of social workers work in the public sector, often at the municipal or county levels. Most of the rest are employed in voluntary agencies (also called 'non-profits'). This is an expanding profession, partly as a result of the ageing population.

Useful organisations and publications

National Association for Social Workers, 7981 Eastern Avenue, Silver Spring, MD 20910. Offers voluntary certification ACSW.

Intercristo, PO Box 33487, 19303 Freemont Ave N, Seattle, WA 98133. A Christian organisation which offers a job placement and job information service. It publishes a quarterly newsletter *On the Job* and operates *Prospectus*, a database of 40,000 openings in non-profit Christian organisations. However it is not in a position to arrange jobs for people living outside the US.

Community Jobs, 1520 16th Street NW, Washington, DC 20036.

Employment Listings for the Social Services, 10 Angelica Drive, Framingham, MA 01701.

National Employment Listing Service for the Criminal Justice System and Social Services, Criminal Justice Center, Sam Houston State University, Huntsville, TX 77341.

Careers in the Non-Profit Sectors, T. Mc Adam, ed, Taft Group, 5130 MacArthur Blvd NW, Washington DC 20016.

Profitable Careers in Non-Profits, W. Lewis and C. Milano (John Wiley)

Taft Directory of Non-Profit Organisations S. E. Elnick, ed (Taft Group).

Sport and recreation

Around half of leisure workers are in the public sector. The rest work in commercial and voluntary organisations, some of them quite small affairs. There is plenty of seasonal vacation work available, much of it carried out by students (see Chapter 3). There is also an increasing need for experienced groundsmen.

Useful addresses and publications

National Recreation and Park Association, 3101 Park Center Drive, Alexandria, VA 22302. Publishes a twice-monthly bulletin of job openings.

American Camping Association, Bradford Woods, 5000 State Road 67 N, Martinsville, IN 46151.

Professional Golfers Association, PO Box 12458, Palm Beach Gardens, FL 33410.

US Professional Tennis Association, 1620 Gulf of Mexico Drive, Longboat Key, FL 33548.

Athletics Employment Weekly, Box 86, Warsaw, IL 62379.

Major employers

Bally Manufacturing Corp, 8700 W Bryn Mawr Avenue, Chicago, IL 60631. Amusement parks.

Walt Disney Productions, 500 South Buena Vista, Burbank, CA 91521. Disneyworld.

YMCA National Office, 101 N Wacker Street, Chicago, IL 60606.

Teaching and lecturing
(See also **Religion**)

If your principal objective is to gain teaching experience for up to one year in the USA, your best plan would be to go to the US on an exchange programme. Among the organisations that organise teacher/ lecturer exchanges are the Central Bureau and the Fullbright Commission. Chapter 3 deals with exchanges in more detail.

For longer periods your employer will normally need to apply for labor certification, unless you are pre-eminent in your field. School teachers wishing to teach in the public sector need to have their credentials accepted by the teaching certification department of the state in which they wish to teach, and this applies to US teachers as much as to foreign ones. The addresses are given in Appendix G. In some states, you need to be a US citizen in order to become a teacher in a state school, notably the District of Columbia, Florida, Idaho, Indiana, Maryland, Mississippi, Nevada, New Jersey, North Dakota, Pennsylvania, Nebraska, South Dakota, Texas, Washington, South Carolina and West Virginia.

Lists of schools and school districts are obtainable from the relevant state department of education (which is listed in Appendix G). Some state education departments maintain a placement bureau that you can contact, but more often than not recruitment is the responsibility of the school district or individual school. There are also teacher placement agencies which may charge a fee.

Teachers seeking posts in private schools do not usually need to meet the same certification requirements as those seeking posts in public sector schools. Applications should normally be directed to the principal of the school in question.

Useful addresses and publications
The National Association of State Directors of Teacher Education Certification (NASDTEC), PO Box 2431, Sacramento, CA 95814. Publishes the *Manual on Certification and Preparation of Educational Personnel in the US.*
Association of School College and University Staffing (ASCUS), Box 4411, Madison, WI 53711. Publishes the *Directory of Public Schools Systems in the US* and *A Job Search Handbook for Educators.*
National Association of Teachers' Agencies, PO Box 223, Georgetown, MA 01833. Can provide a list of teacher placement agencies.
The Handbook of Private Schools, Porter Sargent Publishers, Inc, 11 Beacon Street, Boston, MA 02108.
Independent Educational Services, 20 Nassau St, Princeton, NJ 08542. Teacher recruitment agency.

Foreign and Domestic Teachers Bureau, PO Box 1063, Vancouver, WA 98666. Teacher recruitment agency.

National Education Selection, 189 Clifford St, Newark, NJ 07105. Publishes a teachers' vacancy list nine times a year.

Modern Language Association, 65 Fifth Ave, New York, NY 10011. Publishes job information lists, which include teaching posts.

American Association of University Professors, 1012 14th Street, Washington, DC 20005.

The US-UK Educational Commission, 6 Porter Street, London W1M 2HR. Tel: (071) 486 1098. Has a small library and can provide further information on the US educational system.

Telecommunications
(See also **Electronics**)
Job opportunities in this sector look set to decline.

Useful addresses
Telecommunications International Union, Box 5462, Hamden, CN 06518.

United States Independent Telephone Association, 1801 K St NW, Suite 1201, Washington, DC 20006.

Major employers
AT & T Technologies, 550 Madison Avenue, New York, NY 10022.

GTE Corporation, 1 Stamford Forum, Stamford, CT 06904.

United Telecommunications Inc, PO Box 11315, Kansas City, MO 64112.

Recruitment
Moxon Dolphin Kerby.

Transport

Useful addresses
Air Transport Association of America, 1709 New York Ave, NW, Washington, DC 20006.

Air Line Pilots Association, 1625 Massachusetts Avenue NW, Washington, DC 20036.

American Trucking Association Inc, 1616 P St, NW, Washington, DC 20036.

Official Guide to Travel Agent and Travel Careers and *Official Guide to Airline Careers*, International Publishing Co of America, 665 La Villa Drive, Miami Springs, FL 33166.

United Nations
The headquarters of the UN and a number of its agencies are based in the United States, and if you land a job here your visa problems will be solved. Some of the posts will involve foreign travel and

possibly postings outside the US. There are two kinds of posts:

- Professional posts: specialists in economics, science, data processing, etc; translators, interpreters, précis writers, etc.

- General service posts: secretarial, administrative, information, clerical, accounting, etc.

Useful addresses
Professional Recruitment Service, Room 2465, UN Secretariat, New York, NY 10017.
United Nations Children's Fund (UNICEF), 866 UN Plaza, 6th Floor, New York, NY 10017.
United Nations Institute for Training and Research, 801 UN Plaza, New York, NY 10017.
International Monetary Fund, 700 19th Street NW, Washington, DC 20006.
World Bank, including International Bank for Reconstruction and Development, International Development Association, International Finance Corporation, 1818 H Street NW, Washington DC 20433.

Veterinary medicine
There are good prospects for vets. However you will need a licence to practise; this is gained through taking a two day state board proficiency examination.

Useful address
American Veterinary Medical Association, 930 N Meacham Road, Schaumburg, IL 60196.

Writing
(See also **Publishing and Media**)
Society for Technical Communication, 815 15th Street NW, Suite 516, Washington, DC 20005. Technical writers' association.
Career Opportunities for Writers, R. Guiley (Facts on File)
Writers Market (annual), Writer's Digest Books, 1 Dana Ave, Cincinnati, OH 45207. Distributor: Freelance Press Services, Cumberland House, Lissadel Street, Salford M6 6GG. Tel: (061) 745 8850.

Further information
A more comprehensive list of professional and trade associations is provided in:

Encyclopedia of Associations, (Gale Research).

Career Guide to Professional Associations—A Directory of Organizations by Occupational Field, C. N. Shramek, ed (Carroll Press).

Professional and Trade Association Job Finder—A Directory of Employment Resources offered by Associations and other Organisations: S. N. Feingold and A. Nicholson (Garrett Park Press).

Appendix B

UK RECRUITMENT ORGANISATIONS

Anders Glaser Wills
4 Maddison Court, Maddison Street, Southampton, SO1 0BU. Tel: 0703 223511. Fax: 0703 227911.
Job sectors: Petrochemical engineering.
Type of employer: Multinational engineering and construction firms.
Method of recruitment: Advertising, candidate register.
Advertising media used: Daily Telegraph
Qualifications and experience required: Experienced engineers from within petrochemical industry with at least five years' experience.
Additional information: Operates in conjunction with International Staffing Consultants Inc. PO Box 19688, 19762 MacArthur Blvd, Irvine, CA 92715. More than 100 American placements annually; also recruits for Middle East and elsewhere (FRES).

Angel International Recruitment
50 Fleet Street, London EC4Y 1BE. Tel: 071 583 1661. Fax: 071 353 8538.

Job sectors: Nursing.
Type of employer: Hospitals and private clinics.
Method of recruitment: Advertising, candidate register, recommendation.
Advertising media used: Nursing Times, national newspapers.
Qualifications and experience required: Trained nurses only who have passed CGFNS; at least two years' post-qualification experience.
Additional information: Places between 50-100 annually in US; also recruits for other countries. (FRES).

Beechwood Recruitment Ltd
221 High Street, London W3 9BY. Tel: (081) 992 8647.
Job sectors: Computing (hardware and software).
Type of employer: Most, particularly multinationals, manufacturers and defence industry.

Method of recruitment: Advertising, candidate register, recommendation.
Advertising media used: National press, trade press, local papers.
Qualifications and experience required: Minimum HNC level; 22-45 age range.
Additional information: Salaries range from £12,000 to £40,000. Also recruits for other countries worldwide. (FRES).

British Nursing Association (BNA) International
443 Oxford Street, London W1R 2NA. Tel: (071) 629 9030.
Job sectors: Healthcare (nursing, physiotherapy, occupational therapy).
Type of employer: Hospitals
Methods of Recruitment: Advertising, recommendation.
Advertising media used: Nursing Times, Nursing.
Qualifications and experience required: RGNs and enrolled nurses with theatre or ITU certificate.
Additional information: Operates in association with US subsidiary. Also recruits for Europe and Middle East. (FRES).

Computer People
VLI House, 68-69 St Martin's Lane, London WC2 4JS. Tel: (071) 836 8411.
Job sectors: Information technology.
Type of employer: Large commercial organisations.
Method of recruitment: Advertising, candidate register, executive search, Recommendation.
Advertising media used: *Computing, Computer Weekly*
Qualifications and experience required: Various levels of skill required, particularly with experience of Unix, IBM and CASE technology. Young, single people preferred.
Additional information: Handles 150 placements on average per year; network of 12 offices in USA; salary range $30,000 to $100,000 (FRES).

DGH Management and Recruitment Consultants
Yew Tree Cottage, Yew Tree Green, Horsmonden, Kent TN12 8HR. Tel: (0892) 722987.
Job sectors: Sales and marketing.
Type of employer: Multinationals.
Method of recruitment: Executive search.
Qualifications and experience required: Degree in Science or Business preferred; age 30-40; at least 5 years' experience in IT, data communications or telecommunications sales.
Additional information: Also recruits for Europe and the Far East.

Grafton International
94 High Street, Belfast BT1 2BG. Tel: (0232) 242824. Fax: (0232) 242897.
Job sectors: Healthcare (nurses).
Type of employer: Private and university hospitals.
Method of recruitment: Advertising and candidate register.

Advertising media used: Nursing Times, OSJ, Telegraph.
Qualifications and experience required: RGN plus 2 years' postgraduate experience and CGFNS.
Additional information: Recruits more than 100 annually. Age range 21-60. Salary range: £20,000-£50,000. (FRES).

Harrison Willis
Cardinal House, 39/40 Albermarle Street, London W1X 3FD. Tel: (071) 629 4463. Fax: (071) 491 4705.
Job sectors: Accountancy (normally main-stream audit).
Type of employer: Accountancy practices.
Method of recruitment: Advertising, candidate register, executive search, recommendation.
Advertising media used: Accountancy.
Qualifications and experience required: Full ACA qualification, majority of posts are for people in their twenties with up to three years' post qualification experience.
Additional information: Also recruits for positions worldwide. (FRES).

James Baker Associates
Park House, Wick Road, Egham, Surrey TW20 0HW. Tel: (0784) 473347. Fax: (0784) 438181.
Job sectors: IT, High technology.
Type of employer: Multinational and large national companies.
Method of Recruitment: Advertising.
Advertising media used: Computer Weekly, Computing, etc.
Qualifications and experience required: Technical graduates aged up to 30 with a minimum of three years' experience; normally highly specialist computer skills are required.
Additional information: Also recruits for Europe and the Middle East.

Kennedy Stephens
20 Cousin Lane, London EC4R 3TE. Tel: (071) 236 7307.
Job sectors: Financial: financial market specialists, notably salesmen, sector analysts, fund managers, and strategists.
Type of employer: Merchant banks and securities houses.
Method of recruitment: Executive search, recommendation, advertisement.
Advertising media used: Financial Times, Institutional Investor, Futures and Options World, and *International Financing Review.*
Qualifications and experience required: Graduates or MBAs earning in the region of £75,000.
Additional information: Works in association with its New York affiliate (G Z Stephens Inc). Also recruits for France, Spain, Germany and Scandinavia. Affiliated consultancies in the UK include: Vicky Mann Associates specialising in financial PR and the media; De Lisle Stephens (insurance); A & M Stephens (computers).

Medic International

4 Thameside Centre, Kew Bridge Road, Brentford, Middlesex TW8 oHB. Tel: (081) 568 4300. Fax: (081) 568 5920.

Job sectors: Medical (occupational therapists and physiotherapists).

Type of employer: Various.

Method of recruitment: Advertising, recommendation, candidate register.

Advertising media used: Professional journals.

Qualifications and experience required: British qualifications normally acceptable but may need to be assessed by US Registration Board.

Additional information: Works closely with the Texas based Healthcare Staff Resources; three-week orientation programme provided by HSR; also recruits for countries worldwide. (FRES).

Miller, Brand & Co Ltd

36 Spital Square, London E1 6DY. Tel: (071) 377 5661.

Job sectors: Healthcare.

Type of employer: Public and private sector hospitals.

Method of recruitment: Advertising, candidate register.

Advertising media used: Nursing Times, Nursing Standard, BMJ.

Qualifications and experience required: Qualified nurses and medical practitioners with UK registration and entry qualifications to the USA.

Additional information: Around 100 placements annually; all age ranges and salaries; also recruits for the Middle East, Far East and Australasia.

Morson International

Stableford Hall, Monton, Eccles, Manchester M30 8AP. Tel: (061) 707 1516. Fax: (061) 788 8372.

Job sectors: Engineering, especially oil and gas construction, petrochemicals, aerospace.

Type of employer: Multinational.

Method of recruitment: Advertising, Candidate register.

Advertising media used: National press.

Qualifications and experience required: At least a degree or HND in engineering. Multidisciplinary experience (eg electrical, mechanical, piping, instrumentation).

Additional information: Places around 100 engineers a year in US at salaries in £25,000—£50,000 range. Office in the US: 5353 West Alabama, Suite 525, Houston, TX 77056. Also recruits for Europe. (FRES).

Moxon Dolphin Kerby Ltd

178-202 Great Portland Street, London W1N 6JJ. Tel: (071) 631 4411.

Job sectors: Hi-tech: electronics, aerospace, semiconductors, telecommunications.

Type of employer: Multi-nationals, major corporations, R and D facilities.

Method of recruitment: Advertising; executive search; register.

Advertising media used: Daily Telegraph, Sunday Times, Electronics Weekly, New Scientist.

Qualifications and experience required: At least a first degree plus three to four years' experience in relevant disciplines.

Additional information: Places between 50 and 100 people annually; also recruits for Canada, Europe and the Middle East; four offices in the United States.

Quarry Dougall

9 Brownlow Street, London WC1V 8JD. Tel: (071) 405 6062.

Job sectors: Law (lawyers and paralegals).

Type of employer: Partnerships, national and multinational companies, institutions.

Method of recruitment: Advertising, candidate register, recommendation.

Advertising media used: Times, The Lawyer, Law Society Gazette.

Qualifications and experience required: Legal qualification and ideally also admitted in the US; specialist experience in an area of the law with similar application in the USA.

Additional information: Operates in association with Mestel & Co, Inc; also recruits for other countries worldwide. (FRES).

Randall Massey Consultants

7 Dorcan Business Village, Murdock Road, Dorcan, Swindon SN3 5HY. Tel: (0793) 614700.

Job sectors: Electronics, IT.

Type of employer: High-tech vendors and users.

Method of recruitment: Advertising, executive search.

Advertising media used: Sunday Times; Daily Telegraph.

Qualifications and experience required: Degree in electronics or computer science; 25-35 years old; unique skill set (eg in mobile communications or semi-conductors).

Additional information: Also recruits for Europe and Hong Kong.

Track International

PO Box 292, High Wycombe HP13 5XS. Tel: (0494) 451692.

Job sectors: IT.

Type of employer: Various.

Method of recruitment: Advertising.

Advertising media used: Teletext, Computer Weekly.

Qualifications and experience required: Graduates in the appropriate discipline aged up to 35.

Additional information: Also recruits for Europe and South Africa.

VIP International

17 Charing Cross Road, London WC2H oEP. Tel: (071) 930 0541. Fax: (071) 930 2860.

Job sectors: Hotel and catering management.

Type of employer: Public sector and multinational companies.

Method of recruitment: Advertising, candidate register, executive search, recommendation.

Advertising media used: Hotel Management, Caterer, Evening Standard, etc.

Qualifications and experience required: At least 23 with appropriate qualifications and ideally junior management experience in first class establishments.

Additional information: Few management positions in the US itself, but hundreds of opportunities on board US-based luxury cruises handled by VIP Luxury Cruise Management and Recruitment Division. (FRES).

Organisations which occasionally recruit for the US

Barnett Consulting Group, Providence House, River Street, Windsor, Berks SL4 1QT. Recruits for a variety of sectors.

Beament Leslie Thomas, 107-111 Fleet Street, London EC4A 2AB. Tel: (071) 353 5606. Places taxation specialists and management consultants with firms of accountants and consultants. Professional qualifications and relevant experience are required. Age range: mid 20s to early 30s. (FRES).

British Mining Consultants, PO Box 18, Mill Lane, Huthwaite, Sutton in Ashfield, Notts NG17 2NS. Recruits geologists, mining engineers and mine managers in association with a US subsidiary.

Cambridge Recruitment Consultants, 11 King's Parade, Cambridge CB2 1SJ. Tel: (0223) 311316. Recruits for various sectors.

DM Management Consultants Ltd, 19 Clarges Street, London W1Y 7PG. Tel: (071) 499 8030. A specialist in direct marketing and mail order appointments. The normal requirement is for graduate senior and general managers in their 30s and 40s.

Hunterskil, Project House, 110-113 Tottenham Court Road, London W1P 9HG. Tel: (071) 383 3888. Fax: (071) 387 2048. Recruits analyst programmers with a minimum of three years' commercial experience for IT contracts. Advertises in *Computer Weekly* and *Freelance Informer*. (FRES).

Insurance Personnel Selection, Lloyd's Avenue House, 6 Lloyd's Avenue, London EC3N 3ES. Tel: (0761) 481 8111. Fax: (071) 481 0994. Places skilled insurance and reinsurance staff qualified to ACCI standard with multinational insurance brokers and companies. The majority of candidates come through recommendation. (FRES).

Knight Chapman, 11 Garrick Street, London WC2E 9AR. Tel: (071) 379 7879. Specialises in: A) pharmaceutical and healthcare appointments and B) advertising planners for advertising agencies. Requirements: A—high calibre, well qualified people for a wide range of technical, marketing and general management positions from middle to very senior levels; B— British trained experts with at least three years' experience. (FRES).

MDA Computer Group (Dart Resourcing Group), Sceptre House, 169/173 Regent Street, London W1R 7FB. Tel: (071) 439 1776. Fax: (071) 439 7871. Recruits experienced and qualified IT specialists through advertising, candidate register and executive search. Branches in Birmingham, Bristol, Manchester and Slough. (Member of Computing Services Association).

Merton Associates, Merton House, 70 Grafton Way, London W1P 5LE. Tel: (071) 388 2051. Recruits around ten senior managers a year for the United States using executive search methods. Salaries are normally in excess of $75,000. Founder member of Transearch International, an international organisation of independent executive search consultants.

NPA Management Services Ltd, 12 Well Court, London EC4M 4DN. Tel: (071) 248 3812. Recruits high level international banking specialists in the 25-50 age range for foreign exchange and treasury operations and corporate finance. Normally requires degree in relevant discipline (eg law, accountancy) plus experience.

Profile Management & Specialist Recruitment Ltd, 201 Haverstock Hill, Belsize Park, London NW3 4QG. Tel: (071) 431 1616. Fax: (071) 794 4229. Recruits senior management for hotels and restaurants. Positions are not advertised. (FRES).

Wrightson Wood Ltd, 11 Grosvenor Place, London SW1X 7HH. Tel: (071) 245 9371. Executive search agency specialising in industrial manufacturing and engineering. A member of International Executive Search Associates (INESA), a consortium which includes Gilbert Tweed Associates in the US.

Notes
FRES: Member of the Federation of Recruitment and Employment Services.
ASSC: Member of Association of Search and Selection Consultants.
Both at 36-38 Mortimer Street, London W1N 7RB. Tel: (071) 323 4300.

The information in this chapter is based on the replies to a questionnaire circulated to international recruitment agencies in late 1991, and their recruitment requirements may change. The list does not claim to be comprehensive and inclusion in this section does not imply recommendation by the author or publisher.

Appendix C

US RECRUITMENT ORGANISATIONS

Executive recruitment

This is a select list of executive recruitment consultancies with offices in the British Isles and the United States—and often other countries too. It is important to realise that the British or Irish office listed will not necessarily recruit for jobs in the United States, nor will US branches be equipped to deal with applications from abroad. Please refer to the relevant sections in Chapters Four and Six. The Executive Grapevine produces a directory of executive recruitment consultants in North America: 79 Manor Way, London SE3 9XG.

Abbott Smith Associates, PO Box 318, Millbrook, NY 12545; 2D Pennybank Chambers, Great Eastern Street, London EC2A 3EJ. Tel: (071) 377 6837. Training Professionals. Also Chicago.

Bernard Hodes Overton, 555 Madison Avenue, New York, NY 10022; Monaco House, Bristol St, Birmingham B5 7AS. Tel: (021) 622 3838. Also Arlington, Chicago, Atlanta, Dallas, Denver, Houston, Irvine, Palo Alto, Philadelphia, San Francisco.

Boyden International Inc., 260 Madison Ave, New York, NY 10022-3574; 148 Buckingham Palace Road, London SW1W 9TR. Tel: (071) 730 5292. Also Atlanta, Boston, Cleveland, Dallas, Fort Lauderdale, Houston, Los Angeles, Minneapolis, Morristown, Pittsburg, San Francisco, Stamford, Washington.

Caldwell Partners International, 101 Park Avenue, Suite 4315, New York, NY 10178; 59 Catherine Place, London SW1E 6DY. Tel: (071) 834 7966. Also Atlanta, Chicago, Cleveland, Dallas, Tampa.

Canny Bowen, 425 Park Ave, New York, NY 10022-3574; Amrop

International, Federation House, Canal Road, Dublin 6. Tel: (Dublin) 966855. Also Boston.

Carré Orban & Partners, 825 Third Ave, New York, NY 10022; 7 Curzon St, London W1Y 7FL. Tel: (071) 491 1266.

DPSC, 24 Wyckoff Avenue, Waldwick, NJ 07463; PO Box 38, Tadworth, Surrey, KT20 7UR. Tel: (0737) 814116. Also Wellesley (MA).

EAL International, 2001 Spring Road, Suite 655, Oakbrook, IL 60531; 18 Grosvenor St, London W1X 9FD. Tel: (071) 499 0518. Also Los Angeles, New York.

Robert Half International, 522 5th Ave, New York, NY 10036- 7660; Walter House, Strand, London WC2R 0PT. Tel: (071) 836 3545. One hundred and forty offices throughout US.

Heidrick & Struggles, 245 Park Ave, New York, NY 10147-0152; 100 Piccadilly, London W1V 9FN. Tel: (071) 491 3124. Also Atlanta, Boston, Chicago, Cleveland, Dallas, Greenwich (CT), Jacksonville (FL), Menlo Park, Minneapolis, San Francisco, Washington.

AT Kearney Inc, 222 S Riverside Plaza, Chicago, IL 60606-5904; Stockley House, Wilton Road London SW1V 1LQ. Tel: (071) 834 6886. Also Alexandria (VA), Atlanta, Chicago, Dallas, Denver, Los Angeles, Miami, New York, Scottsdale (AZ).

Korn Ferry International, 237 Park Av, New York, NY 10017- 3142; Pepys House, 12 Buckingham St, London WC2N 6DF. Tel: (071) 930 4334. Also Atlanta, Boston, Chicago, Denver, Houston, Los Angeles, Minneapolis, Newpoer Beach, Palo Alto, San Francisco, Seattle, Stamford, Washington.

KPMG Peat Marwick Executive Recruiters, 345 Park Ave, New York, NY 10154-0111; 70 Fleet St, London EC4Y 1EU. Tel: (071) 236 8000. Branches throughout US.

Marlar International, 410 Severn Ave, Suite 403, Annapolis, MD 21403-2524; 14 Grosvenor Place, London SW1X 7HH. Tel: (071) 248 9614. Also Los Angeles.

Norman Broadbent International, 200 Park Ave, 18th Floor, New York, NY 10166; 65 Curzon St, London W1Y 7PE. Tel: (071) 629 9626.

Russell Reynolds Associates, 200 Park Avenue, 23rd Floor, New York, NY 10166-0105; 24 St James's Square, London SW1Y 4HZ. Tel: (071) 839

7788. Also Atlanta, Boston, Chicago, Cleveland, Dallas, Los Angeles, Minneapolis, San Francisco, Stamford, Washington.

Spencer Stuart & Associates, 52 E 52nd St, New York, NY 10055- 0001; Brook House, 113 Park Lane, London W1Y 4HJ. Tel: (071) 493 1238. Also Atlanta, Chicago, Dallas, Houston, Los Angeles, Philadelphia, San Francisco, Stamford.

TASA, 875 3rd Ave, Suite 1501, New York, NY 10022; Stephenson Cobbold, 84 Palace Court, London W2 4JE. Tel: (071) 727 5335. Also Palo Alto.

Egon Zehnder International Inc, 55 E 59th St, 14th Floor, New York, NY 10022-1112; Devonshire House, Mayfair Place, London W1X 5FH. Tel: (071) 493 3882. Also Atlanta, Chicago, Los Angeles.

Ward Howell International (Whitehead Mann), 99 Park Avenue, New York, NY 10016; also 44 Welbeck Street, London W1M 7HF. Tel: (071) 737 8736. Also Barrington (IL), Chicago, Dallas, Encino (CA), Houston, Los Angeles, San Francisco, Stamford.

Whitney Group, 12 E 49th St, Tower 49, New York, NY 10017; 35 Hill St, London W1 7FD. Tel: (071) 495 3222. Financial sector.

Temporary help services and other employment agencies
To list all such agencies and their branches would require a book several times the size of this one. Normally, you would apply to such an agency once you have arrived in the United States, and the best policy is to thumb through the Employment Agency section of the local *Yellow Pages*. Some telephone directories list agencies according to their specialisation.

The agencies listed below are just a sample of what is available. Most of them have several branches.

Careers Unlimited, 1401 E Lansing Drive, E Lansing, MI 48823.
CDI Temporary Services, 10 Penn Center, Philadelphia, PA 19103.
Integrated Engineering Resources, 411 Seventh Ave, Suite 1403, Pittsburgh, PA 15219.
Kelly Services, 999 W Big Beaver Road, Troy, MI 48084.
Lloyd Personnel Consultants, 10 Cutter Mill Road, Great Neck, NY 10021.
Manpower Inc, PO Box 2053, Milwaukee, WI 53201.
Manus Services Corp, Manus Building, PO Box 440406, Seattle, WA 98114.
Norrell Temporary Services, 3535 Piedmont Rd NE, Atlanta, GA 30305.
Olsten Corporation, 1 Merrick Ave, Westbury, NY 11590.
Personnel Recruiters Inc, 150 Morris Ave, Springfield, NJ 07081.

Scientific Placement Inc, PO Box 19949, Houston, TX 77224.
Temporaries Inc, 1015 18th Street, Suite 504, Washington, DC 20036.
Uniforce Temporary Services, 1335 Jericho Turnpike, PO Box 5055, New Hyde Park, NY 11040.
Victor Temporary Services, 500 Skokie Boulevard, Northbrook, IL 60062.
Watsco Inc, 2665 S Bayshore Drive, Suite 901, Coconut Grove, FL 33133.
Western Temporary Services, 301 Lennon Lane, Walnut Creek, CA 94598.
Wordforce Inc, 902 Broadway, New York, NY 10010.

Trade associations
There are a number of trade associations to which many of these organisations belong; They include:

- National Association of Temporary Services
- Association of Executive Recruiting Consultants
- National Association of Personnel Consultants

Directories
Among the directories that list recruitment agencies are:

Executive Employment Guide, The American Management Association Inc., 135 W 50th Street, New York, NY 10020.
Directory of Executive Recruiters, Consultant News, Templeton Road, Fitzwilliam, NH 03447.
Directory of Personnel Consultants by Specialisation, National Association of Personnel Consultants.

Appendix D

NEWSPAPERS AND SPECIALIST JOURNALS

Key W: weekly; F: fortnightly; M: monthly; B: bi-monthly; Q: quarterly; A: annual.

UK expatriate newspapers and magazines
Jobtrac USA, Suite 10, 29 Harper Road, London SE1 6AW. Tel: (081) 461 5938. A 12-page fortnightly job list devoted to a wide variety of jobs in the US. Other publications which carry advertisements for posts abroad, but not exclusively in the US:

Overseas Jobs Express, F, PO Box 22, Brighton, BN1 6HX. Tel: (0273) 440220.

Nexus, M, Expat Network, PO Box 380, Croydon CR9 2ZQ. Tel: (081) 760 5100.

Careers International, F, PS Publishing, Speer House, 40-44 The Parade, Claygate, Surrey KT10 9QE. Tel: (0372) 68833.

Job Finder, F, Overseas Consultants, PO Box 152, Douglas, Isle of Man.

Home & Away, M, Expats International, 62 Tritton Road, London SE21 8DE. Tel: (081) 670 8304.

The Expatriate, M, First Market Intelligence Ltd, 56A Rochester Row, London SW1P 1JU.

Some of the publications above offer financial advice for expatriates. The following also have financial articles:

EXPATXTRA, M, PO Box 300, Jersey, Channel Islands. Tel: (0534) 36241.

Resident Abroad, M, Financial Times Business Information, 101-108 Clerkenwell Road, London EC1M 5SA.

US national newspapers
Virtually all US newspapers are regional papers. The few exceptions are:

Christian Science Monitor, 1 Norway Street, Boston, MA 02115; Eggington House, 25-28 Buckingham Gate, London SW1E 6LD. Tel: (071) 630 8666.

USA Today, 1000 Wilson Boulevard, Arlington, VA 22209.
Wall Street Journal, 200 Liberty Street, New York, NY 10281. Has four
   regional editions.

US local and regional newspapers
This is a selection of the leading newspapers state by state. Addresses
are given in Appendix G:
Alabama: *Birmingham Post Herald, Huntsville Times, Montgomery Advertiser*
Alaska: *Anchorage Daily News*
Arizona: *Arizona Republic, Arizona Daily Star*
Arkansas: *Arkansas Democrat*
California: *Bakersfield Californian, Fresno Bee, Press Telegram, Los Angeles
   Times, Oakland Tribune, Sacramento Union, San Diego Union, San
   Francisco Chronicle, San Francisco Examiner, San Jose Mercury News,
   Orange County Register*
Colorado: *Denver Post, Rocky Mountain News*
Connecticut: *Hartford Courant, New Haven Register*
Delaware: *News Journal*
District of Columbia: *Washington Post, Washington Times*
Florida: *Fort Lauderdale News Sun Sentinel, Miami Herald, Orlando Sentinel,
   Palm Beach Post*
Georgia: *Atlanta Constitution, Atlanta Journal*
Hawaii: *Honolulu Advertiser*
Idaho: *Idaho Statesman*
Illinois: *Chicago Tribune, Peoria Journal-Star*
Indiana: *Indianapolis News, Indianapolis Star*
Iowa: *Des Moines Register*
Kansas: *Wichita Eagle-Beacon*
Kentucky: *Louisville Courier Journal*
Louisiana: *New Orleans Times-Picayune*
Maine: *Bangor Daily News*
Maryland: *Baltimore Sun*
Massachusetts: *Boston Globe, Boston Herald*
Michigan: *Detroit Free Press, Detroit News, Grand Rapids Press*
Minnesota: *Minneapolis Star Tribune, Saint Paul Pioneer Press Dispatch*
Mississippi: *Clarion Ledger*
Missouri: *Kansas City Star, Kansas City Times, Saint Louis Post Dispatch*
Montana: *Billings Gazette*
Nebraska: *Omaha World-Herald*
Nevada: *Las Vegas Review Journal*
New Hampshire: *Union Leader*
New Jersey: *Newark Star Ledger*
New Mexico: *Albuquerque Journal*
New York: *Albany Times-Union, Buffalo News, New York Post, New York
   Times, Rochester Democrat and Chronicle*
North Carolina: *Charlotte Observer*

North Dakota: *Fargo Forum*
Ohio: *Akron Beacon Journal, Cincinnati Enquirer, Cincinnati Post, Cleveland Plain Dealer, Columbus Dispatch, Dayton Daily News*
Oklahoma: *Oklahoman*
Oregon: *Oregonian*
Pennsylvania: *Harrisburg Patriot News, Johnstown Tribune-Democrat, Philadelphia Daily News, Philadelphia Inquirer, Pittsburg Post-Gazette, Pittsburg Press*
Rhode Island: *Providence Journal Bulletin*
South Carolina: *Charleston News & Courier, Columbia State-Record*
South Dakota: *Sioux Falls Argus Leader*
Tennessee: *Memphis Commercial Appeal, Tennessean*
Texas: *Dallas Morning News, Fort Worth Star-Telegram, Houston Chronicle, Houston Post, San Antonio Express-News, San Antonio Light*
Utah: *Salt Lake Tribune*
Vermont: *Burlington Free Press*
Virginia: *Richmond Times-Dispatch, Roanoke Times*
Washington: *Seattle Post-Intelligencer, Seattle Times, Spokane Chronicle, Morning News Tribune*
West Virginia: *Charleston Gazette*
Wisconsin: *Milwaukee Journal, Milwaukee Sentinel*
Wyoming: *Casper Star-Tribune*

Specialist US journals

(For a more comprehensive selection of journals see *Benn's International Media Guide* or *Ulrich's International Periodicals Directory*.)

Advertising Age, W, Crain Communications, 20-22 Bedford Row, London WC1R 4EB.
Air Transport World, M, Technomedia Ltd.
America's Textiles, M, Robert G Horsfield, Daisy Bank, Chinley, via Stockport SK12 6DA. Tel: (0663) 50242.
American Banker, D, One State Street, Plaza, New York, NY 10004.
American Printer, M, Maclean Hunter Publishing, 300 W Adams Street, Chicago, IL 60606.
Architectural Record, M, McGraw-Hill.
Automotive Engineering, M, 400 Commonwealth Drive, Warrendale, PA 15096.
Aviation Week, W, McGraw-Hill.
Broadcasting, W, Cahners.
Building Design and Construction, M, Cahners.
Business Week, W, McGraw Hill.
Byte, M, McGraw-Hill.
CPI Purchasing, M, Cahners. Purchasing for the chemical process industries.
Chemical and Engineering News, W, Technomedia.
Chemical Engineering, F, McGraw-Hill.

Chemical Week, McGraw-Hill.

Civil Engineering, M, E 47th Street, New York, NY 10017.

Coal Week, McGraw Hill. Includes metallurgy, mining and petroleum.

Communication Age, M, Intergroup Communications, 286 West Barnes Lane, New Malden, Surrey. Tel: (081) 949 0354.

Computer Careers, Q, McGraw-Hill.

Computerworld Newspaper, W, CW Communications, Box 880, 375 Cochituate Road, Framlingham, MA 01701.

Construction Equipment, M, Cahners.

Consulting-Specifying Engineer, M, Cahners. Mechanical/electrical/ electronic system design engineers for construction industry.

Contractor, M, Cahners. Airconditioning, heating and plumbing.

Control Engineering, M, Cahners.

Critical Care Nurse, M, Cahners.

Daily Variety, D, Cahners. Entertainment.

Data Communications, M, McGraw-Hill.

Datamation, F, Cahners. Information processing.

Dental Management, Edgell Communications Inc., 7500 Old Oak Blvd, Cleveland, OH 44130.

Design News, F, Cahners. Design engineers in the original equipment market.

Digital Review, W, Cahners. DEC computing.

EDN News Edition, F, Cahners. Electronic technology.

Editor and Publisher, W, McGraw-Hill.

Electric Utility Week, W, McGraw-Hill.

Electric Construction and Maintenance, M, McGraw-Hill.

Electrical World, M, McGraw-Hill.

Electronic Business, F, Cahners.

Electronic Packaging and Production, M, Cahners. Design and production of electronic circuits, products and equipment.

Electronics, W, McGraw-Hill.

Electronics Purchasing, M, Cahners.

Emergency Medicine, F, Cahners.

Engineering News-Record, W, McGraw-Hill.

Farm Journal, 230 W Washington Square, Philadelphia PA 19105.

Furniture Today, W, Cahners.

Graduating Engineer, Q, McGraw-Hill.

Graphic Arts Monthly, Cahners. Printing, typesetting, binding, etc.

Highway and Heavy Construction, M, Cahners.

High Technology, M, Goldhirsch Group, David Todd Associates, 32-33 Skylines, Docklands, London E14 9TS. Tel: (071) 538 5811.

Hospital Medicine, M, Cahners.

Hotels, M, Cahners.

Industrial Distribution, M, Cahners.

Interior Design, M, Cahners.

International Construction Week, W, McGraw-Hill.

Library Journal, F, Cahners.

Modern Materials Handling, M, Cahners.

Modern Plastics, McGraw-Hill.
Nursingworld Journal, M, 470 Boston Post Road, Weston, MA 02193.
Packaging, M, Cahners.
Pharmacy Times, M, 80 Shore Road, Port Washington, NY 11050.
Plant Engineering, F, Cahners.
Plastics World, M, Cahners.
Pollution Engineering, M, Cahners.
Power, M, McGraw-Hill.
Printing News/East, W, Cahners. Printing and allied industries in Greater
    New York.
Publishers Weekly, Cahners.
Purchasing, F, Cahners.
R and D Magazine, M, Cahners.
Restaurants and Institutions, F, Cahners.
Security, M, Cahners. Security and loss prevention operations.
Security Distributing and Marketing, M, Cahners.
Semiconductor International, M, Cahners.
Systems Integration, M, Cahners. Computer systems design, development and
    integration.
Test and Measurement World, M, Cahners. Electronics.
Textile World, M, McGraw-Hill.
Traffic Management, M, Cahners.
Variety, W, Cahners. Entertainment.

Publishers

Cahners Publishing Company is a division of Reed Publishing and has an
    office in the UK: 27 Paul Street, London EC2A 4JU. Tel: (071) 628 7030.
    Its HQ in the USA is 275 Washington Street, Newton, MA 02158. Tel:
    617 964 3030.

McGraw Hill, McGraw Hill House, Maidenhead, Berks SL6 2QL. Tel:
    (0628) 23431.

Ziff-Davis Publishing, One Park Ave, New York, NY 10016 publish a
    number of aerospace titles. Seymour Press, 334 Brixton Road, London
    SW9 7AG. Tel: (071) 733 4444.

Romaine Pierson Publishers, 80 Shore Road, Port Washington, NY 11050
    publish a range of journals of interest to the medical profession.

US job lists

Academic Journal, M, Brookfield Publishing Co, PO Box 221, Brookfield
    Center, CT 06805.
California Connections, F, California Connections Publications, Box 90396,
    Long Beach, CA 90809. Directory of private and public sector employ-
    ment opportunities.

Career Opportunities News, B, Garrett Park Press, PO Box 1901, Garrett Park, MD 20896.

Career Resource Guide and Digest, National College Placement Association, PO Box 5112, Mill Valley, CA 94942.

Community Jobs, M, Community Career Resource Centerm 1516 P Street NW, Washington, DC 20005.

Employment Listings for the Social Services, 10 Angelica Drive, Framingham, MA 01701.

Environmental Opportunities, PO Box 670, Walpole, NH 03608.

Federal Career Opportunities, Federal Research Services, 370 Maple Avenue W, Box 1059, Vienna, VA 22180.

Federal Employment Bulletin, PO Box 11715, Washington, DC 20008.

Insurance and Financial Services Careers, A, Wallace Witmer Co, PO Box 40169, 1509 Madison Avenue, Memphis, TN 34174.

Job Bulletin, M, Association for Women in Science, 2401 Virginia Avenue NW, Suite 303, Washington 20037.

Job Openings, US Government Printing Office, Washington, DC 20402.

Job Openings for Economists, American Economics Association, 1313 21st Avenue, South Nashville, TN 37212.

ML Job Information Lists, Modern Language Association, 62 Fifth Avenue, New York, NY 10011.

National Business Employment Weekly, 420 Lexington Avenue, New York, NY 10170.

National Employment Listing Service for the Criminal Justice System and Social Services, Criminal Justice Center, Sam Houston State University, Huntsville, TX 77341.

NRPA Job Bulletin, National Recreation and Park Association, 3101 Park Center Drive, 12th Floor, Alexandria, VA 22302.

Occupations in Demand at Job Service Offices, Consumer Information Center, Pueblo, CO 81009.

Teacher Vacancy List, M, National Education Selection, 189 Clifford Street, Newark, NJ 07105.

For a more comprehensive list of journals that carry employment advertising, please refer to *900,000 Plus Jobs Annually—Published Sources of Employment Listings*, S. N. Feingold and G. A. Hansard-Winkler (Garrett Park Press).

Miscellaneous

Occupational Outlook Quarterly, Bureau of Labor Statistics, US Dept of Labor. Articles on jobs and job prospects.

Careers Magazine, 1001 Avenue of the Americas, New York, NY 10018. Quarterly magazine aimed at schools.

US Employment Opportunities—Career News Service. Washington Research Associates, 2103 N Lincoln St, Arlington, VA 22207. Annual with quarterly updates.

Appendix E

JOB APPLICATIONS

You may have discovered the ideal job opportunity, but that is only the first step on the road to landing the job. Along the way you have to convince the employer of your suitability for the post, which means presenting yourself in a positive light from the very first contact.

In a competitive jobs market modesty and reticence have to be abandoned if you are to propel yourself to the interview stage. Americans on the whole tend to be good at selling themselves, and you need to take a leaf out of their book.

Get off on the right foot with documentation that looks good and reads well. Use good quality notepaper of A4 size, and either type or word-process your correspondence unless your handwriting is exceptionally neat and legible.

An increasing number of people now understand what it takes to make an effective application. For those who are unsure of the process this section offers a few pointers.

Answering an advertisement

The agency or employer will often request a CV, or 'résumé' in American parlance. You should include a covering letter with it as a matter of course since this gives you an opportunity to draw attention to your strong points.

The letter should set out

- WHY you want the job
- WHAT qualifications and experience you have
- HOW you measure up to the job description.

Tel: 011 44 71 111 9999

20 Balmoral Avenue
London W19 1ZZ
United Kingdom

February 29, 1992

Caroline North
Vice-President, Human Resources
Iowa Investment Bank, Inc.
5432 Maine Street,
Shenandoah, IA 50300
USA

Dear Ms North,

I wish to apply for the post of international business manager of your organisation as advertised in the *Red Oak Daily Tribune*. I believe this is a challenging post which will offer me scope to make full use of my extensive financial skills.

Since graduating in Economics from the London School of Economics I have worked for a prestigious merchant bank in the City of London and have been promoted twice. I have gained experience in share dealing, investment management and international financing, and have made several successful foreign business trips on behalf of the bank, particularly to Brussels, Frankfurt and Paris.

With my sound knowledge of the European banking scene I believe I am well placed to assist you in your plans to increase your international profile. I am, incidentally, familiar with United States banking practice having done a three month placement with the New York firm of Goldschmidt and Silber three years back.

I very much look forward to meeting you in order to discuss your requirements in depth.

Sincerely yours,

James E Stuart

Fig. 18. Sample application letter

CV or résumé?

In the United States you do not submit a CV (personal history) but a résumé, which is almost the same thing, but not quite. Generally speaking, a British style CV offers more information than an American style résumé, because federal and state laws designed to combat discrimination in the workplace restrict the type of information that should be divulged to an employer (eg age, sex, race, religion).

American employers appreciate the much fuller British style CVs, and if you are applying to an address on this side of the Atlantic you should not hesitate to submit a full-blown CV. If you are applying within the US you should proceed with caution; to include details of your age, date of birth, sex and family status, or to enclose a photograph, might contravene state laws on equal employment rights and render your application invalid.

Your CV/résumé should be concise, typed and, if possible, tailored to the job you are after. Ideally, it should cover no more than one sheet of A4 paper. If your career has been rich and varied, you may have to compromise by providing a one-page summary of your career followed by a more extended version.

There are broadly speaking two types of résumé:

● The chronological CV/résumé which details the positions you have held in chronological (or reverse chronological) order and is by far the commoner of the two;

● The functional CV/résumé which presents your work experience in terms of skills and responsibilities.

A typical chronological CV/résumé will contain the following information.

● Your name, address for correspondence and contact telephone number(s).

● Your job objective. This is often included in American résumés as a matter of course, and might be quite a good idea for a speculative application.

● Your career: positions held, employers, dates. It is quite common in the UK to begin with your present job and work backward.

● Your education and qualifications. Make sure that the latter are comprehensible to an American who may not have a clue what

MIMM, FCIS, AIBA or different classes of degree stand for. People near the beginning of their careers may prefer to put details of their education and qualifications before the career section.

- Other details: membership of professional associations, public offices held, hobbies (within reason), additional skills.

Regard your résumé as your personal sales brochure and be prepared to blow your own trumpet. You need to present a positive image to potential employers.

The interview

Before the interview make sure you are fully clued up about the organisation you are going to visit. If details are hard to come by, ring up the public relations officer and ask for a brochure or a copy of the annual report.

There are certain golden rules to observe during the interview:

- be on time
- dress smartly
- be natural
- look at the interviewer
- be polite
- stay calm
- draw attention to your strengths.

Remember that you need to convince your prospective employer that:

- you have a positive attitude to the job and organisation
- you will be both punctual and regular in attendance
- you enjoy good health
- you have relevant experience
- you are a person who can be relied on
- you can adapt to the requirements of the organisation and job.

Follow up letter

Courtesy can pay dividends in the long run. After the interview it is a good idea to send a letter to the interviewer, thanking him for seeing you and confirming that you are still interested in the job. In order to speed up delivery you might consider sending your message by fax.

Owen Gwynedd

Address:	20 Caernarfon Street, Llangarth, Wales LH1 1BB
Telephone:	0123 987654 (evenings and weekends); 0123 456789 (daytime)
Date of Birth:	31st November 1962
Birthplace:	Pwllheli, North Wales
Family Status:	Married with one child
Nationality:	British

Education and Qualifications:

1973—80	Llywelyn Fawr School, Cardiff
	5 'O' Levels; 'A' Levels in Welsh, Physics
1980—82	Bleddyn ap Cynfyn Technical College, Bala
	Higher National Diploma in Mechanical Engineering
1982—83	Institute of Petroleum Studies, Aberdeen
	Certificate in Drilling Rig Maintenance

Employment Record:

1983—87	Welsh Petroleum Co, Harlech, Wales
	Maintenance Engineer on an offshore drilling rig operating off the Lleyn Peninsula
1987—90	Antrim Exploration Ltd, Ballymena, N Ireland
	Chief Driller with the Abu Dhabi project
1990—now	Instructor in oil rig maintenance

Interests:
Rugby Football
Choral Singing
Collecting antiques

Other Information:
Excellent health
Willingness to relocate
Clean PSV driving licence
Member of Professional Society of Oil Rig Operatives
Languages: Welsh, Arabic
Overseas experience: Spain, Abu Dhabi, Oman

Fig. 19. Sample British style CV

Résumé of   14 Leicester Terrace
Elisabeth Mary Tudor   Raleigh
                                                      Essex ES1 2YY
                                                      United Kingdom
                                                      Tel: 011 44 911 98765

JOB OBJECTIVE: Features Editor

EMPLOYMENT
1989-present   Assistant Editor, *Historic Britain* magazine
                Leicester Publishing, Windsor, Berks, UK.
                Edited articles; liaised with printers and designers;
                dealt with enquiries; assisted with promotions
1988-89   Editorial Assistant,
                Boleyn Books, Sydney, Australia.
                Assisted with copy editing, general office duties, as
                well as promotional work.

ADDITIONAL EXPERIENCE
                Reporter for college newspaper.
                Vacation employment as assistant manager of a
                fashion boutique in Raleigh.
                Vacation employment as a market research
                interviewer.

EDUCATION
1987-88   Greenwich Polytechnic, London, UK
                Diploma in Publishing.
1983-1987   University of St Albans, UK
                BA in History
1976-1983   Shakespeare High School, Southwark, London, UK
                General Certificate of Education A Levels
                (equiv. post-high school diploma) in History,
                Latin, Mathematics and Zoology

ADDITIONAL INFORMATION
                Fluent in French and Italian
                Typing speed: 50 words a minute
                Driving licence
                Member of Guild of Publishing Assistants

Fig. 20. Sample chronological résumé

Richard Gloucester

HOME ADDRESS
26 Clarence Drive
Buckingham, BX90 9XX
Great Britain
Tel: 011 44 111 22222

CURRENT ADDRESS
9872 York Blvd
Bosworth
OK 98765
Tel: 888 999 7777

JOB OBJECTIVE:
    Senior position in either the sales or training division of a
    progressive telecommunication company.
MANAGEMENT EXPERIENCE
    Managed Middle East sales team of Stanley
    Telecommunications, and increased our exports to the area
    by 50 per cent in three years. Supervised the installation of
    telephone exchanges in Yemen and Qatar.
SALES EXPERIENCE
    Planned several sales campaigns within the UK for
    Brakenbury Industrial which led to a considerable increase in
    profits.
    Streamlined customer after-sales service for Brakenbury which
    led to a significant increase in repeat orders.
    Sold telecommunications equipment to seven countries in the
    Middle East, more than doubling company turnover in this
    area.
TRAINING EXPERIENCE
    Instructed apprentices at Stanley Communications in basic
    electrical skills, gaining a national training award for the firm.
    Lectured part-time in telecommunications engineering at
    Ratcliff Technical College. Several of my students went on to
    higher education.
    Devised and directed training programme for export sales
    department of Brakenbury Industrial.
EDUCATION
    Higher National Diploma in Telecommunications (post high
    school diploma) from Rivers College, Richmond, Yorkshire,
    UK.
    City and Guilds Certificate in Supervisory Management
    (by correspondence).
OTHER DETAILS
    Member of British Institute of Management
    Treasurer of Oxford branch of the Lions Club
    Hobbies: Football, gliding and rallying

Fig. 21. Sample functional résumé

Tel: (555) 666 7777

3605 Sunset Strip
Aquitaine
WV 54321

July 4, 1992

Mr R D Franklin
Adams Lincoln Inc
519 Hayes Blvd
Arcadia
FL 00999

Dear Mr Franklin,

I am a robotics design engineer and keen to make full use of my skills and experience. As I know that Adams Lincoln is a world leader in this field, I wonder if you expect to have any vacancies in the near future.

Let me tell you a little about myself. After graduating in computer science from Oxford University, England, I studied for a Master's degree in Robotics at York University, England. I then took a position as a development officer at the National Robotics Research Institute in Much Hadham, and was involved in pioneering the use of robots in mountain bike manufacture. One of my inventions was a runner up in the European Robotics Awards earlier this year.

I am now keen to apply my knowledge within a commercial organisation and to learn more about the state of robotics technology in the United States. I intend to visit Florida during the coming month and would like to take the opportunity to call on you—with no obligation on either side.

I will telephone you when I arrive in the States to arrange an appointment.

Sincerely yours,

Henry Plantagenet

Enc. Résumé

Fig. 22. Sample speculative letter

Tel: 011 44 987 6543

91 Battlefield Close
Hastings HS9 7JJ, UK
December 16, 1992

Mr T Jefferson
President
Colorado Computing Services
1490 Island Road
Miles City, MT 59600

Dear Mr Jefferson,

Thank you for seeing me yesterday during your visit to London. I enjoyed learning about your organisation and the new developments you are planning, and confirm that I am still keen to join your staff.

I hope that your trip proved worthwhile and you had a pleasant flight back to the US. Please let me know if you require any further information from me.

Yours sincerely,

William Norman

Tel: (123) 456 7890

156 Marlborough Heights
Halle, IL 77755
7/24/92

Mr W Wilson
Director of Human Resources
Alabama Associates
Fort Carolina, TX 12345

Dear Mr Wilson,

Thank you for your letter of July 20 regarding my application for a position.

I enjoyed my visit to your firm which is clearly poised for an exciting future, and would like to thank all those who met me.

I am naturally sorry that you saw fit to appoint another person. Nevertheless, I hope you will keep my details on file in case another vacancy occurs in the future for which I would be better suited.

Sincerely yours,

Fig. 21. Sample follow up letters.

If you know by this time that you have not been selected, mention that you would be glad to be considered for any future vacancies that may occur.

For a more detailed discussion of job applications, refer to *How To Get the Job You Really Want*, Roger Jones (Allborough Publishing, Cambridge; 1990).

Appendix F

USEFUL ADDRESSES: UNITED KINGDOM

American Chamber of Commerce, 75 Brook Street, London W1Y 2EB. Has small reference library, but appointments to use it have to be made in advance.

Amertrans, Bushey Mill Lane, Watford, WD2 4JG. Tel: (0923) 54444. International removers.

Animal Aunts, 45 Fairview Road, Headley Down, Hants GU35 3HQ. Tel: (0428) 712611. Offers pet and house-minding service.

Association of Temporary and Interim Executive Services, 36-38 Mortimer Street, London W1N 7RB. Tel: (071) 323 4300.

BBC Video World Subscription Service, PO Box 177, Basingstoke RG24 0FG, or 3rd Floor, 3-4 Hardwick St, EC1R 4RY. Tel: (071) 837 6897. Produces fortnightly video compilations of BBC programmes.

BBC World Service, PO Box 76, Bush House, Strand, London WC2B 4PH. Tel: (071) 240 7790. Publishes *London Calling*, a monthly bulletin of radio programmes transmitted throughout the world.

Blair Consular Services Ltd, 10 Fairfield Avenue, Staines, Middx TW18 4AB. Tel: (0784) 462831. Visa service.

British American Chamber of Commerce, 10 Lower John Street, London W1R 3PE. Tel: (071) 287 2676.

British Association for Counselling, 37A Sheet St, Rugby CV21 3BX. Tel: (0788) 78328.

British Association of Executive Search Consultants, 36-38 Mortimer Street, London W1N 7RB. Tel: (071) 323 4300.

British Association of Removers, 279 Grays Inn Road, London WC1. Tel: (071) 594 7790.

British Overseas Trade Board (BOTB), Department of Trade and Industry, 1 Victoria Street, London SW1H 0ET. Tel: (071) 215 5000.

BUPA Expacare, 102 Queen's Road, Brighton BN1 3XT. Tel: (0273) 23563. Health insurance.

Career Development Centre for Women, 97 Mallard Place, Twickenham, Middlesex TW1 4SW. Tel: (081) 892 3806.

CBI Employee Relocation Council, Centre Point, 103 New Oxford Street,

London WC1A 1DV. Tel: (071) 379 7400. Advises companies moving staff; publishes *Relocation News*.

Centre for International Briefing, Farnham Castle, Surrey GU9 0AG. Tel: (0252) 721194.

Christians Abroad, 1 Stockwell Green, London SW9 9HP. Tel: (071) 737 7811. Advice and contacts for people moving abroad.

Citihealth International, Citycorp, 30-33 Minories, London EC3N 1DD. Tel: (071) 488 1388. Health insurance.

Company Pension Information Centre, 7 Old Park Lane, London W1Y 3JL.

Council for the Accreditation of Correspondence Colleges, 27 Marylebone Road, London NW1 5JS. Tel: (071) 935 5391.

Davies Turner, 334 Queenstown Road, London SW8 4HG. Tel: (071) 622 9361. International removers.

Dean Associates, 51 High Street, Emsworth, Hants PO10 7AN. Tel: (0243) 378022. Educational information on day schooling for the children of families living abroad temporarily.

Department of Health Leaflets Unit, PO Box 21, Honeypot Lane, Stanmore, Middx HA7 1AY. Tel: (0800) 555777.

Department of Social Security, Overseas Branch, Benton Park Road, Newcastle upon Tyne, NE98 1YX.

Department of Trade and Industry, Exports to North America Branch, Kingsgate House, 66-74 Victoria Street, London SW1E 6SW. Tel: (071) 215 4601.

ECIS (European Council for International Schools), 21B Lavant Street, Petersfield, Hants GU32 3EW. Tel: (0230) 68244. Publishes a directory of international schools.

Economist Subscription Fulfilment Service, PO Box 14, Harold Hill, Romfort RM3 8EQ. Tel: (04023) 81555. Fax: (04023) 81211.

Employment Conditions Abroad, Anchor House, 15 Britten Street, London SW3 3TY. Tel: (071) 351 7151. Briefings and country reports.

Europea IMG, Fivash House, 9 Denne Parade, Horsham RH12 1JD. Tel: (0403) 63860. Medical insurance.

Expatriate Advisory Services PLC, 14 Gordon Road, West Bridgeford, Nottingham, NG2 5LN. Tel: (0602) 816572. Financial advisers.

Expat Network, 5th Floor, Carolyn House, Dingwall Road, Croydon CR9 2ZQ. Tel: (081) 760 5100. Fax: (081) 760 0469. Expatriate service organisation.

Expats International, 62 Tritton Road, London SE21 8DE. Tel: (081) 670 8304. Expatriate service organisation.

Exeter HAS, 5 and 7 Palace Gate, Exeter EX1 1UE. Tel: (0392) 75361.

Federation of Recruitment and Employment Services, 36-38 Mortimer Street, London W1N 7RB Tel: (071) 323 4300.

FOCUS Information Services, 47-49 Gower Street, London WC1E 6HR. Tel: (071) 631 4367. Briefing organisation.

Gabbitas Truman and Thring, Broughton House, 6-8 Sackville Street, London W1X 2BR. Tel: (071) 439 2071.

Global International Forwarding Ltd, 16 Perivale Industrial Park, Greenford UB6 7RW. Tel: (081) 997 4321. International removers.

Golden Arrow Shippers, Horsford Kennels, Lydbury North, Shropshire SY7 8AY. Tel: (05888) 240. Pet transportation experts.

Good Book Guide, 91 Great Russell Street, London WC1B 3PS. Mail order book service.

Guardian Publications Ltd, 164 Deansgate, Manchester M60 2RR. Tel: (061) 832 7200. Publishers of *The Guardian Weekly*.

Hall-Godwins (Overseas) Consulting Co, Briarcliff House, Kingsmead, Farnborough, Hants GU14 7TE. Tel: (0252) 5217071. Financial advisers.

Homesitters Ltd, The Old Bakery, Western Road, Tring, Herts HP23 4BB. Tel: (0442) 891188. Caretaking service.

Independent Schools Information Service (ISIS), 56 Buckingham Gate, London SW1E 6AG. Tel: (071) 630 8793.

Inland Revenue Claims Branch, Foreign Division, Merton Road, Bootle L69 9BL.

Inside Tracks, 10 Hartswood Road, London W12 9NQ. Tel: (081) 749 0748. Brief destination profiles of a number of cities in the US and elsewhere.

Institute of Freight Forwarders, Redfern House, Browells Lane, Feltham, Middlesex. Tel: (081) 844 2266.

International Baccalaureate European Office, 18 Woburn Square, London WC1H 0NS. Tel: (071) 637 1682.

International Society for the Protection of Animals (ISPA), 106 Jermyn Street, London SW1Y 6EE. Tel: (071) 839 3066.

Leeson's Employment and Accommodation Data Services (LEADS), 4 Cranley Road, Ilford, Essex IG2 6AG. Employment services for migrants.

Manor Car Storage, PO Box 28, Clavering, Saffron Walden, Essex CB11 4RA. Tel: (0799) 550021.

Mercers College, Ware, Herts SG12 9BU. Tel: (0920) 5926. Correspondence courses for children.

Moran Stahl and Boyer, 136 Bond Street, London W1. Tel: (071) 629 8222. Relocation experts.

Overseas Resettlement Secretary, Board for Social Responsibility, Church House, Dean's Yard, London SW1P 3NZ. Can arrange contacts at destination.

Par Air Services, Warren Lane, Colchester, Essex CO3 5LN. Tel: (0206) 330332. Pet shipping agents.

PPP, Crescent Road, Tunbridge Wells TN1 2PL. Tel: (0892) 40111. Health insurance.

SFIA (School Fees Insurance Agency) Educational Trust Ltd, SFIA House, 15 Forlease Road, Maidenhead, Berks SL6 1JA. Tel: (0628) 34291. Publishers of *The Parent's Guide to Independent Schools*.

Society of Pensions Consultants, Ludgate House, Ludgate Circus, London EC4A 2AB.

UK Expatriates Professional Advisory Services Ltd, 84 Grange Road, Middlesborough TS1 2LS Tel: (0642) 221211. Tax advisors.

United States Embassy, 42 Elgin Street, Ballsbridge, Dublin. Tel: (Dublin) 688777.

United States Embassy, 24 Grosvenor Square, London W1A 2JB. Tel: (071) 499 9000. Visa Branch, 5 Upper Grosvenor Street, London W1A 2JB, and Queen's House, Queen Street, Belfast BT1 6EQ. US Information Service, 55/56 Upper Brook Street, London W1A 2LH.

United States Travel and Tourism Administration, PO Box 1EN, London W1A 1EN. Tel: (071) 439 7433. Fax: (071) 439 1152.

US-UK Educational Commission, 6 Porter Street, London W1M 2HR. Tel: (071) 486 1098.

Women's Corona Society, Room 3/5, 35 Belgrave Square, London SW1X 8QB. Tel: (071) 235 1230. Briefings and country reports.

Worldwide Education Service, 10 Barley Mow Passage, Chiswick, London W4 4PH. Tel: (081) 994 3622. Fax: (081) 747 8376.

Appendix G

USEFUL ADDRESSES: UNITED STATES

National

American Automobile Association, 8111 Gatehouse Road, Falls Church, VA 22042.

American Council on International Personnel, 510 Madison Avenue, New York, NY 10022. Advice on the employment of aliens.

Association of Executive Recruiting Consultants, 151 Railroad Avenue, Greenwich, CT 06830.

Association of Executive Search Consultants, 17 Sherwood Place, Greenwich, CT 06830.

British American Chamber of Commerce, 275 Madison Ave, New York, NY 10016-1128. Similar organisations in California and Florida.

British Embassy, 3100 Massachussetts Ave NW, Washington, DC 20009. British Consulates in California (Los Angeles, San Francisco), Florida (Miami), Georgia (Atlanta), Illinois (Chicago), Massachusetts (Boston), New York, Texas (Dallas, Houston), Washington State (Seattle).

Catalyst, 14 East 60th Street, New York, NY 10022.

Department of Commerce, Washington, DC 20230.

Department of Health and Human Services, 200 Independence Avenue SW, Washington, DC 20201.

Department of Labor, Washington, DC 20210.

Equal Employment Opportunity Commission, 2401 E St NW, Washington, DC 20506.

Health Insurance Association of America, 1025 Connecticut Avenue, NW, Washington 20036-3998. Publications are available from HIAA Fulfillment, PO Box 41455, Washington, DC 20018.

Intercristo, Christian Placement Network, 19303 Fremont Avenue N, Seattle, WA 98133. Job placement service.

Internal Revenue Service, PO Box 25866, Richmond, VA 23289; Rancho Cordova, CA 95743-0001; PO Box 9903, Bloomington, IL 61799. People living outside the US can contact IRS at the nearest US Embassy or the

Assistant Commissioner International, IRS, 950 L'Enfant Plaza South SW, Washington, DC 20024.

International Association of Counseling Services, 2 Skyline Pl, Falls Church, VA 22041.

Irish Embassy, 2234 Massachusetts Avenue NW, Washington, DC 20008. Tel: 202 462 3939.

National Association of Corporate and Professional Recruiters, 4000 Woodstone Way, Louisville, KY 40241.

National Association of Executive Recruiters, 222S Westmonte Drive, Suite 101, Altamonte Springs, FL 32714.

National Association of Personnel Consultants, 3133 Mt Vernon Ave, Alexandria, VA 22305.

National Association of Temporary Services, 119 South Saint Asaph St, Alexandria, VA 22314.

National Employment Counselors Association, 5999 Stevenson Avenue, Alexandria, VA 22304.

National Labor Relations Board, 1717 Pennsylvania Avenue NW, Washington, DC 20570.

National Park Service, Room 1013, US Department of the Interior, 18th and C Street NW, Washington DC 20240.

US Customs Service, PO Box 7118, Washington, DC 20044. Also at US Embassy, London.

US Forest Service, US Department of Agriculture, 14th and Independence Avenue, South Agriculture Building, Washington DC 20250.

US Small Business Administration, PO Box 1000, Fort Worth, TX 76119; 1441 L Street NW, Washington, DC 20416.

By state

Alabama

Birmingham Post Herald, 2200 4th Av N, Birmingham, AL 35203.

Huntsville Times, 2317 S Memorial Pkwy, Huntsville, AL 35801.

Montgomery Advertiser, Box 400, Montgomery, AL 36101.

Department of Economic and Community Affairs, 3465 Norman Bridge Road, Montgomery, AL 36105.

Department of Education, State Office Bldg, Montgomery, AL 36130.

Employment Services Division, Department of Industrial Relations, 649 Monroe St, Montgomery, AL 36130.

Department of Labor, 64 N Union St, Montgomery, AL 36130.

Department of Revenue, Gordon Persons Bldg, Montgomery, AL 36130.

Birmingham Chamber of Commerce, PO Box 10127, Birmingham, AL 35202.

Montgomery Area Chamber of Commerce, PO Box 79, 41 Commerce St, Montgomery, AL 36101.

Alaska
Anchorage Daily News, Box 149001, Anchorage, AK 99514.
INS District Office, Room 401, 632 West 6th Ave, Anchorage, AK 99501.
Alaska Industrial Development Authority, 1577 C St, Suite 304, Anchorage, AK 99501.
Department of Education, PO Box F, Juneau, AK 99811.
Division of Employment Services, Department of Labor, PO Box 3-7000, Juneau, AK 99802.
Department of Labor, PO Box 1149, Juneau, AK 99802.
Department of Revenue, PO Box SA, Juneau, AK 99811.
Anchorage Chamber of Commerce, 415 F Street, Anchorage, AK 99501-2254.
Juneau Chamber of Commerce, 1107 W 8th St, Juneau, AK 99802.

Arizona
Arizona Republic, 120 E Van Buren St, Phoenix, AZ 85004.
Arizona Daily Star, 4850 S Park Ave, Tucson, AZ 85714.
INS District Office, Federal Building, 230 North First Ave, Phoenix, AZ 85025.
Department of Commerce, 1700 W Washington, 4th Floor, W Wing, State Capitol, Phoenix, AZ 85007.
Department of Education, 1535 W Jefferson, Phoenix, AZ 85007.
Employment Services Division, Department of Economic Security, 1300 W Washington, Phoenix, AZ 85005.
Industrial Commission, 800 W Washington, Phoenix, AZ 85005.
Department of Revenue, 1600 W Monroe, 9th Fl, Phoenix, AZ 85007.
Phoenix Metropolitan Chamber of Commerce, 34 W Monroe St, Phoenix, AZ 85003.

Arkansas
Arkansas Democrat, 121E Capitol St, Little Rock, AR 72201.
Department of Education, Capitol Mall, Little Rock, AR 72201.
Employment Security Division, Department of Labor, Capitol Mall, Little Rock, AR 72201.
Department of Labor, 10421 W Markham #100, Little Rock, AR 72205.
Industrial Development Comm, 1 Capitol Mall, Little Rock, AR 72201.
Revenue Division, Ledbetter Bldg, Seventh and Wolf Street, Little Rock, AR 72201.
Greater Little Rock Chamber of Commerce, 1 Spring St, Little Rock, AR 72201.

California
Bakersfield Californian, 1707 Eye St, Bakersfield, CA 93301.
British Weekly, 1626 North Wilcox Ave, #337, Hollywood, CA 90028. UK Rep: Gibbs House, Kennel Ride, Ascot, Berks SL5 7NT.
Fresno Bee, 1626 E St, Fresno, CA 93786.

Press Telegram, 604 Pine Ave, Long Beach, CA 90844.
Los Angeles Times, Times-Mirror Square, Los Angeles, CA 90048.
Tribune, 409 13th St, Oakland, CA 94612.
Sacramento Union, 301 Capitol Mall, Sacramento, CA 95812.
San Diego Union, 350 Camino de la Reina, San Diego, CA 92108.
San Francisco Chronicle, 901 Mission St, San Francisco, CA 94103.
San Francisco Examiner, 110 5th St, San Francisco, CA 94103.
San Jose Mercury News, 750 Ridder Park Drive, San Jose, CA 95113.
Orange County Register, 625 N Grand Ave, Santa Ana, CA 92701.
Union Jack Newspaper, PO Box 1823, La Mesa, California 911944-1823.
Wall Street Journal, 6500 Wilshire Blvd, Suite 1400, Los Angeles, CA 90048.
British Consulates: Suite 312, 3701 Wilshire Boulevard, Los Angeles, CA
    90010. Tel: 213 385 7381; 1 Sansome Street, Suite 850, San Francisco,
    CA 94101. Tel: 415 981 3030.
British American Chamber of Commerce, c/o Barclay's Bank, 3150 California
    Street, San Francisco, CA 94115.
INS Regional Office, Terminal Island, San Pedro, CA 90731.
INS District Offices: 300 N Los Angeles St, Los Angeles, CA 90012; 880
    Front Street, San Diego, CA 92188; Appraisers Building, 630 Sansome
    St, San Francisco, CA 94111.
Department of Commerce, 1121 L Street, Suite 600, Sacramento, CA 95814.
    London Office: 14 Curzon Street, W1Y 7FH. Tel: (071) 629 8211.
Department of Education, 721 Capitol Mall, Sacramento, CA 95814.
Employment Development Department, 800 Capitol Mall, Sacramento, CA
    95814.
Department of Industrial Relations, 455 Golden Gate Ave, San Francisco,
    CA 94102; 1121 L St, Sacramento, CA 95814.
Department of Revenue, PO Box 1468, Sacramento, CA 95807.
Hollywood Chamber of Commerce, 6255 Sunset Blvd, PO Box 2068,
    Hollywood, CA 90028.
Los Angeles Area Chamber of Commerce, 404 South Bixel St, Los Angeles,
    CA 90017.
Metropolitan Sacramento Chamber of Commerce, 917 Seventh St, Sacra-
    mento, CA 95814.
Greater San Diego Chamber of Commerce, 110 West St, Suite 1600, San
    Diego, CA 92101.
San Francisco Chamber of Commerce, 465 California St, San Francisco, CA
    94104.
South Pasadena Chamber of Commerce, 1005 Fair Oaks Ave, South Pasa-
    dena, CA 91030.

Colorado
Denver Post, 1560 Broadway, Denver, CO 80201.
Rocky Mountain News, 400 W Colfax Ave, Denver, CO 80204.
INS, 12027 Federal Office Building, Denver, CO 80202.
Office of Economic Development, 136 State Capitol, Denver, CO 80203.

Department of Education, 201 E Colfax, Denver, CO 80203.
Department of Labor and Employment, 600 Grant St, Suite 900, Denver, CO 80203. Employment services.
Division of Labor, 1313 Sherman St, Denver, CO 80203.
Department of Revenue, 1375 Sherman St, Denver, CO 80203.
Greater Denver Chamber of Commerce, 1600 Sherman St, Denver, CO 80203-1620.

Connecticut
Hartford Courant, 285 Broad St, Hartford, CT 06115.
New Haven Register, 40 Sargent St, New Haven, CT 06511.
INS District Office, 900 Asylum Ave, Hartford, CT 96105.
Department of Economic Development, 865 Brook St, Rocky Hill, CT 06067.
Department of Education, 165 Capitol Ave, Hartford, CT 06106.
Department of Labor, 200 Folly Brook Blvd, Wethersfield, CT 06109.
Department of Revenue Services, 92 Farmington Ave, Hartford, CT 06106.
Greater Hartford Chamber of Commerce, 250 Constitution Plaza, Hartford, CT 06103.

Delaware
News Journal, PO Box 15505, Wilmington, DE 19950.
Development Office, 99 Kings Hwy, Dover, DE 19901.
Department of Public Instruction, Townsend Bldg, Dover, DE 19901.
Office of Personnel, Townsend Bldg, Dover, DE 19903.
Department of Labor, 820 N French Street, Wilmington, DE 19801.
Division of Revenue, Department of Finance, 820 N French Street, Wilmington, DE 19801.
Central Delaware Chamber of Commerce, PO Box 576, Dover, DE 19903.
Delaware State Chamber of Commerce, One Commerce Center, Suite 200, Wilmington, DE 19801.

District of Columbia
Washington Post, 1150 15th St, Washington, DC 20071.
Washington Times, 3600 New York Ave NE, Washington, DC 20002.
INS District Office, 1025 Vermont Ave NW, Washington, DC 20538.
Washington International School, 3100 Macomb Street NW, Washington, DC 20008.
Economic Development Department, 1350 Pennsylvania NW, Washington, DC 20004.
Department of Education, 415 12th St NW, Washington, DC 20004.
Department of Employment Services, 500 C St NW, Washington, DC 20001.
Department of Finance and Revenue, 300 Indiana Ave NW, Washington, DC 20001.
Chamber of Commerce of the District of Columbia, 1411 K St, NW, Washington, DC 20005.

Florida
Fort Lauderdale News Sun Sentinel, 101 N New River Dr E, Fort Lauderdale, FL 33301.
Miami Herald, 1 Herald Plaza, Miami, FL 33132.
Orlando Sentinel, 633 N Orange Drive, Orlando, FL 32801.
Palm Beach Post, 2751 S Dixie Highway, West Palm Beach, FL 33405.
St Petersburg Times, Box 1121, 490 First Ave S, St Petersburg, FL 33731.
Tampa Tribune, 202 S Parker St, Tampa, FL 33601.
British Consulate, Brickell Bay Office Tower, Suite 2110, 1001 S Bayshore Drive, Miami, FL 33131. Tel: 305 374 1522.
British Florida Chamber of Commerce, Suite 550, 2121 Ponce de Leon Blvd, Coral Gables, FL 33134.
INS District Office, Room 1324, Federal Building, 51 SW First Ave, Miami, FL 33130.
Division of Economic Development, Department of Commerce, 501-B Collins Bldg, Tallahassee, FL 32399. London office: 18-24 Westbourne Grove, London W2 5RH. Tel: (071) 727 8388.
Department of Education, The Capitol, Tallahassee, FL 32399.
Labor and Employment Security Department, 300 Atkins Bldg, Tallahassee, FL 32399.
Public Employee Relations Commission, Koger Executive Centre, Turner Building, 2586 Seagate Dr, Tallahassee, FL 32399-2171.
Department of Revenue, Carlton Bldg, Tallahassee, FL 32399-0100.
Fort Lauderdale Area Chamber of Commerce, 208 3rd Ave SE, Fort Lauderdale, FL 33302-4156.
Jacksonville Chamber of Commerce, PO Box 329, 3 Independent Drive, Jacksonville, FL 32201.
Greater Key West Chamber of Commerce, 402 Wall St, PO Box 984, Key West, FL 33040.
Greater Miami Chamber of Commerce, 1601 Biscayne Blvd, Miami, FL 33132.
Tampa Chamber of Commerce, 801 East J F Kennedy Blvd, Tampa, FL 33602.

Georgia
Atlanta Journal-Constitution, 72 Marietta Ave NW, Atlanta, GA 30303.
British Consulate: Suite 2700, Marquis One Tower, 245 Peach Tree Centre Avenue, Atlanta, GA 30303.
INS District Office, Room 406, 1430 West Peachtree St NW, Atlanta, GA 30309.
Department of Industry and Trade, 230 Peachtree St NW, Atlanta, GA 30301.
Department of Education, 205 Butler St SE, Atlanta, GA 30334.
Employment Services Division, Department of Labor, 501 Pulliam St SW, Atlanta, GA 30312.
Department of Labor, 148 International Blvd, Atlanta, GA 30303.

Department of Revenue, 270 Washington St SW, Atlanta, GA 30334.
Georgia State Chamber of Commerce, CCN Center, Atlanta, GA 30303-2705.

Hawaii

Honolulu Advertiser, 605 Kapiolani Blvd, Honolulu, HI 96813.
INS District Office, PO Box 461, 595 Ala Moana Blvd, Honolulu, HI 96809.
Department of Business and Economic Development, 250 S King St, Honolulu, HI 96813.
Department of Education, 1390 Miller St, Honolulu, HI 96813.
Labor and Industrial Relations Department, 830 Punchbowl St, Honolulu, HI 96814.
Department of Taxation, 425 S Queen St, Honolulu, HI 96813.
Chamber of Commerce of Hawaii, 735 Bishop St, Honolulu, HI 96813.

Idaho

Idaho Statesman, PO Box 40, Boise, ID 83707.
Department of Commerce, Statehouse, Boise, ID 83720.
Department of Education, Len B Jordan Bldg, 650 W St, Boise, ID 83720.
Department of Employment, 317 Main St, Boise, ID 83735.
Labor and Industrial Services Department, 277 N Sixth St, Boise, ID 83720.
State Tax Commission, 700 W State St, Boise, ID 83720.
Boise Area Chamber of Commerce, PO Box 2368, 711 W Bannock, Boise, ID 83701.

Illinois

Chicago Tribune, 435 N Michigan Ave, Chicago IL 60611.
Peoria Journal-Star, 1 News Plaza, Peoria, IL 61643.
Wall Street Journal, 1 S Wacker Drive, 21st Fl, Chicago, IL 60606.
British Consulate, 33 North Dearborn Street, Chicago, IL 60602. Tel: 312 346 0810.
INS District Office, Dirksen Federal Office Building, 219 S Dearbon St, Chicago IL 60604.
Department of Commerce and Community Affairs, 620 E Adams, St, 3rd Fl, Springfield, IL 62701.
State Board of Education, 100 N First St, Springfield, IL 62777.
Dept of Employment Security, 401 S State St, Chicago, IL 60605.
Department of Labor, #1 W Old State Capitol Plz, Springfield, IL 62702.
Department of Revenue, 101 W Jefferson St, Springfield, IL 62794.
Chicago Association of Commerce and Industry, 200 North Lasalle, Chicago, IL 60601.
Charleston Area Chamber of Commerce, 501 Jackson St, Charleston, IL 61920.
Greater Springfield Chamber of Commerce, 3 South Old State Capital Plaza, Springfield, IL 62701.

Indiana

Indianapolis News-Star, 307 N Pennsylvania Street, Indianapolis, IN 46204.

Business Development and Marketing Group, Department of Commerce, 1 N Capitol, Suite 700, Indianapolis, IN 46204.

Department of Public Instruction, 227 State House, Indianapolis, IN 46204.

Employment Security Division, 10 N Senate Ave, Indianapolis, IN 46204.

Division of Labor, 1013 State Office Bldg, Indianapolis, In 46204.

Department of Revenue, 202 State Office Bldg, Indianapolis, IN 46204.

Indianapolis Chamber of Commerce, 320 North Meridian St, Indianapolis, IN 46204-1777.

Iowa

Des Moines Register, 715 Locust St, Des Moines, IA 50309.

Department of Economic Development, 299 E Grand, Des Moines, IA 50309.

Department of Education, Grimes State Office Bldg, Des Moines, IA 50319.

Department of Employment Services, 1000 E Grand, Des Moines, IA 50319.

Department of Revenue and Finance, Hoover State Office Building, Des Moines, IA 50319.

Chamber of Commerce of Greater Des Moines, 309 Court Avenue, Ste 300, Des Moines, IA 50309.

Cedar Rapids Chamber of Commerce, 424 First Ave NE, PO Box 4860, Cedar Rapids, IA 52407.

Kansas

Wichita Eagle-Beacon, 825 E Douglas Ave, Wichita, KS 67202.

Department of Commerce, 400 SW Eighth St, 5th Fl, Topeka, KS 66612.

Department of Education, 120 E 10th St, Topeka, KS 66612.

Department of Human Resources, 401 SW Topeka Blvd, Topeka, KS 66603.

Department of Revenue, 2nd Fl, State Office Bldg, Topeka, KS 66612.

Kansas City Chamber of Commerce, 727 Minnesota Ave, PO Box 171337, KS 66117.

Topeka Chamber of Commerce, 120 E Sixth St, 3 Townsite Plaza, Topeka, KA 66603.

Wichita Area Chamber of Commerce, 350 W Douglas St, Wichita, KA 67202-2970.

Kentucky

Courier Journal, 525 W Broadway, Louisville, KY 40202.

Commerce Cabinet, Capital Plz Tower, Frankfort, KY 40601.

Department of Education, Capital Plz Tower, Frankfort, KY 40601.

Department of Personnel, Capital Annex, Frankfort, KY 40601.

Labor Cabinet, The 127 Bldg, US 127 S, Frankfort, KY 40601.

Revenue Cabinet, Capitol Annex, Frankfort, KY 40601.

Frankfort Chamber of Commerce, 100 Capital Ave, Frankfort, KT 40601.

Louisville Chamber of Commerce, One Riverfront Plaza, Louisville, KT 40202.

Louisiana

New Orleans Times-Picayune, 3800 Howard Ave, New Orleans, LA 70140.

INS District Office, New Federal Building, 701 Loyola Ave, New Orleans, LA 70113.

Department of Economic Development, PO Box 94185, Baton Rouge, LA 70804.

Department of Education, PO Box 94064, Baton Rouge, LA 70804.

Department of Labor, PO Box 94094, Baton Rouge, LA 70804.

Department of Revenue and Taxation, PO Box 201, Baton Rouge, LA 70821.

Baton Rouge Chamber of Commerce, 564 Laurel St, Baton Rouge, LA 70801.

New Orleans and the River Region Chamber of Commerce, 301 Camp St, New Orleans, LA 70190.

Maine

Bangor Daily News, 491 Main St, Bangor, ME 04401.

INS District Office, 76 Pearl St, Portland, ME 04112.

Department of Economic and Community Development, State House Station #59, Augusta, ME 04333.

Department of Educational and Cultural Services, State House Station #23, Augusta, ME 04333.

Department of Labor, State House Station #54, Augusta, ME 04333.

Bureau of Taxation, State House Station #24, Augusta, ME 04333.

Greater Portland Chamber of Commerce, 142 Free St, Portland, ME 04101.

Maryland

Baltimore Sun, 501 N Calvert St, Baltimore, MD 21278.

INS District Office, Room 124, Federal Building, 31 Hopkins Plaza, Baltimore, MD 21201.

Business and Industrial Development Department, 217 E Redwood St, Baltimore, MD 21202.

Department of Education, 200 W Baltimore St, Baltimore, MD 21201.

Department of Economic and Employee Development, 217 E Redwood St, Baltimore, MD 21202.

Division of Labor and Industry, 501 St Paul Pl, Baltimore, MD 21202-2272.

Treasury Department, Goldstein Treasury Bldg, PO Box 466, Annapolis, MD 21404.

Metropolitan Baltimore Chamber of Commerce, Legg Mason Tower, 111 S Calvert St, Suite 1500, Baltimore, MD 21202.

Bethesda-Chevy Chase Chamber of Commerce, Woodmont Ave, Bethesda, MD 20814.

Massachusetts

Boston Globe, PO Box 2378, Boston, MA 02107.

Boston Herald, 1 Herald Sq, Boston, MA 02106.

British Consulate, Suite 4740, Prudential Tower, Prudential Centre, Boston MA 02199 Tel: 617 437 7160.

INS District Office, John Fitzgerald Kennedy Federal Building, Government Center, Boston, MA 02203.

Office of Economic Development, State House, Boston, MA 02133.

Department of Education, 1385 Hancock St, Quincey, MA 02169.

Department of Personnel Administration, 1 Ashburton PL, Boston, MA 02108.

Department of Labor and Industries, 100 Cambridge St, Boston, MA 02202.

Department of Revenue, 100 Cambridge St, Boston, MA 02202.

Greater Boston Chamber of Commerce, Federal Reserve Plaza, 13th Floor, 600 Atlantic Ave, Boston, MA 02210-2200.

Michigan

Detroit Free Press, 321 Lafayette Blvd W, Detroit, MI 48231.

Detroit News, 615 Lafayette Blvd W, Detroit, MI 48231.

Grand Rapids Press, 133 Michigan St NW, Grand Rapids, MI 49503.

INS District Office, Federal Building, 333 Mt Elliott St, Detroit, MI 48207.

Department of Commerce, PO Box 30225, Lansing, MI 48909.

Department of Education, S Ottawa Bldg, PO Box 30008, Lansing, MI 48909.

Bureau of Employment Relations, Department of Labor, 1200 Sixth St, Detroit, MI 48226.

Department of Labor, 7310 Woodward Ave, Detroit, MI 48202.

Bureau of Revenue, Treasury Bldg, Lansing, MI 48909.

Minnesota

Star Tribune, 425 Portland Ave S, Minneapolis, MN 55388.

St Paul Pioneer Press Dispatch, 345 Cedar St, St Paul, MN 55101.

INS District Office, Room 932, New Post Office Bldg, 180 East Kellogg Boulevard, St Paul, MN 55101.

Department of Energy and Economic Development, 150 E Kellogg Boulevard, St Paul, MN 55101. London office: 16 St Helen's Place, London EC3A 6BT. Tel: (071) 628 4407.

Department of Education, 550 Cedar St, St Paul, MN 55101.

Department of Jobs and Training, 390 N Robert St, St Paul, MN 55101.

Department of Labor and Industry, 443 Lafayette Rd, St Paul, MN 55101.

Department of Revenue, 10 River Park Plz, St Paul, MN 55146.

St Paul Area Chamber of Commerce, 600 North Life Tower, 445 Minnesota St, St Paul, MN 55101.

Greater Minneapolis Chamber of Commerce, 15 S Fifth St, Minneapolis, MN 55402.

Mississippi

Clarion Ledger, 311 E Pearl St, Jackson, MS 39201.

Department of Economic and Community Development, 1201 Sillers Bldg, Jackson, MS 39201.
Department of Education, 501 Sillers Bldg, Jackson, MS 39201.
Employment Security Commission, 1520 W Capitol, Jackson, MS 39203.
State Tax Commission, 102 Woolfolk Bldg, Jackson, MS 39201.
Jackson Chamber of Commerce, PO Box 22548, 201 S President St, Jackson, MS 39225-2548.

Missouri
Kansas City Star-Times, 1729 Grand Ave, Kansas City, MO 64108.
Saint Louis Post Dispatch, 900 N Tucker Blvd, St Louis, MO 63101.
INS District Office, Room 819, US Courthouse, 811 Grand Ave, Kansas City, MO 64106.
Department of Economic Development, PO Box 1157, Jefferson City, MO 65102.
Department of Elementary and Secondary Education, PO Box 480, 205 Jefferson City, MO 65102.
Labor and Industrial Relations Dept, 421 E Dunklin St, Box 59, Jefferson City, MO 65104.
Department of Revenue, Truman Bldg, 416 Belai Dr, Jefferson City, MO 65109-0708.
Greater Detroit Chamber of Commerce, 600 West Lafayette Blvd, Detroit, MI 48226.
Greater Kansas City Chamber of Commerce, 920 Main St, Suite 600, Kansas City, MO 64105.
St Louis Regional Commerce and Growth Association, 100 South Fourth St, Suite 500, St Louis, MO 63102.

Montana
Billings Gazette, 401 N Broadway, Billings, MT 59107.
INS District Office, Federal Bldg, Helena, MT, 59601.
Business Assistance Division, Department of Commerce, 1424 9th Ave, Helena, MT 59620.
Office of Public Instruction, State Capitol, Helena, MT 59620.
Job Service Division, PO Box 1728, Helena, MT 59624.
Department of Labor and Industry, Capitol Station, Helena, MT 59620.
Department of Revenue, Capitol Station, Box 311, Helena, MT 59620.
Montana State Chamber of Commerce, 11th Ave, PO Box 1730, Helena, MT 59624.

Nebraska
Omaha World-Herald, 14th and Dodge Sts, Omaha, NE 68102.
INS District Office, Room 8411, 215 N 17th St, Omaha, NE 68102.
Department of Economic Development, 301 Centennial Mall S, PO Box 94666, Lincoln, NE 68509.
Department of Education, 301 Centennial Mall S, PO Box 94987, Lincoln,

NE 68509-4987; State Board of Education, 623 Service Life Bldg, Omaha, NE 68102.

Department of Labor, PO Box 94600, Lincoln, NE 68509-4600.

Department of Revenue, 301 Centennial Mall S, PO Box 94818, Lincoln, NE 68509-4818.

Lincoln Chamber of Commerce, 1221 North St, Lincoln, NE 68508.

Greater Omaha Chamber of Commerce, 1301 Harney St, Omaha, NE 68102.

Nevada

Las Vegas Review Journal, 1111 W Bonanza Rd, Las Vegas, NV 89106.

Commission on Economic Development, 600 E William, Suite 203, Carson City, NV 89710.

Department of Education, 400 W King St, Carson City, NV 89710.

Employment Security Department 500 E Third St, Carson City, NV 89710.

Labor Commission, 505 E King St, Carson City, NV 89710.

Department of Taxation, 1340 S Curry St, Carson City, NV 89710.

Carson City Chamber of Commerce, 1191 South Carson St, Carson City, NV 89701.

Las Vegas Chamber of Commerce, 2301 E Sahara Ave, Las Vegas, NV 89104.

New Hampshire

Union Leader, PO Box 780, Manchester, NH 03105.

Department of Resources and Economic Development, PO Box 856, Concord, NH 03301.

Department of Education, State Office, Park S, Concord, NH 03301.

Department of Employment Security, 32 S Main St, Concord, NH 03301.

Department of Labor, 19 Pillsbury St, Concord, NH 03301.

Department of Revenue Administration, PO Box 467, Concord, NH 03301.

Greater Manchester Chamber of Commerce, 889 Elm St, Manchester, NH 03101.

New Jersey

Star Ledger, 1 Star Ledger Plaza, Newark, NJ 07101.

INS District Office, Federal Bldg, 970 Broad St, Newark, NJ 07102.

Commerce and Economic Development Department, 33 W State St, CN 823, Trenton, NJ 08625.

Department of Education, 225 W State St, Trenton, NJ 08625.

Division of Employment Services, Department of Labor, John Fitch Plz, Trenton, NJ 08625.

Department of Labor, CN 110, Trenton, NJ 08625-0110.

Division of Taxation, CN 240, Trenton, NJ 08625.

Greater Newark Chamber of Commerce, 40 Clinton St, Newark, NJ 07102.

Trenton Chamber of Commerce, 214 West State St, Trenton, NJ 08607.

New Mexico

Albuquerque Journal, 7777 Jefferson St NE, Albuquerque, NM 87109.

Armand Hammer United World College of the American West, PO Box 248, Montezuma, NM 87731.
Department of Economic Development and Tourism, 1100 St Francis Dr, Santa Fe, NM 87501.
Department of Education, Education Building, Santa Fe, NM 87501-2786.
Department of Labor, 401 Broadway NE, Albuquerque, NM 87102.
Department of Taxation and Revenue, Joseph Montoya Bldg, Santa Fe, NM 87503.
Greater Albuquerque Chamber of Commerce, 401 Second St NW, Albuquerque, NM 87102.

New York State
Times-Union, 645 Albany-Shaker Road, Albany, NY 12211.
Buffalo News, 1 News Plaza, Buffalo, NY 14240.
New York Post, 210 South St, New York, NY 10002.
New York Times, 229 W 43rd St, New York, NY 10036.
Democrat and Chronicle, 55 Exchange Blvd, Rochester NY 14614.
British Consulate, 845 Third Avenue, New York, NY 10022. Tel: 212 593 2258.
INS District Offices: 68 Court St, Buffalo, NY 14202; 26 Federal Plaza, New York, NY 10007.
Anglo-American School, 18 West 89 Street, New York, NY 10024.
United Nations International School, 24-50 East River Drive, New York, NY 10010.
Department of Commerce, 1 Commerce Plz, Albany, NY 12245. London office: 25 Haymarket, London SW1Y 4EN. Tel: (071) 839 5079.
Department of Education, Education Bldg, Albany, NY 12234.
Department of Labor, Campus, State Office Bldg, Albany, NY 12240.
Department of Taxation and Finance, Campus, Tax and Finance Bldg, Albany, NY 12227.
Empire State Chamber of Commerce, 518 Broadway, Albany, NY 12207.
Greater Buffalo Chamber of Commerce, 107 Delaware Ave, Buffalo, NY 14202.
New York Chamber of Commerce and Industry, 200 Madison Ave, New York, NY 10016.

North Carolina
Charlotte Observer, 600 S Tryon St, Charlotte, NC 28202.
Durham Morning Herald, 115-119 Market St, Durham, NC 27702.
News and Observer of Raleigh, S McDowel St, Raleigh, NC 27601.
Business and Industry Development, Department of Commerce, 430 N Salisbury St, Raleigh, NC 27603.
Department of Public Instruction, 116 W Edenton St, Raleigh, NC 27603-1712.
Employment Security Commission, 700 Wade Ave, Raleigh, NC 27605-1167.
Department of Labor, 4 W Edenton St, Raleigh, NC 27601-1092.

Department of Revenue, 2 S Salisbury St, Raleigh, NC 27602-1348.
Charlotte Chamber of Commerce, PO Box 32785, 129 West Trade Center, Charlotte, NC 28232.
Raleigh Chamber of Commerce, 800 South Salisbury St, Raleigh, NC 27601.

North Dakota
Forum, PO Box 2020, Fargo, ND 58107.
Economic Development Commission, 604 E Blvd, State Capitol Grounds, Bismarck, ND 58505.
Department of Public Instruction, 11th Fl, State Capitol, 600 E Blvd, Bismarck, ND 58505.
Job Service ND, PO Box 1537, Bismarck, ND 58502.
Department of Labor, 5th Fl, State Capitol, 600 E Blvd, Bismarck, ND 58505.
Tax Department, 8th Fl, State Capitol, 600 E Blvd, Bismarck, ND 58505.
Fargo Chamber of Commerce, 321 N Fourth St, PO Box 2443, Fargo, ND 58102.

Ohio
Akron Beacon Journal, 44 E Exchange St, Akron, OH 44328.
Cincinnati Enquirer, 617 Vine St, Cincinnati, OH 45202.
Cincinnati Post, 125 E Court St, Cincinnati, OH 45202.
Plain Dealer, 1801 Superior Ave E, Cleveland OH 44114.
Columbus Dispatch, 34 S 3rd St, Columbus, OH 43216.
Dayton Daily News, 45 S Ludlow St, Dayton, OH 45401.
INS District Office, Room 1917, Federal Office Bldg, 1240 E 9th St, Cleveland, OH 44199.
Department of Development, 30 E Broad St, Columbus, OH 43266.
Department of Education, 65 S Front St, Columbus, OH 43266-0308.
Bureau of Employment Services, 145 S Front St, Columbus, OH 43266-0308.
Department of Industrial Relations, 2323 W Fifth Ave, Columbus, OH 43266-0567.
Department of Taxation, 30 E Broad St, Columbus, OH 43266-0420.
Greater Cincinatti Chamber of Commerce, 120 W Fifth St, Cincinatti, OH 45202.
Greater Cleveland Growth Association International Trade and Business Development, 690 Huntingdon Building, Cleveland, OH 44115.
Columbus Area Chamber of Commerce, 37 North High St, Columbus, OH 43215.
Toledo Area Chamber of Commerce, 218 Huron St, Toledo, OH 43604.

Oklahoma
Daily Oklahoman, 500 N Broadway, Oklahoma City, OK 73102.
Tulsa World, Box 1770, Tulsa, OK 74102.
Department of Commerce, 6601 Broadway Ext, Oklahoma City, OK 73116.
Department of Education, 2500 N Lincoln Blvd, Oklahoma City, OK 73105.

Office of Personnel Management, B-22 Jim Thorpe Bldg, 2101 N Lincoln Blvd, Oklahoma City, OK 73105.
State Department of Labor, 1315 Broadway Pl, Oklahoma City, OK 73103.
Tax Commission, 2501 N Lincoln Blvd, Oklahoma City, OK 73194.
Oklahoma City Chamber of Commerce, One Santa Fe Plaza, Oklahoma City, OK 73102.
Metropolitan Tulsa Chamber of Commerce, 616 S Boston Ave, Tulsa, OK 74119.

Oregon
The Oregonian, 1320 SW Broadway, Portland, OR 97201.
INS District Office, Room 333, US Courthouse, SW Broadway and Main St, Portland, OR 97205.
Department of Economic Development, 595 Cottage St NE, Salem, OR 97310.
Department of Education, 700 Pringle Pkwy SE, Salem, OR 97310.
Department of Human Resources, 875 Union St NE, Salem, OR 97301.
Bureau of Labor and Industries, 1400 SW Fifth Ave, Portland, OR 97201.
Department of Revenue, 955 Center St NE, Salem, OR 97310.
Portland Chamber of Commerce, 221 NW Second Ave, Portland, OR 97209.
Salem Area Chamber of Commerce, 220 Cottage ST NE, Salem, OR 97301.

Pennsylvania
Harrisburg Patriot News, 812 King Boulevard, Harrisburg, PA 17101.
Tribune-Democrat, 425 Locust St, Johnstown, PA 15907.
Philadelphia Daily News/Inquirer, 400 N Broad St, Philadelphia, PA 19130.
Pittsburgh Post-Gazette, 50 Boulevard of the Allies, Pittsburgh, PA 15222.
Pittsburgh Press, 34 Boulevard of the Allies, Pittsburgh, PA 15222.
INS District Office, Room 1321, US Courthouse, Independence Mall W, 601 Market St, Philadelphia, PA 19106.
Department of Commerce, 433 Forum Bldg, Harrisburg, PA 17120.
Department of Education, 10th Fl, Harristown Bldg #2, Harrisburg, PA 17108.
Employment Security Division, Department of Labor and Industry, 1720 Labor and Industry Bldg, Harrisburg, PA 17120.
Department of Labor and Industry, 1700 Labor and Industry Bldg, Harrisburg, PA 17120.
Department of Revenue, Strawberry Square, 11th Fl, Harrisburg, PA 17101-2290.
Greater Philadelphia Chamber of Commerce, Broad and Chestnut St, Philadelphia, PA 19107.
Greater Pittsburgh Chamber of Commerce, 3 Gateway Center, Pittsburgh, PA 15222.

Rhode Island
Providence Journal Bulletin, 75 Fountain St, Providence, RI 02902.

Department of Economic Development, 7 Jackson Walkway, Providence, RI 02903.
Department of Education, 22 Hayes St, Providence, RI 02908.
Department of Employment Security, 24 Mason St, Providence, RI 02903.
Department of Labor, 220 Elmwood Ave, Providence, RI 02907.
Division of Taxation, 289 Promenade St, Providence, RI 02903.
Providence Chamber of Commerce, 30 Exchange Terrace, Providence, RI 02903.

South Carolina
News and Courier, 134 Columbus St, Charleston, SC 29403.
State-Record, 1401 Shop Rd, Columbia, SC 29201.
State Development Board, PO Box 927, Columbia, SC 29202.
Department of Educacation, Rutledge Bldg, 1429 Senate St, Columbia, SC 29201.
Employment Security Commission, 1550 Gadsden St, PO Box 995, Columbia, SC 29202.
Department of Labor, 3600 Forest Dr, Landmark Ctr, Columbia, SC 29204 SC.
Tax Commission, 301 Gervais St, Columbia, SC 29201.
Greater Columbia Chamber of Commerce, 1308 Laurel St, Columbia, SC 29201.
Greater Greenville Chamber of Commerce, PO Box 10048, 24 Cleveland St, Greenville, SC 29603.

South Dakota
Argus-Leader, 200 S Minnesota Ave, Sioux Falls, SD 57012.
Office of Economic Development, Captol Lake Plz, Pierre, SD 57501.
Department of Education, 700 Governor's Drive, Pierre, SD 57501.
Division of Job Services, Department of Labor, 116 W Missouri Ave, Pierre, SD 57501.
Department of Labor, Kneip Bldg, Pierre, SD 57501.
Department of Revenue, 700 Governor's Dr, Pierre, SD 57501-2276.
Sioux Falls Chamber of Commerce, 315 S Phillips, Sioux Falls, SD 57102.

Tennessee
Commercial Appeal, 475 Union Ave, Memphis, TN 38103.
The Tennessean, 1100 Broadway, Nashville, TN 37202.
Department of Economic and Community Development, 320 Sixth Ave N, Nashville, TN 37219.
Department of Education, 100 Cordell Hull Bldg, Nashville, TN 37219.
Department of Employment Security, 504 Cordell Hull Bldg, Nashville, TN 37219.
Department of Labor, 501 Union Boulevard, Nashville, TN 37219.
Department of Revenue, 927 Andrew Jackson Bldg, Nashville, TN 37219.

Memphis Area Chamber of Commerce, 22 N Front St, PO Box 224, Memphis, TN 38101.
Nashville Area Chamber of Commerce, 161 Fourth Ave N, Nashville, TN 37219.

Texas
Austin American-Statesman, 308 Guadelupe St, Austin, TX 78767.
Dallas Morning News, 508 Young St, Dallas, TX 75202.
Fort Worth Star-Telegram, 400 W 7th St, Fort Worth, TX 76102.
Houston Chronicle, 801 Texas St, Houston, TX 77002.
Houston Post, 4747 SW Freeway, Houston, TX 77027.
San Antonio Express-News, Ave E and 3rd St, San Antonio, TX 78205.
San Antonio Light, 420 Broadway, San Antonio, TX 78205.
Wall Street Journal, 1233 Regal Row, Dallas TX 75247.
British Consulates: 813 Stemmons Tower West, 2730 Stemmons Freeway, Dallas TX 75207. Tel: 214 637 3600; Suite 2250, Dresser Tower, 601 Jefferson, Houston, TX 77002. Tel: 713 659 6270.
INS District Offices: Room IC13, Federal Bldg, 1100 Commerce St, Dallas, TX 75202; Room 343, US Courthouse, PO Box 9398, El Paso, TX 79984; Federal Bldg, US Courthouse, PO Box 61630, 515 Rusk Ave, Houston, TX 77208; US Federal Bldg, Suite A301, 727 Durango, San Antonio, TX 78206.
Department of Commerce, 816 Congress, 12th Fl, Austin, TX 78711.
Texas Education Agency, 1701 N Congress Ave, Austin, TX 78701.
Employment Commission, 101 E 15th St, Austin, TX 78778-0001.
Department of Labor and Standards, Box 12157, Capitol Station, Austin, TX 78711.
Public Accounts, LBJ Bldg, Austin, TX 78774.
Austin Chamber of Commerce, 901 W Riverside Drive, Austin, TX 78704.
Greater Dallas Chamber of Commerce, 1201 Elm St, Suite 2000, Dallas, TX 75270.
El Paso Chamber of Commerce, PO Box 9738, 10 Civic Center Plaza, El Paso, TX 79901.
Greater Houston Chamber of Commerce, 1100 Milam Bldg, 25th Floor, Houston, TX 77002.
Greater Marshall Chamber of Commerce, 213 W Auston St, PO Box 520, Marshall, TX 75670.
Greater San Antonio Chamber of Commerce, 602 East Commerce St, San Antonio, TX 78205.

Utah
Salt Lake City Tribune, 143 S Main St, Salt Lake City, UT 84111.
Salt Lake City Deseret News, Box 1257, 30 E First South St, Salt Lake City, UT 84110.
Community and Economic Development Department, 6290 State Off Bldg, Salt Lake City, UT 84114.

Office of Education, 250 E Fifth St S, Salt Lake City, UT 84111.
Department of Employment Security, 174 Social Hall Ave, Salt Lake City, UT 84147.
Industrial Commission, 160 E 300 S, PO Box 45802, Salt Lake City, UT 84145-0802.
Tax Commission, 160 E 300 S, Salt Lake City, UT 84134.
Salt Lake Area Chamber of Commerce, 175 E 400 St, Salt Lake City, UT 84111.

Vermont
Burlington Free Press, 191 College St, Burlington, VT 05402.
INS District Office, Federal Bldg, PO Box 591, St Albans, VT 05478.
Agency of Development and Community Affairs, 109 State St, Montpelier, VT 05602.
Department of Education, 120 State St, Montpelier, VT 05602.
Department of Employment and Training, Green Mountain Drive, Montpelier, VT 05602.
Department of Labor and Industry, 7 Court St, Montpelier, VT 05602.
Department of Taxes, 109 State St, Montpelier, VT 05602.
Lake Champlain Regional Chamber of Commerce, PO Box 453, 209 Battery St, Burlington, VT 05402.

Virginia
Times-Dispatch, 222 E Grace St, Richmond, VA 23219.
Roanoke Times, 201 W Campbell Ave, Roanoke, VA 24011.
Department of Economic Development, 1000 Washington Bldg, Richmond, VA 23219.
Department of Education, PO Box 6-Q, Richmond, VA 23216.
Employment Commission, 703 E Main St, Richmond, VA 23219.
Department of Labor and Industry, PO Box 12064, Richmond, VA 23219.
Department of Taxation, PO Box 6-L, Richmond, VA 23282.
Hampton Roads Chamber of Commerce, 420 Bank St, Norfolk, VA 23510.
Richmond Metropolitan Chamber of Commerce, 201 East Franklin St, Richmond, VA 23219.

Washington State
Seattle Post Intelligencer, 101 Elliott Ave W, Seattle, WA 98119.
Seattle Times, 1120 John St, Seattle, WA 98109.
Spokane Chronicle, 999 W Riverside Ave, Spokane, WA 99201.
Morning News Tribune, 1950 S State St, Tacoma, WA 98405.
British Consulate, 820 First Interstate Center, 999 Third Avenue, Seattle, WA 98104. Tel: 206 622 9255.
INS District Office, 815 Airport Way S, Seattle, WA 98134.
Department of Trade and Economic Development, 101 General Administration Building, M/S: AX-13, Olympia, WA 98504.

Department of Public Instruction, Old Capitol Bldg, M/S: FG-11, Olympia, WA 98504.

Department of Employment Security, 212 Maple Park, M/S: KG-11, Olympia, WA 98504.

Department of Labor and Industries, General Administration Bldg, M/S: HC-901, Olympia, WA 98504.

Department of Revenue, General Administration Bldg, M/S: AX-02, Olympia, WA 98504.

Greater Seattle Chamber of Commerce, 600 University St, Suite 1200, Seattle, WA 98101.

West Virginia

Charleston Gazette/Daily Mail, 1001 Virginia St E, Charleston WV 25301.

Governor's Office of Community and Industrial Development, Rm 146, State Capitol, Charleston, WV 25305.

Department of Education, 1800 Washington St E, Bldg 6, Charleston, WV 25305.

Division of Employment Security, 112 California Ave, Charleston, WV 23505.

Division of Labor, State Capitol Complex, Bldg 3, Charleston, WV 25305.

Department of Revenue, State Capitol Complex, Bldg 1, Charleston, WV 25305.

Charleston Chamber of Commerce, 106 Capitol St, Suite 100, Charleston, WV 25301-2610.

Huntington Area Chamber of Commerce, 522 Ninth St, PO Box 1509, Huntington, WV 25716.

Wisconsin

Milwaukee Journal, PO Box 661, Milwaukee, WI 53201.

Milwaukee Sentinel, 918 N 4th St, Milwaukee, WI 53202.

Bureau of Business Expansion and Recruitment, Department of Development, PO Box 7970, Madison, WI 53707.

Department of Public Instruction, 125 S Webster St, PO Box 7841, Madison, WI 53707.

Job Service Division, Department of Industry, Labor and Human Relations, PO Box 7903, Madison, WI 53707.

Department of Industry, Labor and Human Relations, 201 E Washington Ave, PO Box 7946, Madison, WI 53707.

Department of Revenue, 125 S Webster, Madison, WI 5302.

Greater Madison Chamber of Commerce, 615 E Washington Ave, Madison, Wisconsin 53701.

Metropolitan Milwaukee Chamber of Commerce, 756 N Milwaukee St, 4th Floor, Milwaukee, WI 53202.

Wyoming
Casper Star-Tribune, PO Box 80, Casper, WY 82602.
Economic Development Stabilization Board, Herschler Bldg, Cheyenne, WY 82002.
Department of Education, Hathaway Bldg, Cheyenne, WY 82002.
Employment Security Commission, PO Box 2760, Casper, WY 82602.
Department of Labor and Statistics, Herschler Bldg, Cheyenne, WY 82002.
Department of Revenue and Taxation, Herschler Bldg, Cheyenne, WY 82002.
Cheyenne Chamber of Commerce, 301 W 16th St, Cheyenne, WY 82001.

Note
Where two branches of a state department of labor are listed the first is likely to provide a placement service and job advice while the second administers and enforces the state's labour laws.

Appendix H

BIBLIOGRAPHY

Reference books
(UK publications are asterisked)

Allied Dunbar Expatriate Tax Guide, (Longman)*

The Almanac of American Employers, J.W.Plunkett (Contemporary Books Inc, 1985), 0-8092-5407-7.

The American Almanac of Jobs and Salaries, J.W.Wright, ed (Avon Books).

Career Guide to Professional Associations—A Directory of Organisations by Occupational Field, C.N.Shrameck (Carroll Press).

Careers Encyclopedia (VGM Career Books), 0-8442-8692-3.

CEPEC Recruitment Guide (Centre for Professional Employment Counselling, Kent House 41 East Street, Bromley, Kent BR1 1QQ).*

Cities of the United States, M. R. McCall, ed *(Gale Research)*.

Computer Industry Almanac (8111 LBJ Freeway, 13th Floor, Dallas, TX 75251).

Consultants and Consulting Organisations (Gale Research).

Directory of Counselling Services (International Association of Counseling Services, 2 Skyline Pl, Falls Church, VA 22041).

Directory of Executive Recruiters (Consultant News, Templeton Road, Fitzwilliam, NH 03447).

Directory of Franchising Organisations (Pilot Books).

Directory of Home Study Schools (National Home Study Courses, 1601 18th St NW, Washington, DC 30009).

Directory of Personnel Consultants by Specialisation (National Association of Personnel Consultants).

Directory of US Subsidiaries of British Companies (British-American Chamber of Commerce, 275 Madison Avenue, Suite 1714, New York, NY 10016).

Dun & Bradstreet's Million Dollar Directory (Dun & Bradstreet).

Dun & Bradstreet's Middle Market Directory (Dun & Bradstreet).

Dun's Employment Opportunities Directory (Dun & Bradstreet).

The Economist Business Travel Guide: United States (Economist Publications Ltd).*

Employment and Earnings (US Department of Labor).

Encyclopedia of Associations (Gale Research).

Encyclopedia of Medical Organisations and Agencies (Gale Research).

Encyclopedia of Second Careers, G.R.Hawes (Facts on File, 1984), 0-87196-692-1.

Executive Employment Guide (The American Management Association, Inc., 135 W 50th Street, New York, NY 10020).

The Executive Grapevine (79 Manor Way, London SE3 9XG).*

Expatriate Compensation Reports (Business International, 40 Duke Street, London W1A 1DW).*

The Fourth of July Guide to Careers, Internships and Volunteer Opportunities in the Non-Profit Sector, D.C.Smith, ed (Garrett Park Press).

Franchise Opportunities Handbook (US Industry and Trade Administration, US Government Printing Office, Washington, DC 20402.

Guide to American Directories (Klein B Publications).

Handbook of Trade and Technical Careers (National Association of Trade & Technical Schools, 2021 K St NW, Washington, DC 20006.

Harvard Guide to Careers M.P.Leape and S.M.Vacca (Harvard University Press).

Immigration Law and Practice (ALI-ABA, 4025 Chestnut Street, Philadelphia, PA 19104).

Information Please Almanac (Houghton Mifflin).

International Pay and Benefits Survey (PA Personnel Services, Hyde Park House, 60A Knightsbridge, London SW1X 7LE).*

MacMillan Directory of Leading Private Companies (National Register Publishing).

National Directory of Addresses and Telephone Numbers (General Information).

National Directory of State Agencies (Cambridge Information Group).

National Trade & Professional Associations of the United States (Columbia Books).

Thomas Register of American Manufacturers (Thomas Publishing).

Occupational Outlook Handbook, US Department of Labor (VGM Career Books), 0-8442-8562-5.

Offbeat Careers—The Directory of Unusual Work, Sacharov A (Ten Speed Press).

Professional & Trade Association Job Finder—A Directory of Employment Resources Offered by Associations and Other Organisations, S.N.Feingold and A.Nicholson (Garrett Park Press).

Summer Employment Directory of the United States (Writer's Digest Books).

The Traveller's Handbook, M.Shales, ed (WEXAS, 45 Brompton Road, London SW3 1DE).*

Ulrich's International Periodicals Directory (R R Bowker).

US Government Jobs (US Office of Personnel Management, 1900 E Street NW, Washington DC 20415).

US Government Manual, Office of Federal Register, National Archives and
  Record Administration, Washington DC 20408.
VGM's Careers Encyclopedia, C.T.Norback, ed (VGM Career Books).
The World Almanac and Book of Facts, (Pharoah Books).
When Can You Start? The Complete Job Search Guide for Women of All Ages,
  Catalyst (Macmillan, 1981).
Working Abroad, D.Young (Financial Times Business Information).*
Yearbook of American and Canadian Churches (Abingdon Press).
Yearbook of Recruitment and Employment Services (Federation of Recruitment
  & Employment Services (AP Information Services Ltd, 33 Ashbourne
  Avenue, London NW11 0DU).*

Database reference of US companies

Available from Dialog Information Service, Woodside, Badger Lane,
Hinksey Hill, Oxford OX1 5AU. Tel: (0865) 730275; Datastar
Marketing, Plaza Suite, 114 Jermyn Street, London SW1Y 6HJ.

Disclosure Database: 12,000 records:	Dialog 100
	Datastar (disc)
Dun's Electronic Yellow Pages: 8.5m records	Dialog 515
Dun's Market Identifiers: 2.25m records	Dialog 516
Dun's Million Dollar Directory:	
160,000 records	Dialog 517
Moody's Corporate Profiles: 4,000 records	Dialog 555
Standard and Poors Register—	
corporate: 45,000 records	Dialog 527
Thomas's Register On-line: 1.3m records	Dialog 535
Trinet Establishment Database: 1.5m records	Dialog 517
Trinet Company Database: 2.9m records	Dialog 532

General books

(UK titles are asterisked)
American Ways, G.Althen (Intercultural Press), 0-933662-68-8.
Coping with America, Peter Trudgill (Blackwell, 1985), 0-631-14324-6.*
Destination USA, K.K.Singh (Park Publications, 1 Park Close, London NW2
  6RQ), 0-9507708-1-7.*
Dream Jobs—A Guide to Tomorrow's Top Careers, R.Bly and G.Blake (Wiley
  Press), 0-471-89204-1.
Doing Business in the USA, R.Starr and R.B.Donin (Oyez Publishing).*
Emerging Careers—New Occupations for the Year 2000 and Beyond, S.N.
  Geingold and N.R.Taylor (Garrett Park Press), 0-912048-32-8.
Executive Jobs Unlimited, C.R.Boll (Macmillan Inc).
Finding a Job in the United States J.E.Friedenberg and C.H. Bradley (Passport
  Books), 0-8442-6686-8.
Finding the Right Job at Mid-life, J.F.Allen and J.Gorkin (Fireside Books),
  0-67155548-0.

Getting into America, H.D.Deutsch (Random House/Coronet 1986), 0-340-36935-3.*

Handbook for Foreign Students and Professionals (office of International Education and Services, University of Iowa, 200 Jefferson Building, Iowa City, IA 52242).

How To Get a Job Abroad, R.Jones (How To Books, 1991).*

How To Get the Job You Really Want, R.Jones (Allborough Press, Cambridge, 1990).*

How To Teach Abroad, R.Jones (How To Books, 1989).*

Internships (Writer's Digest Books).

The Job Hunters' Guide to Eight Great American Cities: Atlanta, Boston, Denver, Phoenix, Portland, San Diego, San Francisco, Seattle. (Brattle Publishing), 0-918938-00-7.

Job Hunting with Employment Agencies, E.Gowdy (Barron), 0-8120-0610-0.

Jobs and How To Get Them, H.W.Koch (Ken Books), 0-910553-05-X.

Jobs—What They Are, Where They Are, What They Pay, R.O. and A.M. Snelling (Simon & Schuster).

How to Live and Work in America, S.Mills (How To Books, 1988), 0-7463-0330-0.*

Living in the USA, A.R.Lanier (Intercultural Press, 1988), 0-933662-10-6.

Long Stays in America: R.W.Hicks and F.Schulz (David & Charles/ Hippocrene 1986), 0-7153-8730-8.*

Merchandising Your Talents, US Department of Labor (US Government Printing Office).

Newcomers' Guide to the USA (Self-Counsel Press Inc).

Résumés That Get Jobs: Résumé Service (Arco Publishing), 0-668-05210-4.

The New York Times Career Planner—A Guide to Choosing the Perfect Job for the 101 Best Opportunities of Tomorrow, E.W. Fowler (Times Books/ Random House).

Planning Your Career of Tomorrow, A.Paradis (Passport Books), 0-8442-6678-7).

Predeparture Orientation Handbook for Foreign Students and Scholars Planning to Study in the USA, M.Ernst, ed (Bureau of Education and Cultural Affairs, USIA, Washington DC 20547).

Telesearch—Direct Dial to the Best Job in Your Life, J.Truitt (Facts on File, 1983).

US Immigration Made Easy—The Insider's Guide, M.A.Siegel and L.A. Canter (Sheridon Chandler, Tucson, Arizona).

What Color is Your Parachute?, R.N.Bolles (Ten Speed Press).

Work Your Way Around the World, S.Griffith (Vacation Work).

For a more extensive bibliography of American careers and employment titles, consult:

Where to Start Career Planning: Essential Resource Guide for Career Planning and Job Hunting, Carolyn Lloyd Lindquist (Cornell University Career Center: distributed by Peterson's Guides), 0-87866-384-3.

US Publishers

The following list includes publishers which publish careers books aimed at Americans, particularly young Americans, yet offer insights into different careers in the USA and give useful contact addresses. Where no distributor is stated, your local bookseller should be able to obtain any North American book through the specialist US wholesalers Baker & Taylor International, Northdale House, North Circular Road, London NW10 7UH. Tel: (081) 453 3627. Numbers in final position denote ISBN designation.

Abingdon Press, 201 Eighth Ave S, Nashville, TN 37202. ISBN 0-687.

Arco Publishing, 1230 Ave of the Americas, New York, NY 10020. Publishers of a series of careers guidance books entitled *Your Career In . . .* Designed principally for high school students. A subsidiary of Simon & Schuster. ISBN 0-688

Avon Books, Hearst Corporation, 105 Madison Avenue, New York, NY 10016. 0-380.

Ayer Co Publishers, PO Box 958, Salem, NH 03079. ISBN 0-405, 0-8369, 0-8337, 0-8434.

Bob Adams Inc, 260 Center St, Holbrook, MA 02343. Publisher of *The Job Bank* series for Northern California, San Francisco, Boston, Metropolitan New York, South West. ISBN 0-937860, 1-55850.

Barron Educational Series, 256 Wireless Boulevard, Happauge, NY 11788; UK rep: D Services, Euston Street, Freeman's Common, Leicester LE2 7SS (Tel: 0533 547671). ISBN 0-8120.

R.R.Bowker Co, 245 W 17th St, New York, NY 10011; Borough Green, Sevenoaks, Kent TN15 8PJ. Tel: (0732) 884567. ISBN 0-8352.

Brattle Publishing, 190 North Lake Avenue, Troy, NY 12180. Publishers of *The Job Hunters' Guide* series: eight American cities, the Rocky Mountain region, the Sunbelt. ISBN 0- 918938.

Cambridge Information Group Directories Inc, 7200 Wisconsin Avenue, Bethesda, MD 20814). ISBN 0-942189; 0-916234.

Career Press Inc, Box 34, 62 Beverley Rd, Hawthorne, NJ 07507. UK rep: Gazelle Book Services, Falcon House, Queen Sq, Lancaster LA1 1RN. Tel: (0524) 68765. Publishers of the *Career Directory* series. ISBN 0-934829.

Carroll Press, 43 Squantum Street, Cranston, RI 02920. ISBN 0-939805.

Columbia Books, 1212 New York Ave NW, Suite 330, Washington, DC 20005.

Contemporary Books Inc, 180 North Michigan Avenue, Chicago, IL 60601; UK rep: Gazelle Book Services, Falcon House, Queen Square, Lancaster LA1 1RN. ISBN 0-8092.

Dun & Bradstreet, 299 Park Ave, New York, NY 10171; 26-32 Clifton Street, London EC2P 2LY; Tel: (071) 377 4377. ISBN 0-942526.

Facts on File, 460 Park Avenue South, New York, NY 10016, USA. Tel: 212 683 2244; Collins Street, Oxford OX4 1XJ. Tel: (0865) 728399. Fax:

(0865) 244839. Publisher of the *Career Opportunities* series which includes writing, music, TV, cable and video, advertising and PR, art, robotics. ISBN 0-8160.

Fireside Books, 8356 Olive Blvd, St Louis, MO 63132. ISBN 0-87527.

Gale Resarch Inc, 835 Penobscot Building, Detroit, MI 48226; North Way, Walworth Industrial Estate, Andover, Hants SP10 5YE. Tel: (0264) 334446. ISBN 0-8103.

Garrett Park Press, Box 190, Garrett Park, MD 20896. 0-912048. ISBN 0-912048.

General Information Co, 11715 North Creek Parkway S, Bothell, WA 98011. ISBN 0-941841.

Houghton Mifflin Co, 215 Park Ave S, New York, NY 10003. ISBN 0-555132.

Intercultural Press Inc, PO Box 700, Yarmouth, ME 04096. ISBN 0-933662.

Ken Books, 56 Midcrest Way, San Francisco, CA 94131. ISBN 0-910553.

Klein B Publications, 10119 Sample Road, Coral Springs, FL 33065. ISBN 0-87340.

Kendall Hunt Publishing, 2460 Kerper Boulevard, Dubuque, IA 52001. UK Distr: WCB International Group, Holywell House, Oxford OX2 0ES. Publishers of three guides for college students: *Career Planning Today; Your Career; Training for Life*. ISBN 0-8403.

Lerner Publishing, 241 First Avenue, N Minneapolis, MN 55401. UK rep: Ruskin Book Services. Publishers of the *Career In . . .* series. ISBN 0-8225.

Macmillan Inc, 866 Third Avenue, New York, NY 10022. ISBN 0-02.

McGraw-Hill Book Co, 1221 Avenue of the Americas, New York, NY 10020. Tel: 212 512 2000; McGraw-Hill House, Shopenhangers Road, Maidenhead, Berks SL5 2QL. Tel: 0628 23432. Distributes *Harvard Business School Career Guides* in Management Consulting, Marketing and Investment Banking (Harvard Business School Press). ISBN 0-07.

National Register Publishing, 3004 Glenview Road, Wilmette, IL 60091. Subsidiary of Macmillan Inc. ISBN 0-87217.

National Textbook Co, 4255 W Touhy Avenue, Lincolnswood, IL 60646. Publishes under the VGM imprint the *Opportunities In . . .* series, the *Careers for You* series, the *Professional Résumés* series, the *Professional Careers* series, a *Careers Encyclopedia* and the comprehensive *Occupational Outlook Handbook* compiled by the US Department of Labor. Publishes under the Passport Books imprint *Finding a Job in the United States*. ISBN 0-8442; 0-8325.

Passport Books (see National Textbook Co).

Peterson's Guides, PO Box 2123, Princeton, NJ 08543. ISBN 0-87866.

Pharaoh Books, 100 Park Avenue, 6th Floor, New York, NY 10166.

Pilot Books, 103 Cooper Street, Babylon, NY 11702. Publishes a series of guides on careers, small businesses and franchising. ISBN 0-887576.

Raintree Publications, 310 W Wisconsin Avenue, Mezzanine Level, Milwaukee, WI 53203. Publishers of the *Careers In . . .* series. ISBN 0-8172.

Random House Inc, 201 E 50th St, New York, NY 10022; 30-32 Bedford Square, London WC1B 3SG. Tel: (071) 255 2393. ISBN 0-394.

Richards Rosen Press, 29 East 21st Street, New York, NY 10010. Publishes around 100 careers titles in the *Your future In . . .* series. ISBN 0-8239.

Self-Counsel Press Inc, 1704 N State St, Bellingham, WA 98225. ISBN 0-88908.

Simon & Schuster, 1230 Ave of the Americas, New York, NY 10020; 66 Wood Lane End, Hemel Hempstead, Herts HP2 4RG. Tel: (0442) 23155. Simon & Schuster subsidiaries Cambridge Books, Julian Messner, Prentice Hall all publish a number of careers titles. ISBN 0-691.

Surrey Books, E Ohio Street, Suite 120, Chicago, IL 60611. Publishes a *How To Get a Job In . . .* series for Los Angeles, Dallas/Fort Worth and Chicago. ISBN 0-9609516, 0-940625.

Ten Speed Press, Box 7123. Berkeley, CA 94707. UK rep: Airlift Book Co, 26-28 Eden Grove, London N7 8EF. Tel: (071) 607 5792. Publishers of *Who's Hiring Who?; Offbeat Careers—The Directory of Unusual Work; What Color is Your Parachute?.* ISBN 0-913668;0-89815.

Thomas Publishing, 1 Penn Plaza, 26th Floor, New York, NY 10119, 0-937200.

VGM Careers Books (see National Textbook Co).

Walker & Co, 720 Fifth Avenue, New York, NY 10019. Publishers of *Career Choices for the Nineties*, a series of career guides for students arranged according to different fields of study. ISBN 0-8027.

Franklin Watts, 730 Fifth Avenue, New York, NY 10019; 96 Leonard St, London EC2A 4RH. Tel: (071) 739 32929. Publishers of the *Career Concise Guide* series of some 50 titles.

John Wiley & Sons Ltd, 605 3rd Avenue, New York, NY 10158; Baffins Lane, Chichester, West Sussex PO19 1UD. Tel: (0243) 779777. Publishes a number of careers books including *The Job Finder's Library*. ISBN 0-471.

Writer's Digest Books, 1 Dana Ave, Cincinnati, OH 45207; UK rep: Vacation Work Publications, 9 Park End St, Oxford OX1 1HJ. ISBN 0-89879; 0-911654.

Index